ARTISAN BREADS

atHome with
THE CULINARY INSTITUTE OF AMERICA

ARTISAN BREADS

ERIC KASTEL
CATHY CHARLES

THE CULINARY INSTITUTE OF AMERICA®

WILEY

JOHN WILEY & SONS, INC.

This book is printed on acid-free paper. ∞

THE CULINARY INSTITUTE OF AMERICA

President	Dr. Tim Ryan '77
Vice President, Dean of Culinary Education	Mark Erickson '77
Senior Director Continuing Education	Susan Cussen
Director of Publishing	Nathalie Fischer
Editorial Project Manager	Lisa Lahey '00
Editorial Assistant	Erin Jeanne McDowell '09
Recipe Tester	Lauren Elliot

Published by John Wiley & Sons, Inc., Hoboken, New Jersey
Published simultaneously in Canada

Library of Congress Cataloging-in-Publication Data:

Kastel, Eric.
 Artisan breads at home with the Culinary Institute of America / Eric Kastel, Cathy Charles.
  p. cm.
 Includes index.
 ISBN 978-0-470-18260-4 (cloth)
 1. Bread. I. Charles, Cathy, 1964- II. Culinary Institute of America. III. Title.
 TX769.K295 2010
 641.8'15--dc22
                     2009039247

Printed in China

10 9 8 7 6 5 4 3 2 1

Contents

Acknowledgments

Eric Kastel

To endeavor to write a book takes the combined skills of many people. I have been fortunate to have been part of a talented team that has helped me to complete mine. I owe a lot of thanks to Lisa Lahey, editor at The CIA, for first putting the idea in my head that I could actually do this and for her direction at all times, even when we disagreed.

I am a baker and by no means a writer, so I give great thanks to Cathy Charles, my writer, for her amazing ability to translate my love, care and enthusiasm for bread baking through all of our e-mails, phone calls and classes together into the words on these pages.

To the administration, faculty, staff and students of The Culinary Institute of America who have helped me on this journey: To Tom Vacarro who lent support however and whenever he could and made the road much smoother. To my colleagues in the baking and pastry department for their willingness to give support, advice and critical analysis, whether it was asked of them or not. To my teaching assistant, Lauren Elliot, who I could always count on to take care of the biggest and smallest of matters. She has a deep passion for bread baking and became my most diligent and dedicated recipe tester and worked tirelessly to help prepare breads for the photos. To students Tea Mamut, from Croatia, and Akshay Batra, from India, who helped to develop bread recipes from their homelands. I also thank the great team of diligent student workers who helped with the never-ending production needs of the photo shoots: Stacey Coates, Megan Faillace and Rachel Oliver.

My deepest gratitude to Ben Fink, a truly amazing and gifted photographer, who enjoys his profession and brings this energy with him to work every day and leaves it everlastingly in his beautiful photographs.

To the team at John Wiley & Sons, Inc., who put this book together with great care and concern for every aspect.

I also must thank the following companies that have contributed equipment and supplies: Chicago Metallic, Super Peel, FibraMent baking stone, Epicurean cutting surfaces, Central Milling flour and Tulikivi for the beautiful soapstone for photography.

To the countless people who have influenced my development as a baker: Daniel Leader, Raymond Calvel, Carsten Kruse, George Eckerd, Didier Rosada, Tom Gumpel, Andrew Meltzer, Nick Greco, Jeffrey Hammelman and Ciril Hitz.

For my parents, who gave me support and direction so that I could find my path.

I would also like to thank my children, Angelica, Dylan and Luke, for baking and tasting bread with me.

And lastly, but most of all, to my wife, Erika Kastel, who gave me the love, care, support and time I needed to work on this ever-consuming project.

Cathy Charles

I would like to thank Kate McBride, Chef Eric Kastel and Lisa Lahey for hiring me. It was a pleasure to work on this project. Lisa, I appreciate your wise counsel about the book and so many other things. Eric, I enjoyed every minute in your classroom. Thank you for being so generous with your knowledge, materials, time and friendship. Thanks also to Chef Richard Coppedge, Jr., for continuing to be my friend and mentor. To all of the students I met at The CIA, your questions and personal insights about bread were so valuable to me, and I enjoyed the many conversations we had about baking, life and philosophy.

I want to thank my parents-in-law, Bernard and Evelyn Kaye, for helping my family pack and move while I was writing, as well as minding the boys and encouraging me a great deal. To my own parents and step-parents, Bill Charles, Carolyn Cavallone, Colette Matsui and Joe Cavallone: Thank you for being there for me. Adele Cohen, you are a fearless babysitter, aunt and friend. Thanks as well to the rest of my extended family for supporting me, including my siblings, siblings-in-law and their children.

To my own children, Evan, Lucas and Maxwell: Your presence in my life is both joyous and humbling. You motivate me in so many ways.

And finally, there is my husband, Steve Kaye. Steve, you are the greatest. Thank you.

INTRODUCTION TO
Artisan Bread

What exactly is artisan bread? Picture someone working entirely by hand for several days with stone-ground organic flour, wild yeast starter that's been nurtured for weeks (or even years), pure spring water and sea salt. The baker skillfully mixes, kneads, ferments, shapes, ferments some more and finally scores symmetrical cuts into the dough. The rustic loaves, ripe and ready for baking, go into a wood-burning brick oven on a long-handled peel. The kitchen is hot and filled with a tantalizing aroma, while the loaves rise even more in the oven, and then finally emerge—perfectly burnished and delicious.

CHAPTER ONE

IS THAT ARTISAN BREAD? It certainly is. Is that the only way to do it?

No.

You can make fine artisan bread at home, without being an expert. All it takes to make a quality loaf of bread is the knowledge of ingredients, equipment and techniques that you will learn from this book. Most home bakers don't have a fancy brick oven, and many people stiffen up at the mere mention of the word *yeast*. The words *sourdough starter* can make the blood run cold. Maybe you are one of those people thinking, "Who me? I can't control yeast. And besides, who has time for that?"

For one thing, commercial yeast is easier than ever to use. Thanks to the development of instant dry yeast, you can blend the yeast granules with the flour you are using and you don't have to proof it first. Then, it's just a matter of controlling the temperature. It is simple enough to use a thermometer to determine the room temperature. If it is hotter or colder than usual, you can adjust the temperature of the liquids you are using so that the yeast is within its comfort zone. Now, who is in control? You. You are a fully evolved human. You can conquer a single-celled organism.

If you think baking bread will be hard to fit into your schedule, there are lots of ways you can do it. Many doughs—such as pizza and sweet rolls—benefit from being mixed the night before and allowed to slowly ferment in the refrigerator until the next day, which often can make meal preparation easier as a portion of the meal (the dough) is prepared in advance. Or you can choose to prepare a dough that does not require a prolonged fermentation period and with just the basics: flour, water, yeast and salt; within a few hours you will be pulling a crusty, satisfying loaf out of the oven. Perhaps you've found the time to bake bread at home by using a bread machine. There is no shame in that. But now you may want to take the next step, and this book is here to hold your hand. Or maybe you used to bake bread and want to get back into it again, perhaps try your hand at that elusive sourdough? You can do it! Have a good time. The last thing baking bread should be is stressful or onerous. There are too many things in life that are not fun, and bread baking should not be one of them. Let the process of baking and breaking bread add enjoyment to your life. If you can't shake the memory of past disasters, then try to look at it in a different way. Instead of feeling scarred by "failures," let what you've learned motivate you.

A Brief Overview of Bread

If you are new to bread baking, some of the above-mentioned terms may sound unfamiliar. Here is a summary of what happens during the bread-making process, with more detail to follow in later chapters.

There are four basic elements of bread: flour, water, yeast and salt. When wheat flour is combined with water or another liquid, the two proteins contained in the wheat combine to form **gluten.** As the dough is alternately worked and allowed to rest, the gluten gradually goes from being a shaggy mass to forming long, stretchy strands. During the rest periods, known as **bulk fermentation,** the yeast is busy **fermenting,** meaning it consumes the sugars in the flour and creates ethyl alcohol and carbon dioxide gas. As these gases expand, the stretchy gluten formed by the wheat is able to both trap the gas and expand with it.

Periodically, the dough should be folded, never "punched down," contrary to what you may have heard or done before. **Folding** achieves at least four things, listed here in sequential order: 1) it expels some of the gases and provides more oxygen; 2) it redistributes the yeast's food supply; 3) it equalizes the dough's temperature;

FINDING THE BAKER WITHIN

Bread baking lends itself to all personality types. If you are a perfectionist or tend to be analytical, this trait comes in handy when you need to keep track of temperatures and times, and when you are trying to make symmetrical shapes. If you are more of a right-brain person, you can let your intuition take over, sensing when it's time to move on to each step. But don't let genetics restrain you. Who says you have to be one thing or the other? Baking is an art and science that calls upon all your facets. The artist in you may be overtaken by the heady perfume of a well-balanced sourdough starter. The scientist in you may find it cool that you can apply a formula to something and it actually works. Relax, and let yourself become one with the yeast. Marvel as the gluten strengthens and develops. Bread really is one of those everyday miracles.

WHY BAKE BREAD?

Baking and eating a good-quality loaf of bread links you to something humans have been doing for thousands of years. There is a reason wheat has long been referred to as the "staff of life." In ancient times, in the area of the Middle East known as the Levant, wild grasses that were the precursors of wheat were harvested and used as nourishment when other foods could not be found.

At around 4000 BCE, the Egyptians invented what we now think of as bread baking. It was probably by accident: Someone may have left flatbread dough sitting for too long, saw that it had puffed up, baked it anyway and liked the result. It wasn't long before special ovens were created and a wide range of bread types evolved. People also learned that reserving a piece of the previous day's dough could help leaven the next batch, and that fermented beverages such as beer could also serve as leaveners. Bread was made in essentially the same way for centuries. It wasn't until the 1800s, however, that bakers understood the role of yeast.

In modern times, commercial yeast was developed. Flours changed: It became easier to separate the bran from the white flour, and flour was bleached to prevent millers from having to age their product, so that they could get the flour to market faster. (Flour had been previously aged to allow it to oxidize naturally, which enabled it to hold moisture; see "Why the Flour You Choose Makes a Difference" on page 14.) Eventually, however, bakers learned that nutrients had to be added back in to the flour to prevent vitamin deficiencies in consumers. The advent of mechanized bakeries, including bread-slicing machines, meant that human hands could have almost no contact with the product. Bread was convenient and in good supply, but the quality had changed for the worse.

Nowadays, there are lots of people who try to avoid eating bread, either because they think the carbohydrates found in it will pack on the pounds, or because they just haven't found a bread as high in quality as they like. The "convenient"-style breads still abound on grocery store shelves, but there is a greater range of products now—many of which contain whole grains. If you are lucky enough to live near a good bakery, it may be easy to obtain quality bread made in the timeless artisan style. Then of course, there is you. You can make fine artisan bread yourself, once you know how.

For those who are carbohydrate conscious, try thinking of it this way: If there are no health reasons stopping you from eating bread, you can always enjoy it in moderation. Just cut a thinner slice, or eat only one roll. A little bit of something good is better than a lot of something bland, or nothing at all.

and 4) it promotes gluten development. Once the bulk fermentation period is over, the dough is **divided** into roll-sized portions or individual loaves. There are several reasons for making enough dough to divide. It tends to be easier to work with a double-sized portion of dough and, if you are already going to the trouble of making bread, you might as well get more than one loaf out of it. You might even want to make more than one type of bread, if you are in the kitchen anyway.

After **dividing,** the dough is gently coaxed into a precursor of its final shape in a process called **preshaping.** Next it is allowed to relax once more in a stage that professionals call **bench rest.** Then comes the **final shaping** (i.e., into a round boule, blunt bâtard, or elongated baguette), followed by **final fermentation,** also known as **proofing,** where the shaped dough rises one last time. During final fermentation, the dough is covered to ensure it does not form a skin, so that the bread can expand to its fullest potential during baking. Alternatively, the dough can be put into a **proof box** at this stage, where the right temperature (85–90°F) and humidity (about 80 percent) help it to expand without forming a skin. Just before baking, most breads are scored with a razor (or **lame**). **Scoring** is done to help control where the crust will break, and, in the case of rye bread, to help the loaf expand more than it would otherwise.

Once the loaf goes into the hot oven, the yeast has a last hurrah and the dough rises one more time, in a phenomenon called **oven-spring.** (Many professionals use steam at this point. You will learn how to do this at home in later chapters.) When the temperature of the dough reaches about 140°F, the yeast dies off. As the internal temperature gets hotter, the starches form a firm structure, the alcohol is expelled and the sugars in the crust help it to become brown. For larger loaves of enriched bread (1 pound or more), the bread is done once it has reached 195–205°F inside and has developed a rich golden color. To check the doneness of lean breads, we check for crust development and color as well as a hollow-sounding thump when the loaf is tapped on the bottom. The finished loaf is then pulled out of the oven to cool before eating.

Bread Styles

The most basic breads contain just the four simple ingredients of flour, water, yeast and salt. These are referred to as lean breads and tend to have crusty exteriors, such as a baguette. Enriched breads are ones in which fats and/or sugar have been added, such as milk, eggs, oil, butter or shortening. Good examples of these are challah, which contains egg, sugar and oil; and brioche, made with egg, milk, sugar and butter. Lean and enriched breads sometimes contain what professional bakers used to call garnishes, but now refer to as inclusions, which are mixed into the dough. These can include presoaked grains, chunks of cheese, sautéed vegetables, dried fruit, olives or nuts, to name a few examples.

Basic **flatbreads** may contain yeast (pizza being one of the most popular), or no yeast at all, in the case of corn or flour tortillas. Breadsticks, pita, naan and lavash also fall under the flatbreads category.

HOW TO USE THIS BOOK

When you get a new cookbook it's natural to want to jump right in and start making something from it. But if you are a novice baker and want to have a reasonable chance at having success, you should give yourself time to read through the chapters in this book first. Absorb the techniques and the rationales behind them. Knowing why something is recommended is half the battle. The information you glean can help you make informed choices on your baking journey.

Here are some points to consider:

WEIGHING IS BETTER THAN MEASURING

Many home bakers rely on measuring cups to portion out their recipe ingredients by volume. It is probably what you were taught to do, and it may seem to work well enough. Professional bakers, however, are always looking for consistent results and they search for various ways to control the end product. Knowing that the amount of flour in a measuring cup can and does vary (due to humidity, settling, how and when the flour was milled, the type of cup being used and the way the cup was filled), professional bakers remove those variables by weighing their ingredients. Since they use scales to do this, it is called *scaling*. Scaling is more accurate and is the recommended method in this book. (For more information on how to use a scale, see page 27.) If you don't have a scale or aren't ready to give up your measuring cups, volume measurements are also provided in the recipes.

BAKERS' PERCENTAGES

As mentioned above, professional bakers tend to be very exacting and often rely on mathematical formulas to help them produce large volumes of baked goods. One way they do this is with an ingenious set of numbers called "Bakers' Percentages." You may never want to bake bread for forty people, but you may want to slightly scale up or down the number of servings in a recipe. Here's how it works: Since flour is usually the major ingredient in bread, bakers refer to the total amount of flour in the recipe as 100 percent. If you are using half as much water as flour in the recipe, then your water would be 50 percent, salt might be 2.3 percent, yeast might be 0.8 percent and so on. Because the flour is always 100 percent, your total percentage will add up to more than 100 percent. Once you have the percentages worked out, you can use them to scale a recipe up or down. Looking at the Bakers' Percentages column in a recipe is also a good way to assess the type of bread you will be making. Some breads, such as brioche, will contain a high percentage of fat (an enriched dough) compared to a baguette, which has no added fats (a lean dough).

USE MALTED BARLEY

Malted barley is called for in many of the recipes in this book (as malt syrup). Non-diastatic malted barley contains an enzyme that helps break down the flour's carbohydrates into sugars, making them more available to the yeast. This allows the yeast to do a better job fermenting, generally making for a lighter and tastier loaf of bread. It also helps the bread's color. Diastatic malted barley does not contain enzymes and won't work the same way. If you can't find non-diastatic malted barley

Then there are breads using **preferments.** This is a fancy way of describing a range of methods (including sourdough) where flour, water and yeast (either wild or commercial) are allowed to ferment for a longer period of time before being added to the actual bread dough. Preferments require more time than **straight development** doughs, where the whole process takes only a few hours. The payoff from using a preferment is a more complex taste, better texture and better keeping properties for the bread. Think of the differences between a slice of plain white bread and a slice of sourdough. One is straightforward, while the other has more depth of flavor and a more interesting texture. Chapter 6,

Advanced Artisan Bread Making (page 114), will break down the various preferment techniques and their best uses, including **pâte fermentée** (pronounced the French way: PAHT fehr-men-TAY or just PAHT FUR-ment), **sponge, biga** (BEE-gah), **poolish** (poo-LEESH) and the aforementioned **sour.**

Sounds complicated? Maybe you want to put down this book and just go buy some bread. Well, eating bakery-made bread while you learn about making bread yourself is not actually a bad thing. Just keep reading, keep trying and give yourself a chance to learn. Start with something simple. Once you get comfortable, you can go on to create a vast array of breads. There is no limit to what you can do.

right away, you can make the bread recipes without it. Once you locate it, however (see Resources, page 332), you will see a difference. It comes in syrup or powdered form. You can use either. The syrup should be added to your liquids. The powder should be mixed in with the flour.

USE INSTANT DRY YEAST

We recommend instant dry yeast for the recipes in this book. It comes in packets or in bulk, and does not require proofing in warm water before you use it. You simply mix it with the flour before adding other ingredients. Instant dry yeast is often labeled as "Bread Machine Yeast" or "Rapid Rise." If the label isn't clear, check the instructions for how to use the yeast granules. If they say to combine the granules with the dry ingredients, you've found the right yeast. Unlike "active" dry yeast, instant dry yeast will not make your bread turn out gummy. (For more detailed information on yeast, see pages 15–16.)

USE A THERMOMETER

Successful bread making requires controlling the dough's temperature so the

yeast can have an ideal environment in which to ferment. The easiest way to do this is to control the temperature of the liquids in your recipe. A long-stemmed instant-read thermometer is easy to use and doesn't have to be expensive to do the job. Some people like probe thermometers that come with a timer (see Resources, page 332).

PREHEAT AT A HIGHER TEMPERATURE

The recipes in this book call for preheating your oven from 25–50°F higher than the temperature at which you intend to bake. Here's why: When you open the oven door to load your bread, it can take a minute or two to get it in there, and a considerable amount of heat is lost while the oven door is open. Preheating at a higher temperature can compensate for this loss of heat. Once the bread is in and the oven door is closed, you can adjust the controls to the lower baking temperature and your oven will be hot enough from the start.

Before you even get to the baking part, though, it helps to know your oven. Read the manual if you haven't already, to see how it works. Use an oven ther-

mometer to test for hot spots. If something seems off, have a professional come to service the oven.

STEAM

Some of the recipes in this book instruct you to steam the bread once it's in the oven. You may wonder whether you really need to do this, especially if—like most home bakers—you do not have a steam-injected oven. Steam, in the early stages of baking, helps prevent the crust from forming too early, therefore allowing the bread to rise as high as it can. Steam also makes for a better-quality crust that is thin, crisp and glossy. It's easy to get steam into a regular oven: Select a cast-iron skillet or an old rimmed cookie sheet that you don't mind warping. Fill it halfway with water and place it in the bottom of the oven while you are preheating, or for about 15 minutes before you plan to bake. This will produce steam when you need it. Using ice cubes by throwing them into a hot pan just as you put in the bread is not recommended. They don't melt fast enough to produce the steam you need for oven-spring.

Equipment

Bread baking, like life, can be done simply or elaborately. If you choose, you can make bread with a few basic ingredients (flour, water, yeast and salt) and without a lot of gadgetry. At the very least you need equipment to weigh or measure the ingredients, a clean work surface, hands for kneading and shaping, a cloth for covering the dough, a pan or baking stone, a hot oven and an oven mitt to protect your hands from the heat when removing the bread.

CHAPTER TWO

Ingredients for the Artisan Baker

As you stock your pantry, it's important to understand the purpose each ingredient serves. Let's start with flour, which you will use in the greatest proportion.

Flour

THE FUNCTION OF FLOUR

Flour is probably the most important building block in the production of baked goods, and it serves five primary functions in baking: 1) it provides backbone and structure; 2) it provides the characteristic texture and appearance of the finished product; 3) it serves as a binding and absorbing agent; 4) it provides flavor; and 5) it has nutritional value.

1. *Flour provides backbone and structure.* Flour is used in greater quantities than any other ingredient, forming the bulk of most recipes. When combined with water, the proteins in flour combine to form gluten, the stretchy network of fibers that catch the gas created by fermenting yeast and cause bread to rise. One way to look at flour's importance is to consider the "Bakers' Percentages" usually included in a recipe or formula (the term professional bakers use). This column of figures helps the baker accurately increase or decrease the number of servings in a formula.

2. *Flour provides the characteristic texture and appearance of the finished product, based on the variety of flour used.* You can tell the difference between a slice of sandwich bread and a bagel with your eyes closed. The soft sandwich bread is made with bread flour, whereas the chewy bagel contains high-gluten flour. There are many more flour varieties to explore, as you will see on pages 9–12.

3. *Flour serves as a binding and absorbing agent.* Flour does not dissolve when it comes into contact with a liquid; rather, it absorbs it. You've probably noticed this when you've tried to wash dough off of your hands. It adheres like glue and when it does come off, it clogs the sink. If, instead, you stand over your kitchen garbage can (or compost bucket) and rub some dry flour into your hands, you'll have more success at getting the dough off. The very trait that makes wet flour so annoying on your hands is what holds bread together.

4. *Flour provides flavor, derived from the different varieties of flour.* Think of the differences between earthy whole wheat bread, nutty and sweet semolina and hearty rye.

5. *Flour has nutritional value, containing proteins, carbohydrates, vitamins, minerals and fats.* Some flours have more of these naturally occurring nutrients than others, such as unbleached

WHEAT FLOURS SUITABLE FOR BREAD BAKING

FLOUR	PROTEIN CONTENT	ATTRIBUTES	USES
Bread Flour	10.5%–13%	Provides a quality gluten structure	For most bread-baking purposes
Whole Wheat	11%–14%	100% of the wheat kernel; higher in protein, fat and other nutrients than most flours; more prone to rancidity so store in refrigerator or freezer	Whole wheat's bran fibers "cut" gluten strands, so it is usually combined with white bread flour to mitigate this effect; may substitute 15%–25% whole wheat flour for white flour in a recipe without having to increase hydration

The type of bread you are making will dictate the type of flour you need. Choose whole wheat fine or medium milled flour, but not flour that is coarsely ground. A coarse grind introduces an additional set of issues that you are better off avoiding, including the need for more liquid and faster fermentation.

and whole wheat flours. Common bread-making flours also vary in the amount of protein they contain, with each type working best for different bread types. For example, sandwich bread has a lighter and more tender crumb and bite; therefore, it requires less structure and a flour with less strength or protein. Bagels, on the other hand, require more structure and a stronger flour to develop their characteristic tight crumb and chewy texture and allow them to hold their shape during boiling before they are baked.

Flour can be made from a number of grain and vegetable sources, but it is the flour milled from wheat that is most commonly used in bread making; because of its gluten content wheat flour is the only one that can develop a full-gluten matrix. Rye flour has long been a staple in colder climates. No matter what flour you are using, it can vary considerably based on where and when it was grown, how it was milled, the temperature and humidity at which it is stored and so on. Therefore, the results you get will vary, sometimes even with the same brand name.

BREAD FLOUR AT A GLANCE

1. Clockwise from top: All-purpose flour, Bread flour, High-gluten flour, Cake flour

2. Clockwise from top: Whole wheat, Whole white wheat, Wheat bran, Vital gluten

3. Semolina, Durum

4. Clockwise from top: Masa harina, Corn flour, Cornmeal

5. Whole spelt, White spelt

Flour that clumps when squeezed has a greater proportion of starch. Left is cake flour and right is bread flour.

Other Flours for Bread Baking

FLOUR	PROTEIN CONTENT	ATTRIBUTES	USES
Durum	12%–15%	Finely ground; golden color; very hard kernel	For pasta; usually blended with bread flour for semolina bread; sometimes used in pizza dough
Semolina	12%–15%	Coarser grind; made from durum wheat	Can be alternated with durum flour but requires more hydration
High Gluten	13.5%–15%	The strongest form of wheat flour	Although some people choose to add it to boost the gluten and thereby fortify the gluten ability, there is no need for it if you are using the appropriate type of flour for the bread you are making. High-gluten flour tends to dry out the bread and can give the end product a slightly off flavor.
Cake/Pastry/All Purpose	6%–11%	Lower in protein	Can be used to help "weaken" bread flour in certain recipes (i.e., sweet dough, flatbreads such as flour tortillas)

A FEW WORDS ABOUT RYE

"Dense" may be one of the words that comes to mind when you think of rye bread. This is because the rye kernel contains smaller amounts of the proteins that form gluten. It has some gliadin, which allows dough to hold together, but has only trace amounts of glutenin, which makes dough stretchy. Bakers often combine rye flour with wheat flour to lighten the product, but there are breads made solely with rye that hail from the colder regions where rye is grown, such as Canada, Eastern Europe and Russia. Another feature of rye is that it contains a lot of pentosan gums, which means it tends to absorb much more liquid than wheat flour. The oil in rye flour grows rancid more easily than wheat when exposed to air, so you need to be careful about choosing and storing your flour. Be sure to keep it in the refrigerator or freezer.

Pumpernickel, Medium Rye, White Rye

RYE FLOURS SUITABLE FOR BREAD BAKING

FLOUR	ATTRIBUTES	USES
Light or White Rye	75% extraction. Milled from heart of the rye endosperm; lacks flavor; gray in color.	Used mostly by U.S. bakers. Has a lower percent of the bran and germ; therefore, it has less color and flavor.
Medium Rye	87% extraction. Ground from the whole endosperm; slightly higher in protein than light rye; darker color.	For most bread-baking purposes
Whole Rye/Dark Rye	Fine to medium grind; 100% of rye kernel; produces lowest bread volume	For whole-grain rye breads
Pumpernickel	Coarse grind; 100% of rye kernel; strong flavor; darkest in color	For true pumpernickel recipes

CORN FLOURS AND MEAL

TYPE	ATTRIBUTES	USES
Corn Flour	Finely ground; corn is degerminated, not soaked in lime water	For use in yeasted corn bread
Masa Harina	Finely ground; corn is soaked in lime before being milled	Best for corn tortillas
Cornmeal	Coarse grind; available in yellow, white or blue	Adds texture to corn bread

ALTERNATIVE GRAIN FLOURS

FLOUR	ATTRIBUTES	USES
Whole White Wheat	Contains both the bran and the germ, but less color than red whole wheat and less earthy flavor; absorbs more moisture than bread flour	Substitute for whole wheat flour in a recipe or replace 25% of regular bread flour in a recipe and increase the water by 5%
Spelt	Higher in protein than traditional wheat and considered more digestible; lower-quality gluten; available in white or whole spelt flour	May substitute for regular wheat flour; best for pan breads

THE BEST FLOUR FOR THE JOB

Is organic flour better than conventional flour? Yes. Plants grown in soil with lots of organic matter and no pesticides taste better and are believed to be more nutritious. Organic farming is also more sustainable. But you can still make good bread with something that is not organic. At the very least you should try to avoid using bleached flour (see page 14).

Just as there are scores of different bread types, there are lots of different flour types that may be combined in varying ways to achieve a desired effect. The recipe or formula you decide to use will tell you what you need. Bread making in general requires flour with a protein content ranging from 10.5–13 percent, and it is usually made from a hard variety of wheat. All-purpose flour ("AP" flour) is a blend of hard and soft wheats, with a protein content of between 9.5 and 11 percent, too low for most bread-making purposes. You may also find "artisan" flour, which is more suitable for bread making. It is slightly higher in protein than AP flour, with a range of 10.5–12 percent.

Should you choose stone-ground flour, or flour that is traditionally milled with steel rollers? The fact is, it's getting harder all the time to find stone-ground flours because there are fewer mills of this type around these days. Production costs are higher, and the output is lower. If you can get your hands on some stone-ground flour, you should not be afraid to use it. Stone grinding generates less heat than milling with steel rollers, and as a result, there is less damage to the starch. No matter what type of mill processes the flour, you should choose fine or medium grind. Coarsely ground flour absorbs more water and, if it contains 100 percent of the kernel, it tends to be more acidic and cuts the gluten you are trying to develop. This creates a new set of issues that, as a novice bread maker, you will want to avoid.

If you are determined to use flour made with 100 percent of the kernel, such as whole wheat, there are ways to make it work better. If you want to add flavor, fiber and nutrients to your regular loaf of bread, you can substitute 15–25 percent of your total bread flour with whole wheat.

HOW TO SHOP FOR FLOUR

Grocery stores often have a high product turnover and are a good bet for obtaining the freshest flour. If the labels seem confusing, look for "bread flour," "hard wheat" or "artisan flour." You could also check for a protein content falling within the bread-making range of 10.5–13 percent. Some health food stores are hit-or-miss. Since they don't tend to do as much business as larger grocery stores, the packages of flour these niche markets sell may sit on the shelves longer and be prone to rancidity. Avoid buying flour from an open bin: There is no telling how long it has been in there, getting exposed to air and perhaps becoming stale or spoiled.

Once you get more skilled as a bread baker, you may want to try specialty flours that are most easily ordered by mail or purchased online. King Arthur Flour and Bob's Red Mill are examples of these types of businesses (see Resources, page 332).

Since the subject here is flour, there is something else to consider that may improve the way the flour and yeast work together in your recipes. Non-diastatic malted barley, which contains the enzyme amylase, helps break down the starches in flour into sugars, making them more available to the yeast. The yeast can then do a better job producing carbon dioxide and alcohol, which in turn produces better flavor and better baking. Diastatic malted barley, without enzymes, won't harm your bread but it also won't work the same way to improve it. Non-diastatic malted barley is available in syrup form, which you add to the water in the recipe, and as a powder, which is added to the flour. If you can't find it in a local gourmet shop or health food store, you can order it online from King Arthur Flour (see Resources, page 332). It only takes a little malt, anywhere from 0.5–2 percent of the total flour weight. In volume, this would be about ½ teaspoon of malt for two loaves of bread.

Water

THE FUNCTION OF WATER

Water serves four important purposes in bread making: 1) it allows gluten to form; 2) the amount of water in the recipe helps determine the gluten structure, and therefore the crumb structure and texture of the bread; 3) water temperature is easily controlled, helping you to manipulate the final dough temperature; and 4) water converts to steam during baking and helps the bread attain volume.

1. *Water allows gluten to form.* The most important role of water in bread making is to let the two proteins in wheat—glutenin and gliadin—bind together to form gluten. Without water present, flour is just flour. Once water is added, the two proteins start to form strands of gluten, absorbing up to two times their weight in liquid.

2. *The amount of water determines gluten structure.* How much water is present is a factor in the strength of the resulting gluten. A high percentage of water (between 70 and 100 percent) will weaken the gluten and give you a more open crumb structure, such as in ciabatta. (Remember, in Bakers' Percentages,

HOW WHEAT IS CLASSIFIED

Most of the wheat crops grown in North America are varieties of "common wheat," and are named according to the planting season, the hardness of the kernel and its color. Take hard red winter wheat, for example, commonly used to make flour for bread baking. It is planted in the winter and not harvested until the following summer. This type of wheat does well in areas with cold, dry winters: Kansas, Nebraska, Oklahoma and the Texas Panhandle. Another flour commonly made into bread comes from hard red spring wheat. It is grown in the northern Plains states of Montana, Wyoming, the Dakotas and Idaho, where the weather is too severe to plant in the winter, but the region's hot, dry summers and high-quality soil make it ideal for spring planting.

Winter and spring strains of durum wheat are grown in Michigan, New York, Oregon and Washington State. Durum has the hardest wheat kernel of all varieties and the highest protein content. It is milled into semolina flour, which is often mixed with bread flour to make semolina bread.

Soft red winter wheat, which is made into flour for crackers, cakes and cookies, is grown in more humid environments, covering a swath of the United States from central Texas to the Great Lakes and over to the Atlantic. White wheat is the least commonly grown variety in the United States, and produces a quality of flour similar to that of soft red winter wheat.

Source: CommoditySeasonals.com

flour represents 100 percent; therefore, 100 percent water would mean you are using the same amount of water as flour.) Recipes with lower percentages of water (between 50 and 60 percent) have a stronger gluten structure, a dense crumb and a tougher bite, such as bagels and bialys.

3. *Water temperature is easily controlled.* You can heat water on the stovetop or in the microwave. You can cool it off by adding an ice cube or two, or by placing it in the freezer briefly. It's easy to get the water temperature you need for the recipe you are making, and this plays a crucial role in achieving the desired environment for yeast.

4. *Once your bread is in the oven, the water inside the dough turns to steam.* While the carbon dioxide created by the fermenting yeast plays a far greater role in helping bread rise, steam contributes to this as well.

THE BEST WATER FOR BREAD MAKING

The rule of thumb here is that if you enjoy drinking it, you can use it for baking bread. However, there are three important ways water quality can affect your bread quality. The pH level, mineral content and degree of chlorination all play roles.

1. *Chlorine.* Too much chlorine can inhibit or halt the growth of yeast and therefore fermentation. A chlorine level of one part per million is about as high as you can go without detecting chlorine, and at this measure, it will not affect yeast activity. If your tap water has a discernible "swimming pool" odor, though, you don't necessarily need to use bottled water. You could portion out what you need for baking the night before, loosely cover it to keep the dust off, and let the chlorine in it dissipate. You could also try using a water filter designed to remove chlorine.

2. *pH level.* Yeast likes to grow in a slightly acidic environment. If it's been a while since you've thought about the pH scale,

WHY THE FLOUR YOU CHOOSE MAKES A DIFFERENCE

We recommended using organic, unbleached, unbromated flour (see definition of bromating below) for these recipes. Why organic? Lots of studies have tried to prove or disprove that organic foods are more nutritious than conventionally grown ones. It's hard to say what is true. It is easy, however, to make the argument that organic foods taste better, and that there may be unknown beneficial nutrients in a plant that has had to fend off pests and diseases without the assistance of chemicals or pesticides. Better tasting wheat will, in turn, make a better loaf of bread. Organic flour does cost more, and if the higher cost does not fit into your budget, conventional flour will still make a good loaf of bread. But you should avoid using bleached flour because it is less healthful.

Why is flour bleached in the first place? Flour fresh from the mill is considered "green." In other words, it needs time to get exposed to air, which naturally whitens it to a degree, and also further develops its gluten-forming ability. But this takes time, and flour that is sitting around aging is taking up space. Bleaching speeds up the aging process. Bleached flour is processed with benzoyl peroxide or chlorine gas to simulate aging so that the mill producing it can turn out more flour faster. As a negative side effect, the flour's naturally occurring nutrients are lost, so vitamins and minerals must be added back in. In addition, the process bleaches away the flour's natural carotenoid coloring, which also happens to provide the flavor. Who knows what else is lost in the process?

Bleached flour is a bland, sometimes chemical-tasting, snowy white flour. Unbleached flour, on the other hand, is aged naturally with air, and retains its good creamy color, flavor and nutrients. Unbleached organic flour is even better. There are other chemical processes that have been banned in the United Kingdom and Canada that are still practiced in the United States, such as bromating flour. Bromides help to make flour stronger, but some studies suggest that bromides cause cancer. The Food and Drug Administration has asked bakers to voluntarily stop using them, but the agency has not banned the substance.

Source: Electronic code of federal regulations, http://ecfr.gpoaccess.gov

it runs from 0–14, with 7 considered neutral, anything below 7 acidic, and anything above 7 alkaline. Alkaline water can weaken gluten structure and retard fermentation. Water that is too acidic can have a similar effect. How do you know what kind of water you have without performing a litmus test? If your bread is not rising the way you'd like it to, you could try using bottled water (not distilled, however, because it is lacking minerals) and see whether that helps.

3. Mineral content. Soft water, which has a very low mineral content, will hinder the growth of yeast and slow down fermentation. It will also weaken gluten during the mixing stage. It's not hard to tell if you have soft water: Just drink a glass and if it feels slippery in your mouth, then it is soft. If you can taste the minerals, it is hard water. Again, if you think your water mineral content is off, you should try using bottled water, but not distilled water.

When you take all of the above into consideration, the best water for bread making is hard water that is slightly acidic and lacks off odors or flavors (such as sulfur). Some areas of the country are known for their naturally superior bread-making water. New York's Hudson Valley and the Catskills, the Great Lakes region and Colorado have excellent water. If you're not sure about your own water, your taste buds can be your guide.

Yeast

THE FUNCTION OF YEAST

Yeast does three things: 1) it makes bread rise; 2) the alcohol it produces as a by-product adds flavor; and 3) that same alcohol improves the dough.

1. Yeast makes bread rise. People baked bread for thousands of years without knowing exactly why or how fermentation worked. They just knew that if they let their dough sit, it would eventually puff up, or if they saved a piece of dough from a previous batch, or added some alcohol, they could speed up the process. It wasn't until 1859 that the mystery was solved. Louis Pasteur discovered that yeast is a single-celled organism that eats sugars, gives off carbon dioxide gas and alcohol, and multiplies. Once Pasteur identified wild yeast, it wasn't long before commercial yeast was made available to the home baker. The yeast you buy in the store today is different from wild yeast. It is *Saccharomyces cerevisiae*, a strain found to work best for bread baking.

2 and 3. *Yeast produces alcohol, which helps flavor the bread. That resultant alcohol also helps condition the dough (tenderize the gluten structure or protein) to make it easier to handle.*

THE BEST YEAST TO USE

Commercial yeast available to the home baker comes in three forms: fresh compressed yeast, active dry yeast granules and instant dry yeast. Instant dry yeast is the easiest to use and is therefore recommended for the recipes in this book. If you have one of the other types of yeast already on hand, you can use it, but you must refer to a conversion table (see below) to calculate the correct amounts of yeast and water to use for these recipes. If you can avoid active dry yeast, you should. Yeast in this form (granules that are a little smaller than ball bearings) is dried in a way that kills the outer coating of the yeast, producing a chemical called glutathione that makes for a gummy texture in bread.

In the past, fresh compressed yeast was the standard variety used by commercial and home bakers alike. However, today dry varieties are more commonly used because they produce excellent results, are easier to store and have a much longer shelf life.

Active dry yeast should be reactivated in twice its volume amount of water at 105°F for 3–5 minutes, before it is blended with the remaining ingredients in the formula. Combine fresh yeast with some of the milk or water in the formula and blend evenly before adding the remaining ingredients. Instant dry yeast does not have to be activated, but it should not come in direct contact with ice-cold liquids or ice. When converting a formula from fresh yeast to instant or active dry, most manufacturers suggest that the difference in weight be made up with additional water. The additional water will maintain the yield and hydration of the dough.

SUBSTITUTING ONE YEAST FOR ANOTHER

TYPE OF YEAST	PERCENTAGE	EXAMPLE
Fresh Yeast	100%	10 oz/284 g
Active Dry Yeast	40%	4 oz/113 g
Instant Dry Yeast	33%	3½ oz/94 g

The way yeast is packaged and labeled doesn't make it easy to figure out what is what. The best way to determine what you need is to look at the package instructions for how to use the yeast. If you are directed to proof the yeast in warm water ahead of time, then the product is active dry yeast, and you should avoid using it if you can. It will be obvious if you have a cake of fresh compressed yeast: It is crumbly and light tan in color. This type of yeast must be dissolved in water before using. Instant dry yeast, which

Fresh and Instant Yeast

is sometimes labeled "Bread Machine Yeast," or "Rapid Rise," will instruct you to blend the yeast with the dry ingredients. Once you open the package, you will see that the granules are very small. This is the type of yeast that we recommend.

Whatever type of yeast you are using, you need to keep it from directly contacting the salt and sugar in the recipe, at least until the last minute of mixing. So, when using instant dry yeast, blend it with the flour first, before adding the rest of the dry ingredients. Salt and sugar are "hygroscopic," meaning that they tend to draw moisture away from whatever else is there . Keep your yeast away from fats in the recipe too: Eggs, oil or butter will coat the yeast and prevent it from being distributed. Finally, you need to avoid shocking the yeast with cold (below 50°F) or hot (above 120°F) liquids.

To "prove" your yeast, or to check its vitality, you may place it in a small amount of water at 100°F with a pinch of sugar or honey. If it is still viable, it will produce gas displayed by a foamy covering on the surface in 5–10 minutes.

The correct temperature creates the right environment for yeast. The ideal dough temperature falls between 80 and 86°F, but yeast can do its job at temperatures spanning 50–98.6°F. Temperatures below 50°F won't kill the yeast, but will slow or halt its metabolic rate (although some recipes, like pizza dough, call for you to retard the dough overnight in your refrigerator). Yeast starts to die off when temperatures reach between 130 and 140°F.

Finally, remember that yeast is a living organism. If you give it what it wants, it will perform for you. It needs moisture, food and warmth. The moisture (usually in the form of water) activates the yeast. Food, in the form of starches in the flour, is broken down into sugars and digested by the yeast. This food is converted into carbon dioxide gas, which leavens the bread, and alcohol, which flavors the bread, at least until it evaporates during baking. It bears repeating that yeast does well at around 80°F. The ideal temperature will vary with the recipe and, remember, this is something you can control. Try starting with dry ingredients that are at room temperature, and adjust the liquids by heating or cooling as needed.

Salt

THE FUNCTION OF SALT

Salt is an important component in bread making. If you are on a low-salt diet, consider the fact that the amount of salt in a loaf of bread is very small (2–2.3 percent) and performs four crucial functions: 1) it adds flavor to the bread; 2) it helps strengthen the gluten; 3) it controls the activity rate of the yeast; and 4) it contributes to the browning of the crust.

1. *Salt adds flavor.* For thousands of years, people have relied upon salt to bring out the flavor of food. Even when you cannot taste it, it helps to unify the profile of flavors and improve it. Odds are you have forgotten to put salt in soup or some other dish you were making—it probably tasted bland and flat.

2. *Salt strengthens the gluten.* It helps the gluten hold together, preventing it from tearing too much when it stretches. To put it more scientifically, salt helps with the ionic binding of the two proteins in wheat, glutenin and gliadin. It also helps draw the water away from the protein, tightening the gluten structure. This makes the dough easier to handle, and because the gluten can stretch more freely, you'll get a bread with more volume and a better crumb.

3. *Salt controls the activity rate of yeast.* Yes, you want the yeast to ferment, but not too much. That is where salt comes in, as a check and balance. It slows down the metabolic rate of the yeast.

4. *Salt helps brown the crust.* As mentioned above, salt helps to slow down the yeast's consumption of sugars, therefore leaving some of those sugars in the dough to help contribute to crust browning.

The quantity of salt needed in most recipes is very small, between 2 and 2.3 percent. If you use less salt (even in a range from 1–1.5 percent), the yeast will ferment faster and you will get tacky dough. Once your bread is baked, the crust will lack color, and it will taste bland and too yeasty. If you use too much salt (again, the error window is fairly small: 2.8–3.2 percent), your dough will be tighter and the yeast will ferment more slowly. The crust color of your baked bread will be too dark and it will taste too salty.

THE BEST SALT FOR BREAD BAKING

One can make the argument that salt is salt. That may be true if you are weighing your ingredients, but not if you are measuring them. The best salt to use is fine, unprocessed sea salt. Kosher salt is more expensive and, because of its coarseness, it is hard to measure the right amount and difficult to incorporate it well. Try to avoid using iodized salt. It can leave a chemical aftertaste in your bread.

Enrichments

Whenever you add anything to a bread recipe beyond the basics of flour, water, yeast and salt, it is considered an enrichment. Enrichments make the task of developing gluten more challenging. Fats, such as butter, oil and even eggs, can coat the gluten strands and make it harder for them to form a network. But the payoff is a softer, more cake-like product such as challah or soft rolls, and a richer, more flavorful product such as brioche. Enriched breads also keep longer, because the fats and sugars help prevent spoilage.

EGGS

When eggs are added to bread, they help improve the color, flavor and nutritional profile of the product. They also help provide an even texture to the bread by coagulating during baking. You should look for high-quality large Grade AA eggs as they are the best quality you can buy in the store.

FATS

You might say butter is the queen of fats, at least in baking. It smells good, adds rich color, melts in your mouth and tastes wonderful. Butter is often used in sweet breads to make them more tender and adds a richness that is particularly appealing in holiday breads such as panettone and stollen.

Unsalted butter is what professional bakers choose, but you could use salted butter in a pinch. Remember, in bread baking you are trying to carefully control the amount of ingredients, including salt, down to tenths of a percent. So it makes sense that you would not want to add more salt along with your butter. Unsalted butter doesn't keep as long as salted butter, so check whatever you buy carefully and store it in the freezer if you are not going to use it right away. You will also have a choice between European-style butters (84–85 percent fat) and grocery-store brands (80–82 percent fat). Either will work, but the higher-fat product will lend a richer result.

Olive oil is used frequently in flatbreads such as pita and pizza. In the case of focaccia, it is a very visible feature of the finished bread, with the olive oil glistening thickly on the top. This is one example of where you will want to use high-quality extra-virgin olive oil that has good flavor. Otherwise, extra-virgin olive oil does not hold up well under high heat and can even become bitter tasting. When olive oil is an ingredient in the bread dough itself, the quality of the oil is less crucial. You can save money and even use a non-virgin type of olive oil if you wish. Vegetable oil is an ingredient in some of the recipes in this book, and is also good to have around for oiling baking pans. Canola is a good, flavorless choice.

Shortening is 100 percent fat—an engineered product that contains no water. It got its name by the purpose it serves, to "shorten" strands of gluten by coating them with fat. Shortening was originally developed to replace lard and another more expensive ingredient, butter. Nowadays it has become clear that the trans fats created by hydrogenation are actually less healthy than the saturated fat that naturally occurs in animal products. Nevertheless, shortening has its purposes, specifically, in making flour tortillas. Try to find a shortening that is trans-fat free. You could also just use lard if you want to.

SWEETENERS

Sugar's obvious role in baking is to sweeten a product, but it also serves to draw away water. In order for gluten to be formed from the two proteins in wheat flour, water must be present. So it follows that sugar can delay gluten development. But this can work in a baker's favor by producing a softer, more tender product and browner crust. Sugar also extends a bread's shelf life. In sweet breads, sugar is a significant ingredient, sometimes topping 20 percent of the total amount of flour in the recipe. The recipe you are using will tell you what type of sugar you will need. You probably already have granulated sugar on hand, and may keep brown sugar and powdered sugar in your pantry. Some of the breads, such as craquelin, call for sugar cubes in the dough and coarse sugar as a garnish.

Honey is a featured ingredient in challah and whole wheat bread, and is used primarily for its flavoring, but it also helps the product retain moisture. Clover honey is a common choice for baking because it is readily available.

You will also find a few recipes with glazes that call for light corn syrup. The corn syrup helps to promote browning of the crust when used in a large enough quantity.

MILK

Milk is added to bread for a number of reasons: It makes for a softer and browner crust, lends a rich flavor and produces a fine, even crumb. It also adds nutrients to the bread. The recipes in this book call for whole milk, but you will probably not notice much of a difference if you use 2 or 1 percent milk.

FLAVORING

Most of the flavoring in your bread is going to come from the basic ingredients of flour, yeast, salt and any enrichments you may add. But vanilla extract is a key ingredient in some of the sweet doughs, toppings and fillings. Since you are trying to use the finest ingredients in your artisan bread, pure vanilla extract is preferable to artificially flavored vanillin.

Inclusions and Garnishes

Sometimes you bite into a warm piece of bread and are pleasantly surprised by a creamy nugget of cheese, molten pieces of chocolate or a combination of toasty nuts and dried fruit. These are called inclusions. Inclusions can add flavor, texture and color to bread dough. Other examples of inclusions are fresh herbs, sautéed vegetables, olives and spices. Whole or cracked grains are usually soaked in water before they are added to bread dough. Dry grains tend to draw moisture away from the dough, and therefore dry out the bread. They are also generally too hard to eat without softening them first. "Soakers" may include cracked wheat, rye, millet, flaxseeds or sunflower seeds. Alternatively, you can toast (instead of soaking) seeds and nuts to bring out the flavor and draw out the oil, before adding them to already developed bread dough.

Inclusions that are salty, acidic, sugary or sharp could damage or hinder the gluten. These are often added to the dough after the gluten has already had a chance to develop. Fragile inclusions, such as frozen berries or olives, are also usually added at this stage.

Outfitting a Baker's Kitchen

You probably have most of the equipment you need at home already. There are, however, certain things that professional bakers use regularly that can be very helpful for baking at home. Many of these items are reasonably priced and you may find your results are better with some of these tools. You can start with just the minimum. Add helpful items as you learn what will meet your needs.

Scales for Weighing

As mentioned earlier, weighing your ingredients, instead of measuring them with cups, is the best way to get consistent results. You don't need an expensive balance-beam scale to do the job, but it's great if you already have one. A good electronic scale can be had for as little as $35 (see Resources, page 332). Or you could buy the least expensive kitchen scale you can find and see whether you like scaling. If it wears out from use, you'll know a more expensive scale will be worth the investment. Even if you don't have a scale, you can still make the recipes in this book using the volume measurements that are provided. (See also "Scaling," page 27.)

Work Surfaces

The best work surface for making bread is one made of wood, because it does not conduct heat. Marble is too cold, and stainless steel can sometimes suffer from the same effect. If you don't have a butcher block in your kitchen, you could try placing a large wooden cutting board on your counter or table and work on that. Another option is to buy a silicone bread mat from a baking supply store. It won't make a marble surface warmer, but it will make it easier to clean up after yourself (see Resources, page 332).

Mixers

Ancient bakers produced loaves for the multitudes without ever using an electric mixer. But why do it that way if you don't have to? Some breads do well when mixed by hand, such as a lean dough that contains basic ingredients and is developed very quickly before baking. But other types of dough require a longer mixing period to develop the gluten, such as enriched dough, or are simply too difficult to mix well by hand, such as rye. For these, the best way to go is a heavy-duty stand mixer with a dough hook. Even the highest-rated mixers designed for home use must be operated at a low speed and monitored closely to ensure that the motor doesn't burn out during bread mixing. If you are trying to make more than one bread at a time, it may be useful to have two stand mixers, so you can alternate and give their motors a chance to rest. KitchenAid has a line of popular stand mixers (see Resources, page 332). Remember that when making bread, the more horsepower your mixer has, the better. Bread dough is much stiffer than pastry dough, and can put a strain on weaker appliances. You will also want to make sure you have a generous bowl capacity of at least five quarts.

Food Processors

These machines are indispensable in the kitchen, and are helpful for preparing some of the extras you may put in your bread. Food processors are good for pureeing fruit and vegetables, grating cheese and other such tasks. Food processors are not acceptable for mixing bread dough, however, because they defeat the very purpose you are trying to achieve: The food processor blade (even when made of plastic) cuts the strands of gluten you are trying to develop. So even if your owner's manual says you can make bread with it, forget it. For all of the other odd jobs related to bread making that your food processor can do, you will find a midsize or larger cup capacity to be the most useful.

Tools and Supplies

MEASURING CUPS AND SPOONS

If you are going to measure instead of weigh your ingredients, you will need a set of measuring cups and spoons for dry ingredients, and a graduated measure for liquids. Since you will be using a lot of liquid in some recipes, a 4-cup measure is a good choice.

THERMOMETERS

You need to use a thermometer to make a good loaf of bread. You will be checking the temperature of your liquid ingredients and the temperature of your dough. An instant-read thermometer with a long stem works well. Some electronic thermometers come with a probe and a timer. It is also helpful to have an oven thermometer, that is, a thermometer that you can leave in your oven to see whether the temperature you set is the temperature you get (see Resources, page 332).

BENCH SCRAPER

This tool resembles something you might use to spackle a wall or to lay tile. Its blunt rectangular blade has a wooden handle covering one of the long sides, and it is useful for—among other things—scraping flour and dough off of your work surface; gently lifting soft dough, such as ciabatta, when you need to fold it; and dividing or cutting your dough into portions. It is also great for cubing butter. Since the blade is not sharp, there is no risk of cutting yourself. If you don't have a bench scraper, you could use a large, sharp knife to divide your dough, but be careful.

PLASTIC SCRAPER

The shape of this scraper resembles a bench scraper, but it is flexible and made of plastic or silicone. This tool is very useful for mixing dough by hand and helps you to scrape down the sides of your bowl easily with one hand.

BENCH BRUSH

You could pay a lot of money at a kitchen supply store for one of these, or just buy a new plastic dustpan and hand brush, label them, and use them only for bread making. This helps clean flour from your work surface, and can be used to gently brush flour off of the top of your bread.

SPRAY BOTTLE

You don't need anything fancy, just something that sprays water and has an adjustable stream. You want to mist your bread dough, not rain on it.

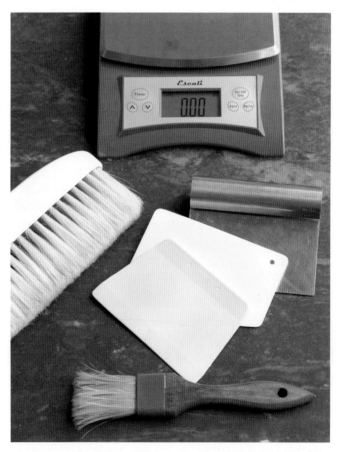

Electronic Scale, Bench and Plastic Scrapers, Pastry Brush, Bench Brush

Rolling Pins

Proofing Baskets, Linens, Couche

ROLLING PINS

Some people like rolling pins with handles. You should pick whatever works best for you, although you will need a dowel-shaped rolling pin with flat ends and no handles for making ring-shaped loaves such as gugelhopf. Picture yourself stabbing the end of the pin into the middle of a ball of dough, then using both hands to rotate the pin very quickly. The centrifugal force you create with this motion will result in a very even-looking ring. That's why you need a dowel. You may also find it handy to have a very large rolling pin for making cinnamon rolls, and a smaller one for rolling out flour tortillas.

BOWLS AND CONTAINERS

Most of the time, it is best to avoid using plastic bowls, unless you are dedicating the bowl or container to one purpose. Plastic absorbs flavors and odors, so whatever the container previously held (such as garlicky tomato sauce) will be transferred to your bread dough. If you use a stainless steel bowl, then you won't have that problem. Once you get to the point where you are developing a sour starter, it is probably worth purchasing a new plastic container with a lid that you use only for that purpose. You will need to make sure it can hold up to three quarts so that your starter can double in size.

COUCHES AND PROOFING BASKETS

A couche—meaning "resting place" in French—acts as a resting place for your shaped dough while it ferments before baking. A tablecloth made of linen or some other lint-free material can be used to create a couche for holding baguettes and batards as they rest during the final fermentation stage. Rectangular or square ones work best. Fold the tablecloth lengthwise so it is manageable, then, as you add the loaves, gently gather up a fold that almost covers the loaf; repeat with successive loaves.

A proofing basket, also known as a brotform or banneton, is made of coiled cane or plastic that bears a woven pattern. It is used for some breads during the final fermentation stage; dusted with flour and sometimes lined with linen, the basket imprints a rustic-looking flour pattern on the top and sides of the dough. The loaf is removed from the basket before baking. You can purchase these from a baking-supply store or order online (see Resources, page 332). Or you can just use a plastic bowl lined with a lint-free cloth.

COVERINGS, WRAPS AND ROLLS

You need to cover dough while it is resting to avoid creating a skin. Plastic wrap is everywhere—in fact, it's easy to argue that it is overused. Plastic provides a quick way to cover something and it wraps things well, but most often people end up throwing it out after one use. Why not go with other, more ecological options when you can?

Razors and Lame for Scoring

A clean, lint-free, moistened towel works well. If you find you are doing a lot of baking, you could go with something durable and reusable—such as a new, well-washed portion of clear plastic sheeting bought from a hardware store. If your dough is in a bowl, you could purchase a new plastic shower cap that will fit nicely around the top of the bowl. Specialty shops sell the same thing but call them plastic bowl covers. Or you could use a piece of waxed paper secured with a rubber band (make sure the piece is large enough to tuck all the way around the dough).

Sometimes, however, plastic wrap is the best choice. An example: the holiday bread stollen. Stollen needs to age at room temperature for one month after you bake it. You need to keep it tightly wrapped to prevent air and moisture from getting in, and waxed paper or foil doesn't really work.

There is one unsurpassed use for foil—to save bread that is browning too fast on the top. You can make a tent out of the foil and cover the top while the middle of the loaf finishes baking.

Last, but certainly not least, in this category is parchment paper. Parchment paper is very useful and is easy to find in your supermarket baking section. Very often it comes in a roll. What you are buying is not sheepskin, but plant-based paper that can stand up to oven heat. It can line sheets and pans, and helps you to move delicate breads from a peel (or from the back of a baking sheet) to a baking stone in the oven. Once the bread has had a chance to develop its crust, you can slide the parchment paper out from under it before the paper starts to burn. If you haven't already discovered it yourself, once you start using parchment paper you will probably wonder how you ever baked without it.

KNIVES AND MORE

Knives are part of every well-equipped kitchen. When you have a good set of knives that are fun to use, it makes every task more enjoyable. If you don't have a bench scraper, you can use a large chef's knife to divide your dough. A paring knife is good for smaller jobs, such as cutting vegetables. It is also a good idea to have a vegetable peeler and citrus zester or Microplane grater. Only a couple of the knives you use should be serrated: a smaller one to cut tomatoes, and a larger, longer one to slice bread (see Resources, page 332).

LAMES

A *lame* (pronounced LAHM, meaning "blade" in French) is a long thin stick made to hold a thin metal razor used to cut, or score, bread dough to help control the expansion of the loaf as it bakes. You can get these from baking-supply stores (see Resources, page 332). Or you can improvise by taking a double- or single-edged razor blade and carefully weaving a plastic or wooden coffee stirrer through the center holes. A box cutter will also work.

MANUAL PASTA MAKER

It is helpful to have a manual pasta machine to make flatbreads. These clamp onto the countertop and are easy to control, once you get the hang of using them. The idea is to roll the dough progressively thinner until you get a flat sheet of dough. These machines can also help you make beautiful, uniform-looking grissini breadsticks. If you don't already have a manual pasta machine, you can roll the flatbreads out with a rolling pin, and manually cut the dough into shapes or strips as directed.

Baking Pans and Molds

Many of the breads in this book turn out best when baked on a baking stone (see page 23). Still other breads work well in a pan, and their formulas are developed to be baked in just that way. The ideal pan will be heavyweight. Chicago Metallic pans (see Resources, page 332), for example, are made of durable, commercial-quality, uncoated aluminized steel. The company will tell you these can be put in the dishwasher, but don't do it! You will just have to buy more pans in less than a year because dishwashers, and any

Baking Pans and Liners

Baking Stone

soap for that matter, will ruin the finish. Don't let the avoidance of soap unnerve you. You will be putting bread dough in these pans and nothing more, and then baking at a high enough temperature to kill any organisms. To preserve the finish, and your pocketbook, you need do nothing more than wipe the pan out with a cloth and some water once you remove the bread.

The pans you need will depend on the bread you would like to make. It is handy to have a standard-sized loaf pan or two for baking pan breads and babka, for example; 10-inch round pans for making cinnamon rolls and sticky buns; a jelly-roll pan you can turn upside down for making some flatbreads; and, if you prefer, perforated baguette pans that look like a wavy piece of metal. If you buy one of these, you will need to make sure it fits into your oven. Another specialty pan you might consider is a Pullman loaf pan. This rectangular pan comes with a sliding lid to create square slices of sandwich bread with a flat top. You may also find it useful to have a square brownie pan.

Some holiday breads, such as panettone, need to be baked in a special pan to achieve their characteristic shapes. Paper panettone molds (see Resources, page 332) may be used in the standard larger size or in miniature; you may also use a coffee can with the top of the can removed. Make sure there are no ragged edges that could cut you. For breads such as babka, which are braided and contain lots of filling that spills out, you will want to use a paper pan liner. These

look like rectangular cupcake holders and you will need ones that fit your loaf pan. Or you could save money and avoid having to go to a specialty shop by using parchment paper. Cut two strips to fit each dimension of your pan both lengthwise and widthwise, running down the sides and across the bottom. Place them in the pan one at a time so that the base of the pan will have two layers of parchment. Crease the paper in the edges where the sides and base meet so that the paper tightly lines the pan.

Ovens, Baking Stones and Peels

Most people already have an oven at home and work with what they have. But what if you could choose a specific type of oven to install in your home for baking? Should you go with gas, electric, convection, steam-injected? Do high-end models work better? It may surprise you that today's electric ovens are among the most consistent for even heating and temperature control. Is convection worth having? Not really. As for steam injection, it is nice to have this feature if you can afford it. Some models come with a well in the oven for adding water to create steam. Others have a steam line that needs to be connected. Some home oven models even have a "proof" setting. You can see whether that would work for you, but there are lots of ways to proof dough without it. If you have no plans to buy a new oven, the most important thing to do is to read

Equipment for Loading the Bread: Oven Peels and Spray Bottle

parchment paper on top. Remember to protect your hands from the heat of the oven with a baking mitt or pot holder.

Commercial bakeries also use something called a loader, a giant conveyor-type device that can roll a number of unbaked loaves onto the floor of an oven. There is a smaller home version of this called the Super Peel. This would be useful to load delicate items onto a stone (see Resources, page 332).

Cooling Racks

Should you really invest in one of these? The answer is yes—if you plan on doing a lot of baking! A wire (or wooden) rack lets the air circulate around the bread and helps the crust stay crisp after baking. You can cool a loaf of bread on a plate or on the counter, but you may find that the bottom, or whichever part of the bread is resting against the surface, gets soggy or gummy. If you don't have a cooling rack, you can try turning the bread every few minutes after you've taken it out of the oven (or out of the pan, if that is the type of bread you've baked) so that no particular side sits for too long.

the manual that came with the oven you have. Invest in an oven thermometer and use it to check whether your oven temperature is accurate and whether there are hot spots. If your oven needs recalibrating, call a professional.

Do you need a baking stone? Not technically, but most bread comes out better when baked on a stone. Placed in the oven before preheating (you need a good hour for it to get hot enough), the stone provides a high amount of bottom heat, helping to push the loaf up. In other words, it helps the loaf attain higher oven-spring. You can use an overturned cookie sheet if you don't have a baking stone yet (see page 332), but you can buy a baking stone without making a big investment. An ideal baking stone is ½–¾ inch thick and can be had for $65–$75 (see Resources, page 332). Or you could try using a pizza stone kit that is widely available at some of the major discount retailers. These are priced as low as $20 and include a pizza peel, which will come in handy when it's time to remove your bread from the oven.

Speaking of peels—these are the large paddles with long handles that bakers use to transfer bread dough into the oven, and to take the finished bread out. Commercial ovens tend to be deep enough that a long-handled peel is necessary. That would be impractical in a home kitchen, however, so it is best to purchase a peel with a shorter handle that feels good in your hand. You can also use the backside of a baking sheet (a cookie sheet with no sides) with some

A Baker's Choices Make a Difference

This chapter has covered a lot of ground, discussing the basic bread-making ingredients as well as enrichments and inclusions, along with key equipment and options that can make the process easier and more successful. There are a lot of details to absorb. One thing you should take away from these pages is this: For every action in baking there will be a reaction. The choices you make at each stage, even before you begin mixing, will affect how your bread turns out. Try to make conscious decisions about the flour, salt and yeast you choose; the water and other ingredients you use; and the tools you employ. If your options are limited by budget, availability or space, make note of what you are using at each stage and try to determine how that impacts your baking. Then adjust where you can. Don't, however, let the weight of each decision keep you from baking. The most important thing is to keep making bread, no matter what your resources. Above all else, it's important to enjoy the process. With that said, it's time now to move on to the next chapter and the basic things you need to know about baking bread. This is where all of your senses, and your analytical sensibility, will be put to good use.

THE BASICS OF **Bread Making**

Once you have filled your pantry and equipped your kitchen, it is time to get down to the business of baking. Earlier, in Chapter 1, you were briefly acquainted with what occurs during the various steps in bread making, and the differences between lean breads (flour, water, salt and yeast) and enriched breads (added fats, eggs and sugar). In this chapter, you will learn more about the overall process of bread making itself, and emerge with the tools to create such classics as baguettes and ciabatta (good examples of lean breads), whole wheat bread and rustic rye. Flatbreads, including pizza and the Italian breadsticks grissini, will also be within your grasp, as well as basic enriched breads such as hamburger buns, savory ham and provolone bread, buttery babka and challah.

CHAPTER THREE

ONCE YOU'VE GAINED SKILLS with these basic recipes, you can go on to tackle the more complicated varieties of bread covered later in this book.

Whether you are making something simple and classic or exotic and complicated, there are a dozen basic steps to bread making.

The Twelve Steps of Bread Making

Before You Begin

Before you do anything, read the recipe you are using so you can make sure you understand the ingredients you need, and the techniques and the timetable you are to follow. Next, it is important to get out your thermometer. With a thermometer, you can make sure the ingredients are at the correct temperature so you can provide the right environment for the yeast. As mentioned in the preceding chapters, yeast generally prefers a temperature of about 80°F. Your recipe will tell you what temperature your liquids should be, and what temperature you should be shooting for once your dough is mixed. The final dough temperature (FDT) is crucial to the outcome of the bread. Depending on the season and conditions of the kitchen, the same dough will have a different FDT during different times of year. This will influence the length of the fermentation process, as the yeast will react differently depending on the temperature of the dough. Lean doughs require slightly cooler temperatures while rye and enriched doughs require warmer temperatures. In calculating the FDT, professional bakers account for a lot of things, including the temperature of the room and the additional heat created by the friction of the mixer. These should be compensated for by the temperature of the water; however, if the FDT is off by a degree or so, your bread will still be okay.

Just be aware that you need to control the temperature of your dough. The best way to do that is to control the temperature of your liquid, and to have the rest of your ingredients at room temperature (if specified). So, for example, take your flour out of the freezer ahead of time, if that is where you store it. If you are making an enriched bread that calls for butter, set it out earlier. If you forget, butter can be microwaved at low power for a very short time to soften it up, but sometimes it is hard to get that right. It is better to just remember to let it come to room temperature naturally.

Next, warm your liquids or cool them, as needed, according to the recipe.

Once you have mixed the dough (again, according to the recipe instructions), consider the environment into which you are placing the dough for the bulk fermentation stage. If it's a cold winter day and the temperature of your dough is cooler than expected, try to put it in a warm area, say, on top of a preheating oven or on top of your refrigerator. Check the dough periodically and move it somewhere else if it is getting too warm. In summertime, if you are in a hot kitchen, you may want to try affecting the outcome before you mix the dough: Make your water slightly cooler than directed to compensate for the ambient heat.

Also, you must keep your instant dry yeast from directly contacting salt and sugar, which pull water away from the other ingredients. Contact will slow down the yeast activity and therefore reduce its leavening ability. Blend the yeast with flour, then add the flour mixture to the mixing bowl. Now you can add the salt and sugar. You also need to make sure the yeast doesn't come into direct contact with fats or eggs in the recipe (at least not until you are mixing), which will coat the yeast granules and make it difficult to incorporate them.

Remember these four T's: Temperature, Taste, Time and Test (the gluten window).

Temperature controls fermentation. You can speed up or slow down fermentation by adjusting the temperature of the ingredients and final dough. This will affect both the flavor and texture of the dough and the final loaf.

Taste your dough to check for salt. If it is too salty, there's nothing you can do except throw it out. However, if you forgot the salt or can't taste it, you can try mixing a bit of salt with a little water first, and then mixing the saltwater with the dough. Don't forget to taste it again.

Time is also something of which you need to be mindful: Record the time you finish mixing and then mark the times you will need to fold your dough on a piece of paper to remind yourself. Use a timer if that helps. Dough ferments faster or slower as the seasons change. Keep an eye on the clock and on your dough.

And: **Test** the gluten window. This means you will periodically check to see how far along your dough's gluten structure has developed during mixing. How to do this will be explained later in this chapter in the "Mixing" section (see page 27).

You may be thinking: "This is the 'Basics of Bread Making' chapter? Twelve steps is a lot of work. Maybe I can skip some of those." DON'T! (Unless, of course, the recipe tells you to do so.) Each one of these steps, and the preparation you need to do beforehand, is important. If you want to make good bread at home, the way professional bakers make it, then you need to carry out each step as directed in your recipe. You can do it! Here's how, starting with step one.

Step 1: Scaling

The advantages of using a scale cannot be overstated. If you like to throw together your ingredients and have a "come what may" attitude, that's okay. But you can't be sure of what kind of bread you will get. Even when you use a scale, sometimes you will get a result you like, and sometimes not. You will not get a consistent result if the amount of flour you are using is not consistent. Even if you are conscientious in your method of measuring with cups and spoons, flour quality, humidity and settling can change the actual amount of flour you are measuring out. Scaling can benefit the novice baker in another important way: If you have weighed your ingredients and double-checked them, you can be confident you've done that part right. And you will be able to resist the temptation to add more flour or water to correct a dough that may look too wet or too stiff, but simply needs more mixing time.

HOW TO USE AN ELECTRONIC SCALE

No matter what kind of scale you are using, the first thing you want to do is read the owner's manual so you understand how it works. Once you are familiar with your scale's particulars, it will make getting started that much easier. Most electronic scales offer a choice between metric and U.S. measurements, so be sure that you have set it to the correct unit. Then you need to make sure you are going to measure the ingredients you are portioning out, and not the vessel into which you are placing them. Let's say you are going to weigh your flour. Once you have placed a bowl onto the scale's pad, you will need to "zero out" the weight of the bowl, then add the flour until the display shows you have reached the desired weight. As you go on to weigh additional ingredients, you could use a different container to scale each one, so you'll need to zero out the scale each time.

Weighing liquids on an electronic scale works the same way. Pick a container that will allow you to easily pour the liquid out once you've weighed it. Place it on the scale, zero out the display, then weigh your water, oil, milk and/or other liquids.

Some people like to weigh all their ingredients into the same bowl, although it's probably a good idea to weigh the dry and wet

Measuring ingredients with a scale is the most accurate method.

ingredients separately. Liquid or solid, you need a steady hand. Zero out the scale after you've measured your first ingredient, then add the second right into the bowl until you reach the desired weight. Zero out again and continue on in this manner until all of your dry or wet ingredients are in there.

Step 2: Mixing

As you mix bread dough, there are several goals you need to keep in mind. It's clear that you are trying to combine the ingredients into a homogenous mass, but that's not all. Proper mixing ensures that the flour absorbs the liquid appropriately and distributes the yeast uniformly. The right mixing technique will incorporate air, develop the gluten and may help shorten the fermentation time, resulting in bread with good volume and a good internal structure.

So what is the right mixing technique? Different types of breads rely upon different methods. There are times when you want very little gluten development, such as when making tortillas, so you mix the dough by hand just until it holds together. Professional bakers call this level of gluten development "short." When the bread you are making requires some gluten development (such as lean bread, semolina and sourdough), it is called "improved" or

Short development of dough: Dough that has reached "short" development will become a homogenous mass, but will fall apart when worked with your hands.

Improved gluten development: Dough that has reached the improved gluten development stage holds together, but tears when you check for the gluten window.

Intense development: The gluten window is transparent enough to see light through it. This means a dough has reached intense gluten development.

"partial" gluten development. You can mix these doughs by hand, as people have done for centuries, or use a mixer to get it going.

Other recipes, however, really do develop better in a mixer because of the long mixing period needed to fully develop the gluten. Bagels, bialys, challah and brioche fall into this category, called "intense" gluten development.

Most of the recipes in this book assume you will be using a heavy-duty stand mixer with a dough hook, and it is worth the investment if you don't yet have one. Hand mixers will not work. The dough gets stuck and you risk burning out the appliance. You should also never use a food processor for mixing: The sharp blade (even a plastic one) will cut the gluten you are trying to develop. Even with a stand mixer, it is a rare occasion when you will operate it on high speed for bread making. You will spend a lot of time on low and medium speeds. If the mixer heaves or walks across your kitchen counter, you need to slow it down. If you notice a burnt or electrical smell, stop what you are doing and let the mixer recover. This is when it is handy to have a similarly styled backup mixer. Then you could just move the mixing bowl to another machine and continue, remembering to use a more moderate speed.

There are several types of mixing methods, depending on the kind of bread you are making. The most straightforward way to mix, used for many lean and enriched doughs, is called "straight mixing." Here you mix all the ingredients at the same time. Gen-erally speaking, you want to put your liquids into the mixing bowl first, then add the dry ingredients on top, unless otherwise directed. This will help get everything incorporated. You will need to scrape the mixing bowl periodically, and flip the dough over in the bowl several times to make sure you don't have dry flour on the bottom of your dough. Flipping is important for another reason: Your mixer, no matter how great it is, is unable to properly mix a bread dough on its own. When you flip the dough over, it helps to pull the dough down off of the hook, allowing this part of the dough to develop as well.

There are other, more involved, mixing techniques (such as autolyse, double hydration and blitz) that will be covered in Chapter 6. But first, you need to learn how to recognize what is happening to bread dough as you mix it, and you need to understand the type of gluten development your recipe requires.

How can you check for gluten development? By looking at the gluten window. Every so often you will need to stop mixing and take a manageable piece of dough from the bowl and dip it in flour, so it will not stick to your hands. Now, rather than pulling or stretching the dough, gently work it out from underneath. If it barely holds together, this is called "short development," which is desirable for tortillas but not for bagels or brioche.

If you are making a lean dough that requires partial or "improved" gluten development, you should continue mixing, then

HAND MIXING: TORTILLAS AND LEAN DOUGH

Hand mixing is done for breads that do not require as much gluten development. Examples are lean doughs and flatbreads.

When you mix corn tortillas, you will simply combine the masa harina (corn flour treated with lime), warm water and salt by hand until it reaches a homogenous mass. Then you cover the dough and let it rest.

For flour tortillas, you will cut shortening into all-purpose flour, adding salt and hot water. You want to keep cutting the dough to expose the moist surfaces of the shortening, but just bring it together, not overwork it. Then cover the dough and let it rest.

To hand-mix lean dough, the process takes longer. The objective is partial gluten development. Put your liquids in first to help incorporate the dry ingredients better. Check the temperature with a thermometer: You will be shooting for 80°F, which will provide a friendly environment for the yeast. Adjust your water temperature as needed. Next, add the flour along with the yeast and stir them up with the water. Add the salt last, mixing by hand all the while. Squeeze and work the dough into the side of the bowl, rolling it around. Using a spoon is not recommended as the dough will just get stuck on it because it's sticky and tacky, which is good. You don't want it to be too dry. Then, gather it up (after lightly sprinkling flour on your work surface), fold in half, turn it 90 degrees, push into it, and don't use too much flour. The objective is to make it smooth, so you need dry hands. When you are done, it should remain smooth and tacky. Again, you want to fold in half, push in, make a quarter turn, and knead in this manner for a minute or two to evenly distribute the ingredients. Now it will have a little structure, but not much, so you want to let it develop during the bulk fermentation/folding stages. To prepare for this: Add ½ tsp vegetable oil to a metal bowl large enough to let the dough double in size, rub dough around in the bowl to fully coat with oil, and flip it over. Cover with a moist cloth, reusable plastic or plastic wrap, but don't let it touch the dough. Record the time mixing is complete and then mark your upcoming folding times, either on a piece of paper, or right on the disposable wrap if that's what you are using. In the wintertime, you could try to let the dough ferment on top of the refrigerator or on top of a preheating oven, or boil some water in the microwave to create warmth, remove, and place your dough in the microwave.

Fold the dough in half.

Press the dough forward and repeat to develop the gluten and incorporate the ingredients.

check the gluten window again periodically. You will know you have reached improved development if the dough holds together more, but tears as you work it.

Some doughs require "intense" development, meaning that you need to keep mixing the dough until it is fully developed. If, as you check the gluten window, the dough doesn't tear and holds a thin membrane you can see through, then the gluten is properly developed.

Checking the gluten window is important, and the stakes get higher when you are making an intensely developed bread. If you overmix the dough, the gluten will break down. The dough will go from smooth and elastic to wet and sticky. Your bread will fail, meaning that it won't rise properly or bake well. On the other hand, if you don't mix the dough enough or mix it improperly, you will also wind up with low volume and poor internal structure. Poorly mixed dough may mean that the flour does not absorb the liquids properly and that the dough turns out irregular. It will have a poor gluten structure, lack elasticity and remain wet and sticky.

One way to know when to check for gluten development is to understand the changes that occur while mixing. There are four separate mixing stages, no matter what mixing method you are using. Each stage shows a clear difference in how far along the dough has developed in gluten structure. You will know when to end the mixing process because the recipe you are using will tell you the level of development you need. Let's say you are mixing a dough that requires intense gluten development, so you are using a stand mixer. Here's what happens, start to finish:

STAGE 1: PICKUP
The pickup stage occurs soon after you have combined the liquid and dry ingredients. As you run the mixer on low speed, the dough will begin to resemble a rough, sticky mass. It will be spread out over the bottom of the mixing bowl.

STAGE 2: CLEANUP OR PRELIMINARY DEVELOPMENT
Once the pickup stage passes, you need to increase the mixer speed to moderate (just above low speed) so you can begin to develop the gluten. You will know you have reached the cleanup stage once the dough starts to form more of a ball. This is the preliminary stage of gluten development. (If you were to check the gluten window during this phase of mixing, it should indicate "short development.")

STAGE 3: INITIAL DEVELOPMENT
To move from preliminary gluten development to the stage of initial development, you need to increase the mixer to medium speed (not high speed, which would overwork the mixer, and over

time could overdevelop the dough). The dough will start to look less rough and will begin to pull away from the sides of the mixing bowl. It begins to become elastic. You will still see some dough sticking to the sides and bottom of the bowl. Checking the gluten window during this phase should reflect "improved" or "partial" gluten development. You will know you've reached this phase if, when you work the dough out for the gluten window, it is thin but won't hold together.

STAGE 4: FINAL DEVELOPMENT
To reach the final development stage, continue running the mixer on medium speed. Look for the dough to become even smoother and more elastic. The sides and bottom of the bowl will be completely clean when the mixer is running. Keep checking the gluten window to see whether you have reached intense gluten development. Again, the dough should form a thin, transparent membrane when worked with your hands. When you push on the window, it should hold.

Since you must keep testing the gluten window while mixing, it makes sense to remind you again that you need to be aware of the Four T's mentioned earlier in this chapter: Temperature, Taste, Time, and Test. When you Test for the gluten window, you will know your dough is where it should be in development. Use a thermometer to take the dough Temperature, so you know whether you need to place it in an especially cool or warm spot to compensate. Taste the dough to make sure the salt level is correct. And be aware of the Time, so you will remember when to fold the dough.

Step 3: Bulk Fermentation

Once you stop mixing, the bulk fermentation stage begins. After you take the dough out of your mixing bowl, you need to work it some more with your hands to make sure it has a smooth surface, and therefore more ability to hold in gas. Fold your dough in half, turn it 90 degrees, and repeat this process until it looks smooth and somewhat tight. Since you are working with a relatively small amount of dough, you need to place it in an oiled bowl during this phase, even if it is stiff enough to hold its own shape. Covering the bowl will help to prevent a skin from forming and it will also help keep the dough warm. Make sure your container is large enough for the dough to double in size and put it in a warm area (such as on top of the refrigerator or on top of the stove while warming up the oven). The goal here is to give the gluten strands a chance to relax, and to let the yeast ferment.

During fermentation, the yeast consumes the sugars in the flour and produces carbon dioxide and alcohol. The alcohol contributes to the flavor of your dough, and in most basic breads, bulk fermentation is the first chance your dough will have to develop flavor as a whole. The time your dough spends in bulk fermentation will help to improve the taste of your bread in the end. The alcohol produced by the yeast also makes the gluten strands more tender, resulting in a more expansive loaf with a yielding and chewy texture. The carbon dioxide produced by the yeast is dispersed in the liquid part of the dough. It will play an even greater role later, when the heat of the oven turns the remaining carbon dioxide into gas.

Bulk fermentation continues on through the folding process, where you will stretch the gluten to help it further develop. Generally you will fold it when the dough has doubled in size, but your recipe will confirm what to do.

Some basic doughs, such as pizza dough, bulk ferment for a short time at room temperature, and are then refrigerated overnight to "retard" or slow the rate of fermentation. Some other enriched and fully developed doughs, such as sweet dough and brioche, are taken directly from the mixing bowl and refrigerated (well wrapped). By fermenting the dough at a much lower temperature for a few hours or overnight, not only will the gluten have more time to relax, but your dough will have more flavor and beneficial acids.

Doughs that do not contain yeast skip the bulk fermentation phase altogether, because there is nothing to ferment. Tortillas, for example, simply rest after mixing and before preshaping. Tortillas also skip the folding stage.

Step 4: Folding

As mentioned earlier, folding occurs during the bulk fermentation phase, usually when the dough has doubled in size. There are several reasons to do this. Folding expels some of the carbon dioxide. It also helps develop the gluten structure, which will allow the dough to retain some of the gases when it bakes and therefore produce a higher, lighter loaf. Additionally, the act of folding redistributes food and warmth for the yeast by moving the temperature and ingredients in the middle of the dough to the outside.

When and how often to fold depends upon how much gluten development your dough has achieved during the mixing phase. For example, lean breads, which are not mixed as much as enriched breads, require more folding to further develop the gluten. Some intensely developed breads are not folded at all: Challah and sunflower rolls fall into this category. Rye dough also skips the folding phase, but it is in its own special category. Rye contains far less gluten than wheat dough and has a high percentage of pentosan

To fold the dough, gently stretch and fold in thirds.

gums, which account for its unique texture. Because you want to avoid overdeveloping rye dough and making it too gummy, rye is mixed only to the "improved" stage of gluten development. It is not folded during bulk fermentation for the same reason.

If folding sounds new to you, perhaps it's because in the past you've "punched down" or "deflated" your bread dough, or heard others describe it that way. This is too rough a treatment for the gluten you are trying to develop. Resist the temptation to pummel the dough: Think of it not as an adversary, but an ally.

So how do you fold? Pretty much exactly as it sounds. You gently stretch the dough to elongate it. Next, fold it into thirds like a sheet or a towel, making sure there is no flour on the dough. You don't want raw flour dispersed into your bread.

Then, for larger pieces of dough, fold the resultant rectangle in half widthwise. Lightly flour it over and under, and place the seam on the bottom.

For soft dough, pick it up gently (so you will not degas it or damage the gluten structure) and set it back down into your bowl. You might need to add a little oil to the bowl to keep it from sticking. If your dough was stiff enough to be resting on the counter, then put it back in its place. And that is it. Cover your dough, and watch the clock until your next scheduled folding time.

Step 5: Dividing

Once bulk fermentation and folding are done, it is time to divide your dough. Most often you will make enough dough for two loaves of bread, or you will prepare rolls or flat breads that need to be divided into appropriately sized pieces. Here again, you need to get out your scale. Eyeballing it can lead to uneven-sized loaves or rolls. Using a bench scraper (which has a wide, blunt blade) is the safest, easiest way to cut up the dough. Look at your recipe and determine how much each piece of dough should weigh. Or, you can weigh the whole dough and then divide the weight by the number of loaves or rolls you want to make. Be accurate. Evenly divided dough looks good and takes a similar length of time to bake.

If the pad on your scale is too small to accommodate the pieces, you could set a plate on it first, but remember to zero out the scale before weighing the dough. Then put some dough on there, and add more or subtract until you get the right weight. Work quickly: When you cut the gluten strands in the dough, they will no longer be able to retain carbon dioxide. The goal is to divide quickly and then preshape as soon as you can, to tighten the gluten back up so it can trap the gas. As you work, make sure you keep the divided pieces covered. If you are making rolls, for example, try to place them in order of when you've divided them. When it is time to start preshaping the pieces, work with the first piece of dough you cut, and continue on until you reach the last piece.

Step 6: Preshaping

Preshaping is the first stage of shaping. The goal is to gently round and seal off the surface of the loaf or roll you are making and give it structure again so it can contain the carbon dioxide gas. As mentioned above, you will want to work in an organized fashion, starting with the first piece you divided, and ending with the last. Almost all doughs receive a preshaping, but there are exceptions. Ciabatta is not preshaped because its dough is very soft and delicate. And sometimes round loaves do not need to be preshaped. Your recipe will tell you if this is the case.

PRESHAPING ROUND LOAVES AND ROLLS

Preshaping is fairly similar for most round breads. Gently pat a piece of dough down, fold it in half and turn it 90 degrees. Repeat two times more: fold in half, quarter turn, fold in half, quarter turn. Next you want to tuck the ends of the dough underneath, making sure the top stays on the top. Now, pull the dough toward you, cupping it with both hands, pinkies outside dragging along the dough against your work surface to tighten it. Make sure you are pulling straight toward yourself and not pulling your hands up and under the dough. Do this three times: tuck, cup, pull and quarter turn. Place your preshaped dough, with the seam side up, back under its cover to avoid creating a skin.

If you are working with smaller rolls, you can use one hand to tighten the dough: Make your hand into a bear claw and place it over the dough so that the ball is pushed up against the fleshy part of your hand. Rotate your hand without rolling the dough over: You are trying to tighten the dough and round it, but not roll it into a ball. It helps to keep the dough in the area between the thumb and the index finger while putting slight downward pressure on it. Make sure your work surface is clean and has no flour on it (again, to avoid incorporating raw flour into your dough). You can moisten the work surface with a little water if you find it too dry.

Preshape to tighten the dough, but cover during resting or fermentation to avoid the formation of a skin.

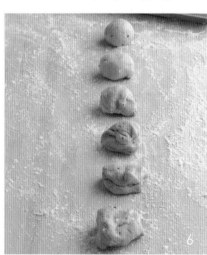

1. Fold one portion of the dough over two thirds. This will help ensure the seam of the bread is in one place on the bottom in the final shape.

2. Fold the new edge of the dough over to meet the other edge.

3. Using one hand, cup the dough between your thumb and forefinger, making sure the bottom of your hand is touching the table. Apply just enough pressure to the top of the dough so that you can feel it is secured in your hand.

4. Move your hand in a clockwise circle, keeping your hand on the table surface at all times. Pinch the dough under when it hits your pinky finger and release pressure slightly when it reaches your thumb. If you

are having difficulty controlling the dough, try lightly dampening the table surface with either water or oil.

5. Space the rolls out evenly on a baking tray lined with parchment paper. The rolls will double in size before being baked, so make sure you leave enough space in between so that they do not run into each other later. You will not want to move the rolls once they are fully proofed.

6. In each step, the main thing to ensure is that there are no seams or creases at the top of the dough. This will help create a beautiful final shape.

The progression of shaping an oblong

Step 7: Bench Rest

Bench rest, also known as intermediate fermentation, is the second time your dough will ferment. Mostly, though, you are letting the gluten relax and rest before you coax it into its final shape before baking. Here, you keep the preshaped dough covered for 10 to 20 minutes.

Step 8: Shaping

In this phase, you are giving your bread its final shape. You want to tighten the outer strands of gluten so that, once in the oven, they will do a better job of holding in the expanding carbon dioxide gas and give you a lighter loaf. What determines shape? Professional bakers use traditional shapes to help identify specific types of bread at a glance in the bakery. Some of these shapes uniquely suit the bread. Rye, for example, lends itself to a more blunt shape because it is a dense bread.

The action of shaping is similar in some ways to preshaping, especially for round loaves and rolls. Remember to avoid using too much flour: Raw flour could get caught up in the seam and end up in the middle of your baked bread. Use as little flour as possible to prevent the dough from sticking. It's good to have some friction with the work surface when you are shaping. Keep your hands as dry as possible.

SHAPING A BOULE

To shape a boule, you will need dough that has been preshaped into a round (see "Preshaping," page 32). The weight of your dough will vary depending on the recipe you are making. Fold the dough in half, then rotate it a quarter turn. Repeat this motion two more times: fold, quarter turn, fold, quarter turn. By doing this you are helping to expel some of the gas. Your next task is to tighten the dough. Tuck under the ends, cup the dough with both hands and pull toward yourself with your pinkies dragging along the bottom side. You should feel some dough under your pinkies as you pull. Repeat this action three to four times, giving a quarter turn each time, so that the dough is smooth and tight. Do not roll the dough over. The objective is to use the resistance of the table to tighten the dough—not to further round it.

Next, flour a basket (you can also use a bowl with a cloth napkin placed inside), lightly roll the dough in the flour, knock off the

PRESHAPING OBLONG LOAVES AND ROLLS

Loaves and rolls that are oblong, such as baguettes and batards, are gently preshaped into a cylinder. Gently stretch the piece of dough into a rectangle—about 10 inches long for a loaf or 3 inches long for a roll. You want the long side of the rectangle to be parallel to your work surface. Fold each of the rectangle's short sides into the middle of the dough, pressing it gently with your fingertips.

Next, fold the long top edge of the dough down to the center, pressing it lightly down.

Fold the top edge again, this time to meet the bottom edge, and seal it along its length with the heels of your hands.

Finally, use your palms to roll the dough into an even cylinder, about 6 inches long for a loaf, and 3 inches long for a roll.

Once you have preshaped your dough, cover it again for the bench rest phase.

1. Lightly flatten the dough and fold the dough in half.

2. Fold the dough in half again to tighten.

3. Fold the dough a third time to further tighten the gluten and the surface of the dough.

4. Place the dough seam-side down on the work surface, and tighten the shape by rotating with cupped hands in a downward circular motion.

5. The progression of shaping a boule from front to back: A scaled piece of dough, folded once, folded twice, rounded with cupped hands.

excess, lightly dust the top of the dough with flour and place the dough in the basket seam-side up (this will eventually be the bottom of your loaf). Cover the dough and let it sit for final fermentation. The basket or bowl allows the dough to maintain its shape.

A dinner roll is a smaller version of a boule. You will probably use dough pieces weighing about two ounces, depending on the recipe. To shape the roll, flatten the ball of dough, fold it in half, then rotate it a quarter turn. Repeat the folding and turning two more times. Since you are using a smaller piece of dough, you can use one hand to tighten it. Make your hand into a bear claw and tuck the dough into the fleshy cave part of your hand. Rotate your

hand without rolling the dough over. Here you want to keep the ball of dough tight against the palm of your hand, exerting downward pressure between your thumb and index finger. This achieves the same end as the tuck, cup, pull action (see page 34). Remember, you are tightening the dough, not trying to round it further, so do not let the dough roll over. Keep the top of the dough at the top, and tighten the ball. If you find the "bear claw" technique is not working for you, you can try using the two-handed method described on page 34 for the larger boule.

SHAPING A BAGUETTE

1. After bench rest, gently press to slightly degas. Pull the top edge down one third of the way and press slightly to secure. Repeat to form a cylinder. On the last fold, pinch down the edge so that the seam doesn't open up when rolling out the dough.

2. Seal the seam of the baguette with the palm of your hand.

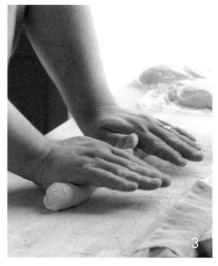

3. To begin rolling, keep both hands in the center of the dough and apply very little pressure. This should be the widest part of the baguette. Continue rocking your hands back and forth evenly along the dough, spreading them apart as you move toward the ends. Try to keep them moving in the same direction at the same time to avoid twisting the dough.

4. As you reach the end of the dough, apply slightly more pressure with the palms of your hands so that the ends are skinnier than the middle. Use the least amount of movement possible so as to avoid overworking the dough and deflating the air pockets.

The progression of shaping a baguette from top to bottom

stone and will allow you to load your bread into the oven easily. You can make a longer and thinner baguette if you use a baguette baking screen that can slide directly into your oven. These baking screens look like wavy, perforated pieces of corrugated metal. Just make sure the screen will fit your oven before you get to this stage.) Next, take the top, long edge of the dough and fold it down to the center, pressing with your fingertips to tighten the dough. Take the newly formed top edge and fold it down to meet the bottom edge, pressing the edges together with the heels of your hands. Try to keep the seam you are making straight. Now, gently roll it into a cylinder about 12 inches long. Once you have the cylinder, elongate it with the palms of your hands, rolling it with even pressure. Place the loaf seam-side up in a couche for the final fermentation stage.

SHAPING A BAGUETTE

To give a baguette its final shape, position your preshaped dough, relaxed from its bench rest, lengthwise along your work surface, seam side up. Gently stretch it into a rectangle about 8 inches long. (This length can be accommodated by the size of your baking

SHAPING A BATARD

To shape an oblong loaf or batard, form a rectangle with your pre-shaped dough, making sure it is seam-side up and horizontal to the edge of the work surface. It will be loose, so grab it at the edge of the rectangle and push against the table three times to elongate it slightly. Then, fold in the two long sides of the dough to meet in the center, pushing your fingers at a 45-degree angle through the dough to the table. Generally, you should apply light pressure,

HOW TO APPLY SEEDS

Why put seeds on the outside of the bread? It looks good. Also, a multigrain bread that has some rolled oats or other seeds scattered on the top helps identify what's inside. Seeds can also change the character and flavor of the bread. Plain semolina bread is earthy and delicious, but if you roll the loaf in sesame seeds before baking, it takes on a nutty and sweet character. A mixture of caraway and salt on the outside of rye bread adds crunch and flavor.

So how do you get the seeds to adhere? You can accomplish this by misting the top of the bread with water, then scattering the seeds. You may also roll the loaf on a moistened towel, and then roll the moistened loaf in a pan filled with seeds (keep the seam side up when you do this so water and seeds don't get trapped in there). You can also apply seeds, such as poppy and sun-flower, after egg washing. Unlike some of the heartier grains that may go inside a loaf of bread, you don't have to soak seeds that are going on the outside.

If salt is part of your bread top-ping, you don't want to spray the salt with water before baking: It will partially dissolve and you won't get the desired effect.

Applying seeds to a shaped piece of bread dough

not too hard or too soft, so you don't degas the dough (unless your recipe directs you to press down tightly). Pull the top edge down one third of the way in the same manner, then the final third in the same way to form a cylinder. With each fold, you should feel the bread getting firmer. Make sure the seam is closed all the way.

Now, with the seam on the bottom, roll the dough with your hands on the edges at a 45-degree angle to tighten the ends. Place it in a couche with the seam side up for final fermentation (for instructions on how to make a couche, see page 20).

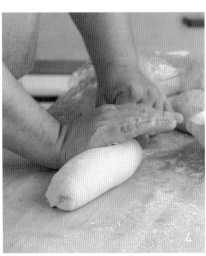

1. Relax the portioned dough by gently pulling it into a rectangle. This will help form the ultimate shape of the dough, making the rest of the forming easier to accomplish.

2. Fold in the two sides of the dough to meet in the center. Press slightly just to secure them.

3. Pull the top edge down one third of the way and press slightly to secure. Repeat to form a cylinder. On the last fold, use the bottom edge of your palm to pinch down the seam so it doesn't open up during baking.

4. Seal the seam of the loaf with the palm of your hand.

5. Roll the dough briefly to taper the edges to give it a nice final shape. Apply slightly greater pressure to the ends as you give them a final roll to seal them closed. Place the dough in a cloth-lined basket to keep the shape during baking.

6. The progression of shaping a batard from bottom to top.

Step 9: Final Fermentation

Final fermentation is the third stage of fermentation. This stage is also known as "proofing." Here again, the dough is kept covered and it is allowed to relax and ferment a while longer before it is scored and placed in the oven for baking. Professionals often use a proofing box that allows them to control the temperature and humidity so that conditions are ideal for the shaped loaf to relax and trap more gas. The ambient temperature, and the temperature of your loaf, will determine how long your bread needs to proof, so you will need to check it frequently. Assuming you don't have a proofing box, you can gently mist your bread with a spray bottle before you cover it to keep it moist. Spray again as needed.

How do you know when you bread is ready to bake? Use the finger test: Upon pressing the dough with a moist finger, it should come back halfway. If the dough comes back all or most of the way, it's not ready. If the indentation you made stays there, your dough has fermented too long.

Top to bottom: Overproofed bread; Properly proofed bread;
Underproofed bread

EGG WASHING

A classic example of an egg-washed bread is challah. Think about this bread's beautiful, glossy braid; its deep brown color; its moist richness and tender crust. The appearance and texture of the challah's crust are due in part to egg washing.

When you egg wash a loaf of bread, you usually do it twice: once after the bread is shaped, to seal it while it is fermenting, and a second time right before the bread goes into the oven. (Remember to cover your shaped and fermenting dough after the initial egg wash. Whether you are using plastic wrap or going with something reusable, spray the wrap with oil so it won't stick to the dough.) In general, breads that are egg washed are not misted before baking, and they are not scored. You can apply seeds to bread that is egg washed. Let's say you are making sunflower rolls. Egg wash the rolls after you form them. Egg wash again after the rolls have proofed, then sprinkle the seeds on top before baking.

A good rule of thumb for making egg wash is to use one whole egg plus one yolk. This gives a better shine due to the additional fat from the yolk. Add a little salt to the egg wash to help break down the proteins in the eggs, which will make the egg more homogenous (the addition of salt will also change the egg wash's color to a deep orange, like orange juice). Add a little water to the wash to make it more pliable. Finally, strain the egg wash through a sifter to remove any parts of the egg that didn't incorporate.

The egg wash can be kept at room temperature for the time you are using it. Make sure not to keep your brush in the egg wash. Set the brush aside on a saucer or spoon rest between applications. After you are finished, wash the brush well and allow it to dry out fully.

Step 10: Scoring

Score a loaf of bread with a razor, sharp knife or scissors just before baking. It helps dictate where the crust will break, and allows for a pleasing appearance and an even crumb. Scoring also lets steam escape and allows the bread to expand more during the crucial first stage of oven-spring. Some breads do not need scoring, such as ciabatta, which is an extremely wet dough. Nor do enriched breads require scoring. The fats and sugars in enriched doughs tenderize the gluten strands enough so that scoring would weaken the dough's structure and soften it too much. But other doughs must be scored—otherwise they will turn out misshapen and denser than they should be.

Scoring can also help identify a type of bread once it is baked. For example, there is no mistaking a classic baguette.

HOW TO SCORE A BAGUETTE

There is definitely a right way and wrong way to do this. You can use a lame or a box cutter (see page 21). Angle the blade at 45 degrees, and make three to five diagonal and overlapping cuts of the same length and depth (about ¼ inch) on the loaf.

You may not get the correct scoring technique the first time you try it. It takes practice, so allow yourself time to practice. "Play dough" is a great tool to help with better scoring. Fashion some dough into a loaf, and practice scoring on it.

Another scoring technique for baguettes is to try cutting down the center of the loaf at a 90-degree angle (which is a common scoring technique for rye bread). This allows the bread to expand more and is an easy way to get variety in appearance.

OTHER SCORING TECHNIQUES

There are plenty of other ways to score bread. When you have a round country loaf, you want to score it evenly over its surface, holding your scoring tool at a 45-degree angle. You can make parallel cuts, hatches or wheat patterns, or come up with your own signature score.

When making an X, it works better if you make one leg of the X a full-length cut, then finish the other leg with two cuts. This is especially true of smaller rolls. Using scissors to cut your X pattern will result in a raised effect.

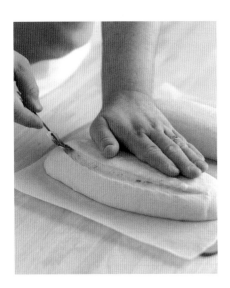

Scoring a batard

Scoring a baguette: If you don't angle the blade, the cuts may gape open. You want to avoid making the loaf look like a striped candy cane. Nor do you want the baguette to have cuts of different lengths, or you will get an irregularly shaped loaf.

Scoring craquelin with scissors

Oblong loaves follow essentially the same principle for scoring, with evenly distributed cuts. Symmetry makes for a pleasing look. You can also follow the curve of the loaf, scoring one side in an elongated C shape.

When scoring rye bread, you are trying to open up the loaf so it can reach its rising potential. Use a 90-degree angle and slash down the middle of an oblong loaf or create an X in the center of the loaf.

After scoring, your bread should go right into the oven. Lean breads benefit from another quick mist from a spray bottle before being loaded onto a baking stone or tray. This will help prevent the crust from forming too early while baking, allowing for a higher loaf.

Step 11: Baking

On the most basic level, when you bake raw bread dough, you are turning it into something edible. The yeast in your dough gently ferments at somewhere between 70 and 80°F during final fermentation, then it encounters a dramatic temperature increase when it starts baking. Depending on the bread, the oven can be as high as 500°F. The jolt in temperature causes "oven-spring," the last stage of fermentation. Steaming helps this along. Here, the yeast amps up its activity, producing even more carbon dioxide and alcohol. The loaf expands very quickly until its internal temperature reaches about 140°F, when the yeast dies off and most of the carbon dioxide is spent. The alcohol, which helps flavor the bread, evaporates.

Meanwhile, enzymes on the outside of the dough help to convert starches into sugars, setting things up for a brown crust later. As the dough temperature heads higher, the starches inside it absorb water in a process called "gelatinization," which helps form the bread's crumb. At the same time, the proteins in the dough are coagulating. What does this mean? The gluten strands you worked so hard to develop, after stretching once more to trap the carbon dioxide gas during oven-spring, will stop this expansion and set the structure of your loaf once the internal temperature approaches 200°F.

Next, your bread's crust has to brown. As the surface of the loaf gets hotter, something called the Maillard reaction occurs. The heat and residual moisture in the oven combine with the proteins and sugars on the outside of the bread to create a pleasing, rich brown color. Caramelization also contributes to browning as the surface temperature of the bread gets even hotter. Your bread is done when the inside of it measures between 195 and 210°F and it is properly browned.

Not all types of bread are baked the same way. Lean doughs, made with just a few ingredients, bake at temperatures between 450 and 500°F. Enriched doughs with added fats and sugars must be baked at lower temperatures (350–400°F), to avoid burning the crust.

When you place your loaf in the oven, either directly on a baking stone or in a pan, try not to leave the door open long. Before you open the door, have your oven mitts on and place your bread on a peel or on the backside of a baking tray. If your recipe calls for a pan bread, then have the pan where you can readily reach it. You will generally preheat at a slightly higher temperature than needed for final baking, so, when ready, place the bread in the oven, close the door, and lower the thermostat to its actual baking temperature.

STEAMING AND VENTING

It is during the first stage of baking, in most cases, that you want to use steam. The steam keeps the outside of the bread moist and allows the loaf to expand more before it is confined by the formation of the crust. Do you really need to steam? If you've gotten this far in the process, why leave things to chance? Why not bake the best bread you can? You don't need an oven with fancy settings to create steam, but if you have one, go ahead and use it. It's safe to say a lot of home bakers have very standard ovens. If you are one of those people, here's what to do: First, preheat your oven. About 15 minutes before you plan to put your bread in, fill a rimmed cookie sheet or cast-iron skillet halfway with water and place it on the bottom rack. This way, you'll have the right amount of steam when it's time to load the bread. You'll need to vent (open) the oven a few minutes later once oven-spring is over (your recipe should tell you when exactly). You can prop open your oven door with a metal spoon (remember to use an oven mitt) to allow the steam to escape if you have no other way to vent it.

HOW TO TELL WHEN IT'S DONE

Short of sticking a thermometer into your bread (which you can do if you choose), you can tell your bread is done if the crust is nicely browned and it sounds hollow when you gently knock it on the bottom.

Once baked, there is one more important step to ensuring you get a good loaf of bread. Let it cool properly.

Step 12: Cooling

When your bread comes out of the oven, you should take it right out of the pan if you are using one. Don't forget to use mitts to protect your hands from burning. If the bread seems stuck in the

USING A PEEL TO LOAD YOUR BREAD

What is a peel? In a professional bake-shop, it is typically a long-handled wooden tool that looks like a flat shovel. The wide part at the end can accommodate one or more loaves of bread, and allows the baker to load bread all the way into the back of the oven and pull it out without burning himself or herself. You don't need to have a peel to bake bread, but using one can make the process easier and safer. Unless your home kitchen is particularly roomy and/or equipped with an extra-deep oven, having a long-handled peel will be awkward and unnecessary. You can use one of those inexpensive wooden pizza peels that are sold at major retailers, or even the back of a sheet tray. The idea is to put your loaf of bread on the wide part of the peel (placing parchment paper underneath the loaf makes it easy to load and unload the bread). Open the oven and, using oven mitts to protect your hands, prepare to load your bread onto the baking stone in the oven. Hold the peel's handle and place the wide part of the peel on the stone. Then give it a gentle forward thrust with your hands and pull back to slide the bread off of the peel and onto the stone. Close the door. Once the bread has had a chance to set up (12–15 minutes), you may use the peel to help remove the parchment paper before it starts burning. Gently slide the paper out from under the loaf and use the peel to keep the bread in place on the stone. Meanwhile, get your cooling rack set up. When the bread is done, put on your oven mitts again. Open the oven door and gently slide the peel under the bread. Use the peel to slide the bread onto your cooling rack.

Professional bakeshops also often use conveyor-type peels. These peels are long and have cloth belts, which are particularly useful for loading delicate breads such as pizza. A smaller, shorter version of this rolling conveyor-type peel (suitable for home bakers) can be ordered online at www.superpeel.com. Also, see Resources, page 332.

Loading baguettes into the oven

pan, tap the pan on the counter a few times and the bread should come right out. Placing the bread on a cooling rack is important. This allows for proper airflow, it lets the crust set up properly, and the bottom of the loaf won't get gummy from being in contact with a solid surface. Cooling is an important step. Resist the temptation to tear right into the warm loaf of bread you just baked—you've made it this far through the process. A cooled loaf of bread will keep its shape and the crust will look good, just as it does in a professional bakery.

When Do We Eat?

Once the bread has cooled, it's time to enjoy it. You've worked very hard, so sit down and savor it. Once you have broken off a piece, or sliced what you want, give yourself a chance to inhale the bread's aroma. Taste it and think about the nuances of its flavor and texture.

How to Slice

Don't try to slice bread that is fresh from the oven. It needs a little time to set up and cool off or it may stick together, tear or fall apart. When you're ready to slice, use a serrated knife. The teeth on the knife allow for even cuts and won't squish the bread as you slice. Remember to keep your fingers out of the way and focus on what you are doing so you don't accidentally cut yourself. Slice gently, without too much of a sawing motion.

To slice bread lengthwise, place your loaf, roll or bagel on a work surface. Hold the top with your nondominant hand. Keeping your fingers out of the way, gently work the knife along the length of the bread. Never slice toward you while holding the bread perpendicularly. This is dangerous.

Storing Baked Bread

Generally, you want to eat your bread within a day or two of baking it. Keep it loosely covered. Some breads stay fresh longer—especially rye bread, sweet breads and breads made with preferments. If you think you have more bread than you need, don't put it in the refrigerator; this will only make it go stale more quickly. You can place extra loaves, portions of loaves, rolls or slices of bread in the freezer, where they will keep for several months if well wrapped in plastic and foil. When you're ready to use the bread, just take it out ahead of time and let it defrost at room temperature. If it was fresh when you put it in the freezer, you won't be able to tell the bread was frozen once it's thawed.

You may also recrisp crusty breads, if needed. Preheat your oven to 450°F with a baking stone in place if you have one. Load the bread onto the stone, close the door, and 8 to 10 minutes later it should be just right.

Become a Better Baker

You now have the keys to making basic loaves of bread and rolls. As you explore the recipes in the next few chapters, think about how your actions affect each outcome. Most important of all, however, is to enjoy baking, enjoy eating and do it often.

Breads and Rolls

Flour. Water. Yeast. Salt. Sometimes it's easy to forget that these four basics are all you need to make a loaf of bread. Many of the loaves in today's grocery aisles have a much longer list of ingredients—some of which are nearly indecipherable. Why? These extras help age and enrich the flour, condition the dough (making it easier for the bakery to turn out more loaves faster), and help the bread stay on the grocery shelf longer, among other things. One of the reasons to bake your own bread is to be able to avoid buying such "bread." It's not snobbish to want something good and honest to eat.

CHAPTER FOUR

You may notice that this chapter has the fewest recipes in the book. It is meant to help you get started with your hands-on bread-baking self-education. Here you will find "straight development" breads, meaning that you mix the dough, let it ferment for a short period of time, and bake it, all within a few hours. These recipes cover the classic lean breads, including crusty baguettes, hearty whole wheat and rustic rye. If you want more fiber in your diet, you can choose to make multigrain or oatmeal bread. And there are two variations of rosemary durum bread, which goes well with a bowl of pasta and a salad. You can also choose to make any of these breads into rolls.

When you steep yourself in the twelve steps of bread baking and master the basics—as you will with these recipes—you may eventually find yourself wanting more. More flavor, more texture, more crustiness. If you go to a fine neighborhood bakery, you may wonder what it is the people who work there are doing that you're not. It is not necessarily that they're using a fancier oven. The truth is, the depth and complexity of flavor and texture in a loaf of bread has a direct relationship with how long the dough ferments and the amount of acidity that develops. Once you get used to eating real bread, your palate will become more attuned to how bread should taste, especially if you are baking your own and comparing your basic efforts to more complex breads made by a professional. This is a good problem to have. Make these basic breads and get confidence, so you can grow into the kind of baker who can make the bread you really want to eat.

Hoagie and Kaiser Rolls

The hoagie sandwich originated in Philadelphia and is usually filled with Italian cold meats and dressings as well as cheese, lettuce and tomato. Today it goes by many names, depending on which area of the country you are in. It makes a great on-the-go meal.

yield: 9 rolls at 4.5 oz | FDT: 82°F

bulk fermentation: 45–60 minutes | final fermentation: 45–60 minutes | bake: 400°F *and* 18–20 minutes

INGREDIENT	OUNCES	GRAMS	VOLUME	BAKERS %
Water, 80°F	13.2	374	1⅔ cups	53.0%
Malt syrup	0.1	2	⅛ tsp	0.3%
Canola oil	0.6	17	3½ tsp	2.4%
Bread flour	25.0	706	5 cups + 3 Tbsp	100.0%
Yeast, instant dry	0.2	6	1½ tsp	0.8%
Salt	0.6	17	2½ tsp	2.4%
Sugar	0.6	17	4 tsp	2.4%
TOTAL	40.3	1139	•	161.3%

1. **PUT** the water, malt and oil in the bowl of a mixer. Add the flour and yeast, then the salt and sugar. Place the bowl on a mixer fitted with a dough hook and mix for 5 minutes on low speed, making sure to scrape down and flip the dough over twice during this time. Then mix for 3 minutes on medium speed, making sure to scrape down and flip the dough over. The dough should have full gluten development and be a little tacky. Place the dough in a lightly oiled bowl large enough for it to double in size and cover with plastic wrap.

2. **ALLOW** the dough to rest and ferment for 45–60 minutes, until when touched lightly the dough springs back halfway.

3. **PLACE** the dough on a lightly floured work surface and divide it into 4.5-oz pieces. Preshape each piece into an oblong about 3 inches in length. Place the rolls on a lightly floured work surface with the seams up and cover. Allow to rest and ferment for 10 minutes, until when touched lightly the dough springs back halfway.

4. **FOR HOAGIES:** Bring the top of each piece of dough toward you one third of the way and tuck in; repeat 2 more times as on page 36. Make sure to tightly pinch the seam closed. Roll the dough out to 6 inches, making sure to taper the ends by holding your hands at a 45-degree angle to the dough, pressing the dough, and rolling. Place the rolls seam-side down on a baking tray with parchment paper, about 6 on a tray.

FOR KAISER ROLLS: Bring the top of each piece of dough toward you one third of the way and tuck in; repeat 2 more times. Make sure to tightly pinch the seam closed. Roll the dough out to 14 inches by applying downward pressure. Lightly flour the dough. Hold the dough piece in your left hand. (See illustrations in Appendix on page 328.)

5. **LIGHTLY** egg wash the rolls (see sidebar on page 50) and cover lightly with plastic wrap. Place in a warm place to relax and ferment for 45–60 minutes, until when lightly pressed the dough comes back halfway.

6. TWENTY MINUTES before the end of the final fermentation, preheat the oven to 450°F.

7. PREPARE hoagies for the oven by egg washing, scoring each one down the length and allowing them to sit for 5 minutes. Prepare the kaiser rolls for the oven by egg washing and sprinkling with seeds, if desired.

8. PLACE the trays in the oven and immediately reduce the temperature to 400°F. Bake for 15 minutes, then rotate the pans and bake for 3–5 minutes more, until they are golden brown.

9. REMOVE from the oven and place the baking trays on a cooling rack.

Hoagie and Kaiser Rolls

EGG WASH

Egg wash may be applied for three reasons: 1) to seal the product to maintain moisture, 2) to give shine and color to the crust of bread as it is baked, and 3) to act as an adhesive for garnish (a sprinkling of seeds, salt, herbs or many other ingredients used to add flavor, texture and a decorative element to breads and rolls).

When applying egg wash, make sure to apply an even, thorough, but thin coating. Areas that are missed by the wash will appear dull, lacking shine and color, and this will detract from the overall beauty of your finished bread or roll.

Egg wash is applied to bread before it is placed in the oven to bake. It also is applied at least twice: before and after final fermentation. Additionally, it may be applied during the final fermentation if the bread dough is appearing at all dry.

Egg wash that has been left to stand before use may turn a bright orange. This is not an indication of a lack of freshness, but is the result of a reaction with the salt.

EGG WASH

1 egg
1 egg yolk
⅛ tsp salt
1 tsp water

Thoroughly whisk all ingredients together. Store in an airtight container in the refrigerator until needed. To ensure the wash is completely homogenous, it may also be put through a fine-mesh sieve before applying.

WHOLE WHEAT BREAD

The warm and comforting flavor of whole wheat takes center stage in this recipe. If you wish, customize the loaf by adding your choice of seeds; this honey-brown bread is a simple delight you'll want to make again and again.

yield: 2 loaves at 24 oz | FDT: 82°F
bulk fermentation: 60–75 minutes | *final fermentation:* 45–60 minutes |
initial bake: 450°F *and* 12 minutes | *final bake:* 425°F *and* 18–20 minutes

INGREDIENT	OUNCES	GRAMS	VOLUME	BAKERS %
Water, 90°F	20.2	572	2½ cups	73.2%
Honey	1.3	36	¼ cup	4.6%
Malt syrup	0.1	2	⅛ tsp	0.5%
Bread flour	16.6	470	3⅓ cups	60.1%
Whole wheat flour	11.0	312	2½ cups	39.9%
Yeast, instant dry	0.2	7	1 tsp	0.8%
Salt	0.6	18	1 Tbsp	2.3%
TOTAL	50.0	1417	•	181.4%
GARNISH				
Seeds, if desired	as needed			

1. **PUT** the water, honey and malt in the bowl of a mixer. Combine the flours and yeast and add to the bowl, then add the salt and place the bowl on a mixer fitted with a dough hook. Mix on medium speed for 8 minutes, making sure to scrape down and flip the dough over twice during this time. After mixing, the dough should have some gluten development but feel slightly tacky. Place the dough in a lightly oiled bowl large enough for it to double in size and cover with plastic wrap.

2. **ALLOW** the dough to rest and ferment in a warm place for 45–60 minutes, until when lightly touched the dough springs back halfway.

3. **PLACE** the dough on a lightly floured work surface and stretch it out slightly. Fold the dough in thirds. Put the dough back into the bowl, re-cover it with plastic wrap, and allow it to rest for 15 minutes.

4. **IF MAKING ROUND LOAVES,** prepare plastic bowls lined with a heavy-duty paper towel, white cloth napkin or white kitchen towel. Flour the lined bowls generously (unless seeds are being applied to the loaves).

IF MAKING 12-INCH OBLONG LOAVES, line baking trays with white cloth napkins or white kitchen towels and generously flour (unless seeds are being applied to the loaves).

5. **PLACE** the dough on a lightly floured work surface and divide it into two 24-oz pieces.

FOR ROUND LOAVES, round each piece against the tabletop. To apply seeds, if using, brush or spray the loaf with water and then roll the top and sides in the seeds. Place the loaf in a prepared bowl with the seam up. Use any extra cloth to cover the loaves and then lightly cover the bowl with plastic wrap.

FOR OBLONG LOAVES, shape each dough piece into a round. Place the rounds seam-side up on the work surface, cover lightly with plastic wrap, and allow them to rest for 10 minutes. Then shape each dough into a 10-inch oblong.

6. PLACE each shaped loaf seam-side up on the prepared tray and bring the cloth up between the loaves. To apply seeds, if using, brush or spray each loaf with water and then roll the top and sides in the seeds. Place the loaves on the prepared tray with the seam sides up. Use any extra cloth to cover the loaves and then lightly cover the tray with plastic wrap.

7. PLACE the dough in a warm place for 45–60 minutes, until when lightly pressed the dough springs back halfway.

8. TWENTY MINUTES before the end of the final fermentation, preheat the oven to 475°F. Ten minutes before baking the loaves, place a tray filled with 3 cups of warm water below the baking area in the oven to help produce steam.

9. PLACE the loaves seam-side down on a peel lined with parchment paper or baking tray. Spray the tops and sides of the loaves with water and let set 5 minutes. Score the top of each loaf once lengthwise, cutting ¼–½ inch deep. Spray the loaves with water again.

10. TRANSFER the loaves with the parchment paper to the baking stone or place directly on an oven rack, and immediately reduce the temperature to 450°F. Bake for 12 minutes. Remove the steam tray and parchment paper, reduce the heat to 425°F, and bake for an additional 18–20 minutes, until the loaf has a dark color and a thick crust. If the crust isn't thick enough at the end of the baking time, turn the oven off and leave the bread in the oven with the door cracked open until the crust does not give when pressed and has a dark color.

11. REMOVE the bread from the oven and place on a cooling rack.

Whole Wheat Bread

OATMEAL BREAD

For a rustic, feel-good bread well suited for breakfast, lunch or dinner, try this lightly honey-sweetened oatmeal loaf. Toasted dry oats are mixed in to accentuate the nutty flavor of rehydrated oats in the dough. For a thicker crust, leave the loaf in the oven, turned off, with the door cracked for a short time after baking.

yield: 2 loaves at 24 oz | FDT: 82°F
soaker: 30 minutes | *bulk fermentation:* 60–75 minutes | *final fermentation:* 60–75 minutes | *bake:* 425°F *and* 20–30 minutes

INGREDIENT	OUNCES	GRAMS	VOLUME	BAKERS %
OAT SOAKER				
Water	5.0	142	⅔ cup	18.3%
Oats, rolled	3.4	96	1¼ cups	12.4%
FINAL DOUGH				
Water, 80°F	12.7	360	1½ cups	46.5%
Oat soaker	8.4	238	•	30.7%
Honey	2.4	67	3 Tbsp	8.6%
Malt syrup	0.1	4	1 tsp	0.5%
Bread flour	20.2	572	4¼ cups	73.8%
Yeast, instant dry	0.3	8	2¼ tsp	1.0%
Salt	0.6	16	1 Tbsp	2.1%
Oats, rolled, toasted	3.8	107	1½ cups	13.8%
TOTAL	48.5	1372	•	177.0%

1. MAKE the oat soaker by bringing the water to boil and pouring it over the oats. Cover with plastic wrap and allow it to sit at room temperature for 30 minutes.

2. TO MAKE THE DOUGH, combine the water, oat soaker, honey and malt in the bowl of a mixer. Place the bowl on a mixer fitted with a dough hook and mix for 2 minutes on medium speed to break down the oat soaker. Add the flour and yeast, then add the salt. Mix the dough on low speed for 4 minutes, making sure to scrape down the bowl and flip the dough over twice during the mixing process. Increase to medium speed and mix for another 3 minutes. At this point, the dough should have developed some gluten

structure and still feel slightly tacky. Add the toasted oats and mix for 1 minute on medium speed, making sure to scrape down the bowl and flip the dough over halfway through mixing. Place the dough in a lightly oiled bowl large enough for it to double in size and cover with plastic wrap.

3. ALLOW the dough to rest and ferment in a warm place for 45–60 minutes, until when lightly pressed the dough springs back halfway .

4. PLACE the dough on a lightly floured work surface, fold it into thirds, then place it back into the bowl, re-cover it, and allow it to rest for another 15 minutes.

5. PREPARE the bowls or trays for fermenting. If making round loaves, you should use small plastic bowls lined with a heavy-duty paper towel, white cloth napkin or white kitchen towel. If making oblong loaves, use a baking tray lined with a white cloth napkin or white kitchen towel. Any cloth liners will also need to be floured (unless oats are being applied to the exterior of the loaf).

6. PLACE the dough on a lightly floured work surface and divide it into two 24-oz pieces.

FOR ROUND LOAVES, round each piece against the tabletop. To apply oats, brush or spray the loaf with water and then roll the top and sides in additional oats. Place the dough in the prepared bowl with the seam up. Use any extra cloth to cover the top of the dough and then lightly cover with plastic wrap. Place the dough in a warm place and allow it to rest and ferment for 60–75 minutes, until when lightly pressed, the dough springs back halfway.

FOR OBLONG LOAVES, make rounds, then place them on the work table seam-side up, cover and allow to rest for 10 minutes. Remove the dough and shape into oblongs. Roll each dough piece until it is 12 inches long. With one hand at each end of the piece at a 45-degree angle to the dough, roll the dough to taper the ends. Place the oblong pieces on a cloth-lined tray with the seams up, and pull the cloth up to create a barrier between the 2 loaves on the tray. To apply oats, brush or spray the loaves with water, then roll the top and sides in additional oats and place the loaves on the prepared tray with the seams up. Use any extra cloth to cover the loaves, then lightly cover them with plastic wrap. Place the dough in a warm place and allow it to rest and ferment for 60–75 minutes, until when lightly pressed, the dough springs back halfway.

7. TWENTY MINUTES before the end of the final fermentation, preheat the oven to 450°F with a baking stone. Ten minutes before baking the loaves, place a tray filled with 3 cups of warm water below the baking area in the oven to help produce steam.

8. PLACE the loaves seam-side down on a peel with parchment paper or baking tray and spray the tops and sides of the loaves with water. Let the loaves sit for 5 minutes before scoring to allow the surface to absorb moisture. With a sharp razor held at a 45-degree angle to the dough, make 1 lengthwise score down the center of the loaf (about ¼–½ inch deep). After scoring, spray the loaves with water again to help create steam in the oven and allow the loaves to expand evenly.

9. TRANSFER the loaves to the baking stone or leave on the tray and immediately reduce the temperature to 425°F. Bake for 10 minutes, then remove the water tray and bake for another 10–20 minutes, to allow the loaves to finish baking and form a crust. If the crust isn't thick enough at the end of the baking time, turn the oven off but leave the bread in the oven with the door cracked open, until the loaves are golden brown and when tapped on the bottom they give a hollow sound.

10. REMOVE the bread from oven and place on a cooling rack.

DURUM AND ROSEMARY ROLLS

Durum flour—a wheat flour high in protein and gluten strength—contributes a slight yellowish hue to these aromatic rolls. Flavors of chopped rosemary and olive oil bring to mind thoughts of the Mediterranean.

yield: 22 rolls at 2 oz | FDT: 82°F
bulk fermentation: 75–90 minutes | final fermentation: 40–50 minutes | bake: 450°F *and* 18–20 minutes

INGREDIENT	OUNCES	GRAMS	VOLUME	BAKERS %
Water, 80–82°F	18.5	524	2⅓ cups	69.8%
Olive oil	0.8	23	2 Tbsp	3.0%
Malt syrup	0.1	4	⅛ tsp	0.6%
Durum flour	16.0	454	3¼ cups	60.4%
Bread flour	10.5	298	2 cups + 3 Tbsp	39.6%
Yeast, instant dry	0.3	9	1 Tbsp	1.1%
Salt	0.6	17	1 Tbsp	2.3%
Rosemary, coarsely chopped	0.3	9	2 Tbsp	1.1%
TOTAL	47.1	1338	•	177.9%

1. **PUT** the water, oil and malt in the bowl of a mixer. Combine the flours and yeast and add to the bowl, then add the salt. Place the bowl on a mixer fitted with a dough hook, and mix on medium speed for 4 minutes, making sure to scrape the bowl and flip the dough over once during mixing. Add the rosemary and mix for another minute on medium speed, making sure to flip the dough over halfway through the mixing time. Place the dough in a lightly oiled bowl large enough for it to double in size and cover with plastic wrap.

2. **ALLOW** the dough to rest and ferment in a warm place for 60–75 minutes, until when lightly pressed the dough springs back halfway.

3. **PLACE** the dough on a lightly floured work surface, and stretch it out slightly. Fold the dough in thirds. Place the dough back into the bowl, re-cover it with plastic wrap, and let it rest for an additional 15 minutes.

4. **PREPARE** a tray with a cloth that is lightly floured with durum flour.

5. **PLACE** the dough on a lightly floured work surface and divide it into 2-oz pieces. Round each piece against the tabletop. Place the rounded pieces seam-side up on the prepared tray, bringing the cloth up between each row of rolls. Cover the tray with plastic wrap and place in a warm place for 40–50 minutes, until when lightly touched the dough springs back halfway.

6. **TWENTY MINUTES** before the end of the final fermentation, preheat the oven to 475°F with a baking stone. Ten minutes before baking the loaves, place a tray filled with 3 cups of warm water below the baking area in the oven to help produce steam.

7. **THE BREAD** will be baked in 2 separate batches. Lightly flour an oven peel and place the rolls on the oven peel. Spray the rolls with water and let them rest for 5 minutes, then spray with water again. Score the tops with an X using a sharp razor blade held at a 90-degree angle to the top of the roll.

8. TRANSFER the rolls to the baking stone and immediately reduce the temperature to 450°F. Bake for 10 minutes, then remove the steam tray and continue baking for an additional 8–10 minutes, until they form a golden brown firm crust.

9. REMOVE the rolls from the oven and place on a cooling rack. Raise the oven temperature and then bake the second batch immediately.

Durum and Rosemary Rolls

DURUM, ROSEMARY AND LEMON ROLLS

Use a citrus zester for the lemons. This tool allows for finer handling of the curves of the lemon and will help to remove the yellow rind without picking up the bitter white pith as well. Wrap the leftover lemons and store in the refrigerator for fresh lemon juice.

yield: 22 rolls at 2 oz | FDT: 82°F

bulk fermentation: 75–90 minutes | final fermentation: 40–50 minutes | bake: 450°F *and* 18–19 minutes

INGREDIENT	OUNCES	GRAMS	VOLUME	BAKERS %
Water, 82°F	19.0	539	2⅓ cups	70.4%
Olive oil	0.8	23	2½ tsp	3.0%
Malt syrup	0.2	4	⅛ tsp	0.6%
Bread flour	10.7	303	2¼ cups	39.6%
Durum flour	16.3	462	3⅓ cups	60.4%
Yeast, instant dry	0.3	9	2½ tsp	1.1%
Salt	0.6	17	1 Tbsp	2.2%
Rosemary, coarsely chopped	0.3	9	2 Tbsp	1.1%
Lemon zest	0.3	9	½ tsp	1.1%
TOTAL	48.5	1375	•	179.5%

1. PUT the water, oil and malt in the bowl of a mixer. Combine the flours and yeast and add to the bowl, then add the salt. Place the bowl on a mixer fitted with a dough hook, and mix on low speed for 4 minutes, making sure to scrape the bowl and flip the dough over once during mixing. Increase to medium speed and mix for 2 minutes more to develop partial gluten structure. Add the rosemary and zest and mix for 1 minute on low speed, making sure to flip the dough over halfway through the mixing time. Place in a lightly oiled bowl large enough for it to double in size and cover with plastic wrap.

2. ALLOW the dough to rest and ferment in a warm place for 60–75 minutes, until when lightly pressed the dough springs back halfway.

3. PLACE the dough on a lightly floured surface, and stretch it out slightly. Fold the dough in thirds. Place the dough back into the bowl, re-cover it with plastic wrap, and let it rest for an additional 15 minutes.

4. PREPARE a tray with a cloth that is lightly floured with durum flour.

5. PLACE the dough on a lightly floured work surface and divide it into 2-oz pieces. Round each piece against the tabletop. Place the pieces seam-side up on the tray , bringing the cloth up between each row of rolls. Cover the tray with plastic wrap and place in a warm place for 40–50 minutes, until when lightly pressed the dough springs back halfway.

6. TWENTY MINUTES before the end of the final fermentation, preheat the oven to 475°F with a baking stone. Ten minutes before baking the rolls, place a tray filled with 3 cups of warm water below the baking area in the oven to help produce steam. You will need to bake the rolls in 2 separate batches.

7. LIGHTLY flour an oven peel and place the rolls on the oven peel with parchment paper. Spray the rolls with water and let them rest for 5 minutes. Score the tops with an X using a sharp razor held at a 90-degree angle to the top of the roll, then spray with water again.

8. TRANSFER the rolls to the baking stone and immediately reduce the temperature to 450°F. Bake for 14 minutes, then remove the steam tray and bake for an additional 4–5 minutes, until the crusts are a deep golden brown and are firm.

9. REMOVE the rolls from the oven and place on a cooling rack. Allow the oven to come back up to 475°F with a steam tray for 10 minutes, then continue from step #7 for the second batch.

Multigrain Bread

MULTIGRAIN BREAD

Do good for your heart and your stomach by eating a piece of bread from this multigrain loaf. A multigrain mixture (see Resources, page 332) is soaked to tenderize the seeds for a pleasing texture on the palate, as well as to hydrate the grains, ensuring that no dough moisture is absorbed by the seeds during baking.

yield: 2 loaves at 24 oz | FDT: 82°F
bulk fermentation: 60–75 minutes | final fermentation: 45–60 minutes |
initial bake: 450°F *and* 15 minutes | final bake: 425°F *and* 12–15 minutes

INGREDIENT	OUNCES	GRAMS	VOLUME	BAKERS %
GRAIN SOAKER				
Water, 80°F	7.1	201	⅞ cup	26.0%
Multigrain mixture	6.6	187	1 cup	24.4%
FINAL DOUGH				
Water, 80°F	11.8	333	1½ cups	42.2%
Honey	1.2	34	2¾ tsp	4.5%
Malt syrup	0.1	2	⅛ tsp	0.5%
Bread flour	15.9	451	3¼ cups	58.4%
Whole wheat flour	4.7	133	⅔ cup	17.2%
Yeast, instant dry	0.2	6	1 tsp	0.8%
Salt	0.6	17	1 Tbsp	2.3%
Grain soaker	13.7	388	•	50.4%
TOTAL	48.2	1364	•	176.3%
GARNISH				
Sesame seeds	as needed			

1. MAKE the grain soaker by mixing the ingredients together. Cover and allow it to soak at room temperature overnight.

2. TO MAKE THE DOUGH, put the water, honey and malt in the bowl of a mixer. Combine the flours with the yeast, add them to the bowl, then add the salt. Place the bowl on a mixer fitted with a dough hook and mix on medium speed for 8 minutes, making sure to scrape down and flip the dough over twice during the mixing process. Add the soaker in two additions, mixing on low speed for 1 minute and and on medium for an additional minute. At this point, the dough will have some gluten development and feel slightly tacky. Place the dough in a lightly oiled bowl large enough for the dough to double in size and cover with plastic wrap.

3. ALLOW the dough to rest and ferment in a warm place for 45–60 minutes, until when lightly touched the dough springs back halfway.

4. PLACE the dough on a lightly floured work surface. Fold it into thirds, then place it back into the bowl, re-cover it, and allow it to rest for another 15 minutes, until when lightly touched the dough springs back halfway.

5. IN THE MEANTIME, prepare the bowls or trays for fermentation. If making rounds, you will need plastic bowls lined with a heavy-duty paper towel, white cloth napkin or white kitchen towel. The lined bowls should also be floured (unless seeds are being applied to the loaves). If making oblong loaves, line a standard baking tray with a white cloth napkin or white kitchen towel and flour the cloth (unless seeds are being applied to the loaves).

6. PLACE the dough on a lightly floured work surface and divide it into two 24-oz pieces.

FOR ROUND LOAVES, round each piece against the tabletop. To apply seeds, if using, brush or spray the loaf with water and then roll the top and sides in the seeds. Place the loaf in a prepared bowl with the seam side up. Use any extra cloth to cover the loaves and then lightly cover the bowl with plastic wrap.

FOR OBLONG LOAVES, shape each dough piece into a round. Place the rounds seam-side up on the work surface, cover lightly with plastic wrap, and allow them to rest for 10 minutes. Then shape each dough into a 10-inch oblong.

7. PLACE the dough in a warm place and allow it to rest and ferment for 45–60 minutes, until when lightly touched the dough springs back halfway.

8. TWENTY MINUTES before the end of the final fermentation, preheat the oven to 475°F with a baking stone. Ten minutes before baking the loaves, place a tray filled with 3 cups of warm water below the baking area in the oven to help produce steam.

9. PLACE the loaves seam-side down on a peel with parchment paper or baking tray and spray the tops and sides of the loaves with water. Let the loaves sit for 5 minutes before scoring. Using a sharp razor held at a 45-degree angle to the dough, score the top of each loaf with 1 lengthwise cut about ¼–½ inch deep. After scoring, spray the loaves with water again. This will help with the steam in the oven and also allow the loaf to expand evenly.

10. TRANSFER the loaves to the baking stone and immediately reduce the temperature to 450°F. Bake for 15 minutes, then remove the water tray and parchment paper. Reduce the heat to 425°F and bake for 12–15 minutes more. This will allow the loaves to finish baking and form a crust. If the crust isn't thick enough at the end of the baking time, turn the oven off and leave the bread in the oven with the door cracked open until the crust is dark in color and firm.

11. REMOVE the bread from the oven and place on a cooling rack.

Soakers

When adding a significant quantity of smaller grains, or any amount of large, whole grains such as wheat berries, it is best to soak the grains first before incorporating them into the final dough. Whole grains added without soaking tend to absorb moisture from the dough and will also damage the developing gluten network. Not to mention that they will be very hard, ruining the texture of your bread, and will not add any flavor.

A soaker can be made using one of two methods: hot or cold. A hot *soaker* pregelatinizes the starch of the soaker's grain, which can improve the crust and decrease the baking time of some whole-grain breads. Hot soakers work faster, but some chefs feel that there is some loss of flavor and quality. To produce a hot soaker, bring the liquid to a boil and then incorporate the grains. Then cook the mixture for about 5 minutes over low heat. Set the soaker aside for at least 1 hour to allow it to cool before adding it to the dough.

A *cold soaker* must be prepared at least a day in advance. For a cold soaker, the grains and liquid are incorporated, covered and allowed to soak overnight. This will have the benefits of a hot soaker without gelatinizing the starches.

Soakers are added to the dough after it has started to develop and are mixed into the dough on medium speed for a few minutes, just until they are fully and evenly incorporated. The exception is with rye breads. Due to their lack of gluten development, any soaker is added at the beginning of mixing.

Soaker before and after absorption

RUSTIC RYE BREAD

This rustic rye uses medium rye flour, which gives the bread a deep yet not overpowering flavor. There are three types of rye flour—dark, medium and light—and each contributes a different amount of flavor.

yield: 2 loaves at 24 oz | FDT: 80°F
bulk fermentation: 40–55 minutes | final fermentation: 40–50 minutes | bake: 425°F *and* 30–34 minutes

INGREDIENT	OUNCES	GRAMS	VOLUME	BAKERS %
Water, 84°F	20.2	573	2½ cups	70.1%
Malt syrup	0.2	4	⅛ tsp	0.5%
Bread flour	19.2	544	4 cups	66.7%
Rye flour, medium	9.6	272	2⅔ cups	33.3%
Yeast, instant dry	0.2	6	1½ tsp	0.7%
Salt	0.7	20	1 Tbsp	2.4%
TOTAL	50.1	1419	•	173.7%

1. PUT the water and malt in the bowl of a mixer. Combine the flours and the yeast and add to the bowl. Add the salt and place the bowl on a mixer fitted with a dough hook. Mix for 4 minutes on low speed, making sure to scrape down and flip the dough over twice during this process. Mix for 2 minutes on medium speed, making sure to scrape down and flip the dough over. The dough should be a little sticky, but with partial gluten development. Place it in a lightly oiled bowl large enough for the dough to double in size and cover with plastic wrap.

2. ALLOW the dough to rest and ferment in a warm place for 30–45 minutes, until when lightly touched the dough springs back halfway.

3. PREPARE a baking tray with a white cloth napkin or white kitchen towel on it. Sift flour onto the cloth.

4. PLACE the dough on a lightly floured work surface and divide it into two 24-oz pieces. Shape each piece into a round and place seam-side up on the baking tray, then cover and allow to rest for 10 minutes, until when lightly touched the dough springs back halfway.

5. REMOVE the dough and shape each round into an oblong. Roll each dough piece until it is 10 inches long. With one hand at each end of the piece at a 45-degree angle to the dough, roll the dough to taper the ends. Place the pieces on the prepared tray seam-side up, and pull the cloth up to create a barrier between the 2 loaves on the tray. Place the loaves seam-side up on the tray. Use any extra cloth to cover the loaves, then lightly cover them with plastic wrap. Place the dough in a warm place and allow it to rest and ferment for 40–50 minutes, until when lightly touched the dough springs back halfway.

6. TWENTY MINUTES before the end of the final fermentation, preheat the oven to 475°F with a baking stone. Ten minutes before baking the loaves, place a tray filled with 3 cups of warm water below the baking area in the oven to help produce steam.

7. PLACE the loaves seam-side down on a peel with parchment paper or baking tray and spray the tops and sides of each loaf with water. Let the loaves sit for 5 minutes before scoring. Score the top of each loaf with a sharp razor held at a 45-degree angle to the dough, cutting ¼–½ inch deep. Spray the loaves with water again. This will help with steam in the oven and allow the loaf to expand.

8. TRANSFER the loaves to the baking stone and immediately reduce the temperature to 425°F. Bake for 20 minutes, then remove the water tray, rotate the loaves if needed, and bake for 10–14 minutes more. This will allow the loaves to finish baking and form a crust. If the crust isn't thick enough at the end of the baking time, turn the oven off and leave the bread in the oven with the door cracked open until the crust is a dark color and does not give when pressed.

9. REMOVE the bread from the oven and place on a cooling rack.

Rustic Rye Bread

BASIC ENRICHED DOUGH

Breads and Rolls

Enrich your life with bread. One of the great things about bread is the fact that it can be almost anything you desire. Plain or fancy, crusty or soft, lean or loaded with enrichments. Enrichments, you say? That means butter, eggs, sugar, milk, honey and oil. These ingredients speak to humans on a most basic level, addressing the voice in our heads that says, "Give me something rich and sweet." And, of course, there are times when we want even more than that. How about seeds? And nuts! Dried fruit! Sautéed vegetables! Cheese! Ham! Herbs! Cinnamon sugar!! If these ingredients are calling your name, you will find recipes here that answer your cravings.

CHAPTER FIVE

BEFORE GETTING TO THOSE RECIPES, though, it helps to remember that whenever you add something beyond just the basic bread ingredients (flour, water, yeast and salt), it changes the baking equation. Fats coat the strands of gluten and make it harder for them to develop. Sugars speed up the action of yeast and serve to liquefy the dough. Sugary or sharp additions such as dried fruits and chopped nuts generally need to be added toward the end of mixing so they don't reduce the leavening ability of the yeast or cut the strands of gluten you've developed—otherwise you will have a denser bread with less volume.

What exactly do enrichments do for a dough? Milk, eggs, oil, sugar and/or honey can make the baked bread's crust softer and its crumb more tender. Think about soft rolls, and you can imagine what this means. You will find a recipe for those, as well as for soft white pan bread (great for sandwiches) and a whole wheat version.

If you are looking for something showy, there are lots of options. Once you know how to make sweet dough, put in a little extra work and you can turn it into tempting cinnamon rolls or sticky buns, simply by adding a filling and rolling the dough up around it. Sweet dough is refrigerated overnight to slow down fermentation. So you could make the dough the night before, as well as prepare your cinnamon pan smear. Then wake up a little early and assemble these rolls for breakfast. Cinnamon-raisin swirl bread, on the other hand, takes about half a day, looks pretty and tastes delicious.

When you want something savory, there is cottage and dill bread, with a hint of horseradish to lend some zing. Add some caraway to your rye bread, or even Cheddar and onion. Ham and provolone are paired in a loaf of soft white bread, and sunflower seed bread (a dough that makes great rolls, by the way) is glossy on the top with a beautiful sprinkling of seeds. Take a bite and there are more seeds inside, adding some tooth to a soft, enriched bread.

So go for it, and most of all, have fun.

SOFT ROLLS

Soft and buttery, these rolls are a classic staple at dinnertime. Follow the recipe's directions to make a knotted design, or simply shape small, traditional rounds. The rolls may be egg washed and garnished with seeds for a more attractive appearance.

yield: 24 rolls at 2 oz | FDT: 80°F
bulk fermentation: 60–75 minutes | final fermentation: 45–60 minutes | bake: 375°F *and* 15–18 minutes

INGREDIENT	OUNCES	GRAMS	VOLUME	BAKERS %
Milk, whole, 80°F	14.0	400	1⅔ cups	51.9%
Eggs	2.6	74	⅓ cup	10.0%
Malt syrup	0.1	2	¼ tsp	0.3%
Bread flour	27.0	765	5¾ cups	100.0%
Yeast, instant dry	0.2	6	1½ tsp	0.8%
Butter, soft	2.6	74	¼ cup	10.0%
Sugar	2.6	74	¼ cup	10.0%
Salt	0.6	17	1 Tbsp	2.3%
TOTAL	49.7	1412	•	185.3%
GARNISHES				
Egg wash	as needed			
Poppy and/or sesame seeds	as needed			

1. COMBINE the milk, eggs and malt in the bowl of a mixer fitted with a dough hook. Combine the flour with the yeast and add it to the ingredients in the mixer bowl, then add the butter, sugar and salt. Mix for 5 minutes on low speed, making sure to scrape down and flip the dough over twice during this time. Increase to medium speed for another 3 minutes, making sure to scrape down and flip the dough. The dough should feel slightly sticky but have full gluten development. Place the dough in a lightly oiled bowl large enough for it to double in size and cover with plastic wrap.

2. ALLOW the dough to rest and ferment in a warm place for 45–60 minutes, until when lightly touched the dough springs back halfway.

3. PLACE the dough on a lightly floured work surface and divide into 2-oz pieces. Preshape the pieces into 3-inch oblongs for knot rolls or round them for dinner rolls. Cover the dough with plastic wrap and allow it to rest for 15 minutes before making the final shape.

4. TO SHAPE KNOT ROLLS, bring the top edge of the oblong piece down one third of the way and tuck it in to create a seam. Bring the top edge down another one third and tuck it in. Then bring the last third down and gently press it along the edge to close the seam tightly. Using a little flour, roll the piece back and forth to 10–12 inches long, then tie the dough into a knot. (See illustrations in Appendix on page 327.)

TO SHAPE DINNER ROLLS, tighten up the rounds by rolling them in a circular motion against the tabletop.

5. PLACE the finished rolls seam-side down on a baking tray lined with parchment paper, lightly egg wash the rolls, and cover with lightly oiled plastic wrap. Allow the dough to rest in a warm place for 45 to 60 minutes, until when lightly touched the dough springs back halfway.

6. TWENTY MINUTES before the end of final fermentation, preheat the oven to 425°F.

7. EGG WASH the rolls again and garnish with seeds, if desired.

8. TRANSFER the tray to the oven and immediately reduce the temperature to 375°F. Bake for 15–18 minutes, or until the rolls are golden brown, rotating the tray three fourths of the way through baking.

9. REMOVE from the oven and place the baking tray on a cooling rack.

Soft Rolls

WHITE BREAD

Deliciously simple, this recipe yields a loaf of white bread that is nothing less than purely tasty. The uses for this old favorite are endless, from sandwiches to toast, but warm out of the oven and simply sliced and buttered may indeed be the greatest way to eat it.

yield: 2 loaves at 28 oz | FDT: 80°F
bulk fermentation: 55 minutes | final fermentation: 60–75 minutes | bake: 375°F *and* 30–35 minutes

INGREDIENT	OUNCES	GRAMS	VOLUME	BAKERS %
Water, 75°F	19.6	556	1 cup + 2½ Tbsp	60.1%
Butter	3.0	84	3 Tbsp	9.1%
Malt syrup	0.2	4	¼ tsp	0.5%
Bread flour	32.7	926	3 cups + 3½ Tbsp	100.0%
Sugar	1.3	38	1 Tbsp + 1 tsp	4.1%
Yeast, dry	0.4	12	1½ tsp	1.3%
Salt	0.9	24	2½ tsp	2.6%
TOTAL	58.1	1644	•	177.7%

1. **PUT** the water, butter and malt in the bowl of a mixer. Add the flour, sugar and yeast, then the salt. Place the bowl on a mixer fitted with a dough hook and mix for 4 minutes on medium speed, making sure to scrape down and flip the dough over during this time. Increase to medium speed and mix for another 4 minutes, making sure to scrape down and flip the dough over. The dough should feel slightly sticky but have good gluten development. Place the dough in a lightly oiled bowl large enough for it to double in size and cover with plastic wrap.

2. **ALLOW** the dough to rest and ferment in a warm place for 45 minutes, until when touched the dough springs back halfway.

3. **PLACE** the dough on a lightly floured work surface and divide into two 28-oz pieces. Round each piece against the tabletop. Cover the rounds with plastic wrap and allow to rest and ferment for 10 minutes.

4. **SHAPE** each round into a 12-inch oblong (see page 72). Place each loaf seam-side down in a well-oiled loaf pan. Egg wash the surface of the loaves, cover lightly with plastic wrap, and allow to rest and ferment in the pans for 60–75 minutes, until when lightly touched the dough springs back halfway.

5. **TWENTY MINUTES** before the end of final fermentation, preheat the oven to 425°F.

6. **EGG WASH** the loaves again, and transfer the pans to the oven. Reduce the oven temperature to 375°F and bake for 30–35 minutes, or until golden brown.

7. **REMOVE** the pans from the oven and allow them to completely cool before removing the bread from the pans.

SHAPING PAN BREAD

1. Shape the dough into an oval. Pull the top over and press it into the center. Repeat with the top. Repeat this step three or four times to ensure a tight shape.

2. Press firmly to seal the seam. The dough should now look similar to a football.

3. Roll the dough gently to form a cylindrical shape. This will help seal the seam as well as make a nice final shape in the pan.

4. Use a lightly floured surface to avoid sticking, but make sure there is not excess flour on the dough before placing it in the pan.

White Bread

WHOLE WHEAT PAN BREAD

Easy to make and even easier to shape, this recipe assures soft, sliceable bread from a beautiful loaf. From toast to sandwiches, the finished bread is chewy, full of flavor and perfect at any meal of the day.

yield: 2 loaves at 28 oz | FDT: 80°F
bulk fermentation: 60 minutes | final fermentation: 60–75 minutes | bake: 375°F *and* 35 minutes

INGREDIENT	OUNCES	GRAMS	VOLUME	BAKERS %
Water, 80°F	21.6	614	1⅓ cups	68.0%
Vegetable oil	2.0	59	2 Tbsp	6.5%
Honey	1.2	35	2 tsp	3.9%
Malt syrup	0.1	4	1 tsp	0.5%
Bread flour	19.1	543	2¼ cups	60.1%
Whole wheat flour	12.6	360	1½ cups	39.9%
Yeast, instant dry	0.2	6	2 tsp	0.7%
Salt	0.8	24	1 Tbsp	2.6%
TOTAL	57.6	1645	•	182.2%
GARNISH				
Egg wash	as needed			

1. PUT the water, oil, honey and malt in the bowl of a mixer. Combine the flours and yeast and add to the bowl, then add the salt. Place the bowl on a mixer fitted with a dough hook and mix on medium speed for 4 minutes, making sure to scrape down and flip the dough over during this time. Mix on medium speed for another 4 minutes, making sure to scrape down and flip the dough over during this time. After mixing, the dough should feel slightly sticky but have fairly good gluten development. Place the dough in a lightly oiled bowl large enough for it to double in size and cover with plastic wrap.

2. ALLOW the dough to rest and ferment in a warm place for 45 minutes, until when touched the dough springs back halfway.

3. DIVIDE the dough into two 28-oz pieces. Place the dough on a lightly floured work surface and round it against the tabletop. Cover lightly with plastic wrap and allow to rest for 15 minutes.

4. SHAPE the round into a 12-inch oblong. Place seam-side down in a well-oiled loaf pan. Egg wash the surface of the loaf and cover the surface lightly with oiled plastic wrap. Allow the dough to rest and ferment in the pan for 60–75 minutes, until when lightly touched the dough springs back halfway.

5. TWENTY MINUTES before the end of final fermentation, preheat the oven to 425°F.

6. REDUCE the oven temperature to 375°F. Transfer the pan to the oven and bake for 35 minutes, or until golden brown.

7. REMOVE the pan from the oven and allow it to completely cool before removing the bread from the pan.

CHEDDAR-ONION RYE ROLLS

Sweetly caramelized onions and sharp Cheddar cheese make this rye bread a delightfully savory snack. Rye flour mixed with wheat flour keeps the texture of the bread light; bake the dough in loaf form for exciting sandwich bread or shape it into rolls for a punchy accompaniment to dinner or a lunchtime bowl of soup.

yield: 24 rolls at 2 oz | FDT: 82°F
bulk fermentation: 45–60 minutes | final fermentation: 30–40 minutes | bake: 450°F *and* 19–21 minutes

INGREDIENT	OUNCES	GRAMS	VOLUME	BAKERS %
Onions, diced	5.0	142	1¼ cups	18.9%
Water, 80°F	15.6	442	2 cups	58.9%
Vegetable oil	2.1	60	¼ cup	7.9%
Molasses	0.5	14	2 tsp	1.9%
Malt syrup	0.2	6	⅛ tsp	0.8%
Bread flour	19.9	564	4¾ cups	75.1%
Rye flour, medium	6.6	187	1¾ cups + 1 Tbsp	24.9%
Yeast, instant dry	0.2	6	2 tsp	0.8%
Sugar	0.5	14	1 Tbsp	1.9%
Salt	0.7	20	1 Tbsp	2.6%
Cheddar cheese, grated	5.0	142	1¼ cups	18.9%
TOTAL	56.3	1597	•	212.6%
GARNISHES				
Salt	pinch			
Cheddar cheese, grated	6.0	170	1½ cups	

1. SAUTÉ the onions with a small amount of oil until caramel brown in color. Set aside to cool.

2. PUT the water, oil, molasses and malt in the bowl of a mixer. Combine the flours and yeast and add to the bowl, then add the sugar and salt. Place the bowl on a mixer fitted with a dough hook. Mix for 4 minutes on low speed, making sure to scrape down and flip the dough over twice during this process. Mix for 4 more minutes on medium speed, making sure to scrape down and flip the dough over. At this point, the dough should be slightly strong with full gluten development. Add the onions and 5 oz of the cheese and mix for 1 minute on low speed, making sure to scrape down and flip the dough over once during this process. Place the dough in a lightly oiled bowl large enough for it to double in size and cover with plastic wrap.

3. ALLOW the dough to rest and ferment in a warm place for 45–60 minutes, until when lightly touched the dough springs back halfway.

4. PLACE the dough on a lightly floured work surface and divide into 2-oz pieces. Round each piece of dough against the tabletop and place the dough pieces seam-side down in 4 rows of 3 on 2 baking trays lined with parchment paper. Cover the tray lightly with lightly oiled plastic wrap and allow the rolls to rest and ferment in a warm place for 30–40 minutes, until when lightly touched the dough springs back halfway.

5. TWENTY MINUTES before the end of final fermentation, preheat the oven to 475°F. Ten minutes before baking the rolls, place a tray filled with 3 cups of warm water below the baking area in the oven to help produce steam.

6. UNCOVER the rolls and spray them with water. Allow the rolls to sit for 5 minutes, then score the tops by making one cut across each center using a sharp razor blade held at a 90-degree angle to the top of the roll. Spray the rolls with water again and sprinkle the tops with salt and cheese.

7. TRANSFER the rolls to the oven and immediately reduce the temperature to 450°F. Bake for 15 minutes, then rotate the tray and bake for another 4–6 minutes, until golden brown.

8. REMOVE from the oven and place the baking tray on a cooling rack.

VARIATION: PAN LOAVES

After step #3 at left:

4. PLACE the dough on a lightly floured work surface and divide into two 28-oz pieces. Preshape the dough pieces by rounding them against the tabletop. Place them seam-side up on the work surface, cover with plastic wrap, and allow to rest and ferment for 15 minutes.

5. SHAPE each round into a 12-inch oblong. Place each loaf in a well-oiled loaf pan seam-side down and lightly cover with plastic wrap. Allow the dough to rest and ferment in a warm place for 60–75 minutes, until when lightly touched the dough springs back halfway.

6. TWENTY MINUTES before the end of final fermentation, preheat the oven to 425°F. Fifteen minutes before baking the loaves, place a tray filled with 3 cups of warm water below the baking area in the oven to help produce steam.

7. SPRAY the loaves with water. Allow the dough to sit uncovered for 5 minutes, then score each loaf directly down the middle from end to end, using a sharp razor held at a 90-degree angle to the bread. Spray the loaves with water again and garnish the tops by sprinkling with salt and cheese.

8. PLACE the loaves in the oven and immediately reduce the temperature to 400°F. Bake for 15 minutes, then remove the steam tray, rotate the pans, and bake for an additional 20–25 minutes, until golden brown.

9. REMOVE from the oven, immediately remove the loaves from the baking pans, and place the loaves on a cooling rack.

Cheddar-Onion Rye Rolls, Pan Loaf and
Ham and Provolone Loaves

HAM AND PROVOLONE LOAVES

A playful take on the ham and cheese sandwich, this soft loaf bread rolls it all into one. Diced ham and provolone cheese are mixed into olive oil–moistened dough to create a savory, filling bread that once cooled from the oven, you'll be tempted to make into a meal in itself.

yield: 2 loaves at 20 oz | FDT: 80°F
bulk fermentation: 60–75 minutes | final fermentation: 45–60 minutes | bake: 400°F *and* 25–30 minutes

INGREDIENT	OUNCES	GRAMS	VOLUME	BAKERS %
Ham steak, cubed	5.2	147	1 cup	31.0%
Provolone cheese	5.2	147	1 cup	31.0%
Water, 80°F	10.0	284	1¼ cups	59.5%
Olive oil	1.7	48	3 Tbsp	10.1%
Butter, soft	0.4	11	2½ tsp	2.4%
Malt syrup	0.1	2	⅛ tsp	1.2%
Bread flour	16.8	476	3¾ cups	100.0%
Yeast, instant dry	0.2	6	1½ tsp	1.2%
Salt	0.3	9	1½ tsp	1.8%
TOTAL	39.9	1130	•	238.2%

1. CUT the ham and provolone into ½-inch dice and reserve at room temperature.

2. PUT the water, oil, butter and malt in the bowl of a mixer. Combine the flour with the yeast and add to the bowl. Add the salt, place the bowl on a mixer fitted with a dough hook, and mix for 4 minutes on low speed, making sure to scrape down and flip the dough over twice during this time. Mix for 2 minutes on medium speed, making sure to scrape down and flip the dough over. At this point, the dough should have developed good gluten structure. Add the ham and cheese, then mix for 1 additional minute on low speed, making sure to flip the dough over once during this time. Place the dough in a lightly oiled bowl large enough for it to double in size and cover with plastic wrap.

3. ALLOW the dough to rest and ferment in a warm place for 45–60 minutes, until when lightly touched the dough springs back halfway.

4. PLACE the dough on a lightly floured work surface and fold it into thirds. Cover the dough with plastic wrap and allow it to rest and ferment for 15 minutes. Prepare small plastic bowls or baskets lined with a heavy-duty paper towel, white cloth napkin or white kitchen towel. Any cloth liners will also need to be floured.

5. PUT the dough on a lightly floured work surface and divide it into two 20-oz pieces. Round the dough pieces against the tabletop, then place each piece in a prepared bowl or basket seam-side up. Cover the dough lightly with plastic wrap and allow it to rest and ferment for 45–60 minutes, until when lightly touched the dough springs back halfway.

6. TWENTY MINUTES before the end of final fermentation, place a baking stone in the oven and preheat the oven with the baking stone to 450°F. Ten minutes before baking the loaves, place a tray filled with 3 cups of warm water below the baking area in the oven to help produce steam.

7. PLACE the loaves on an oven peel with parchment paper. Spray the surface of each loaf with water. Let the loaves sit for 5 minutes before scoring to allow the surface to absorb moisture. With a sharp razor held at a 90-degree angle to the dough, score the loaf in the shape of an X. After scoring, spray the loaves with water again to help create steam in the oven and allow the loaves to expand evenly.

8. PLACE the loaves on the baking stone in the oven and immediately reduce the temperature to 400°F. Bake for 15 minutes. Remove the steam tray and continue to bake for another 10–15 minutes, until the crust is golden brown and doesn't give when pressed.

9. REMOVE from the oven and place the baking tray on a cooling rack.

CORN ROLLS

The kosher salt and cornmeal garnishes on these vibrant rolls lend added texture and flavor to the bread. However, be careful not to put too much on as it could overwhelm the flavor when you take a bite.

yield: 24 rolls at 2 oz | FDT: 82°F
soaker: overnight | *bulk fermentation:* 45–60 minutes | *final fermentation:* 45–60 minutes | *bake:* 425°F *and* 18–20 minutes

INGREDIENT	OUNCES	GRAMS	VOLUME	BAKERS %
CORN SOAKER				
Cornmeal, coarse grind	5.3	150	¾ cup + 1½ Tbsp	21.4%
Milk, whole	22.7	644	2¾ cups, divided	91.6%
FINAL DOUGH				
Corn soaker	28.0	794	•	113.0%
Honey	2.2	62	3 Tbsp	8.9%
Vegetable oil	1.3	35	3 Tbsp	5.0%
Malt syrup	0.1	2	½ tsp	0.4%
Bread flour	16.1	456	3½ cups, divided	64.9%
Corn flour	4.0	113	¾ cup	16.1%
Yeast, instant dry	0.1	2	1 tsp	0.4%
Corn, frozen or fresh	4.0	113	½ cup	16.1%
Salt	0.7	20	2 Tbsp	2.8%
TOTAL	56.5	1597	•	227.6%
GARNISHES				
Egg wash	as needed			
Kosher salt	6.0	170	⅔ cup	
Cornmeal	6.0	170	1 cup	

1. **TO MAKE THE CORN SOAKER,** put the cornmeal in the bowl of a mixer. Bring 1¾ cups of the milk to a hard, rolling boil, then pour over the cornmeal. Stir the mixture and let sit for 2 minutes. Put the bowl on a mixer fitted with a paddle attachment, and mix the cornmeal and milk on high speed for 3 minutes. On medium speed, add the remaining 1 cup milk to the mixture in 3 additions, waiting about 1 minute between each addition. Make sure to scrape down the sides of the mixer with a spatula while mixing. Cover the soaker and refrigerate overnight or for a minimum of 8 hours.

2. **TO MAKE THE DOUGH,** put the corn soaker over a simmering water bath and warm to 85°F. In a mixer fitted with a paddle attachment, add the honey, oil and malt to the soaker and mix on medium speed for 1 minute. Add 3¼ cups of the bread flour along with the corn flour and yeast to the starter mixture. Toss the corn with the remaining ¼ cup bread flour and add to the mixture. Lastly, add the salt. Switch to a dough hook and mix for 6 minutes on low speed, making sure to scrape down and flip the dough over in the bowl twice during the mixing process. Increase the speed to medium and mix for an additional 4 minutes. The dough will be slightly tacky but should have good gluten development. Place the dough in a lightly oiled bowl large enough for it to double in size and cover it with plastic wrap.

3. **ALLOW** the dough to rest and ferment in a warm place for 45–60 minutes, until when lightly touched the dough springs back halfway.

4. **PUT** the dough on a lightly floured work surface and divide it into 2-oz pieces. Round the dough pieces against the tabletop, then place them seam-side down in 3 rows of 4 on 2 baking trays lined with parchment paper. Brush the rolls with egg wash, then lightly cover them with lightly oiled plastic wrap. Allow the dough to rest and ferment in a warm place for 45–60 minutes, until when lightly touched the dough springs back halfway.

5. **TWENTY MINUTES** before the end of final fermentation, preheat the oven to 450°F.

6. **EGG WASH** the rolls again, then sprinkle each one with salt and then with cornmeal.

7. **TRANSFER** the rolls to the oven and immediately reduce the temperature to 425°F. Bake for 15 minutes. Rotate the trays and bake for another 3–5 minutes, or until golden brown.

8. **REMOVE** the rolls from the oven and allow them to cool on the baking pan.

HERB, PEPPER AND CHEESE BUNS

In this recipe, the creaminess of mozzarella's texture and flavor balances the basil, garlic and red pepper. There are several different varieties of cheese that you could use. Be creative with the herbs to match the flavor of the cheese, should you choose to use something other than mozzarella.

yield: 12 buns at 4.5 oz | FDT: 82°F
bulk fermentation: 75–90 minutes | final fermentation: 30 minutes | bake: 400°F *and* 18–20 minutes

INGREDIENT	OUNCES	GRAMS	VOLUME	BAKERS %
Garlic, minced	0.6	17	2 Tbsp	2.1%
Water, 80°F	15.1	428	2 cups	53.0%
Canola oil	0.7	20	1½ Tbsp	2.5%
Malt syrup	0.1	2	½ tsp	0.2%
Bread flour	28.5	808	6 cups	100.0%
Yeast, instant dry	0.2	6	1½ tsp	0.7%
Salt	0.7	20	1 Tbsp	2.5%
Sugar	0.7	20	1½ Tbsp	2.5%
Mozzarella cheese, grated	5.7	162	1½ cups	20.0%
Red pepper, roasted and diced	2.3	65	⅓ cup	8.1%
Basil, chiffonade	0.6	17	½ cup	2.1%
Bread flour	0.8	23	3 Tbsp	2.8%
TOTAL	56.0	1588	•	196.5%
GARNISHES				
Egg wash	as needed			
Mozzarella cheese, grated	4.0	113	1 cup	

1. SAUTÉ the garlic in a small amount of oil over low heat until fragrant and cooked, but not browned. Set aside.

2. PUT the water, oil and malt in the bowl of a mixer. Mix the flour and yeast together and add to the bowl, then add the salt and sugar. Place the bowl on a mixer fitted with a dough hook and mix for 5 minutes on low speed, making sure to scrape down and flip the dough over twice during this time. Then mix for 3 minutes on medium speed, making sure to scrape down and flip the dough over. The dough should have full gluten development and should be a little tacky. Combine the sauteed garlic, cheese, peppers, basil and remaining 3 Tbsp flour in a bowl. Add to the dough and mix for 1 minute on low, then scrape down and flip the dough. Mix for another 30 seconds on low speed. Place the dough in a lightly oiled bowl large enough for it to double in size and cover with plastic wrap.

3. ALLOW the dough to rest and ferment in a warm place for 45–60 minutes, until when lightly touched the dough springs back halfway.

4. PUT the dough on a lightly floured work surface and divide it into 4.5-oz pieces. Round each piece against the tabletop and place the rounds seam-side down in 2 rows of 3 on 2 baking trays lined with parchment paper. Lightly egg wash the buns and cover lightly with lightly oiled plastic wrap. Allow them to relax and ferment in a warm place for 30 minutes, until fully relaxed.

5. UNCOVER and lightly flatten the tops of the buns. Lightly egg wash them again, then cover and allow to ferment another 30 minutes, until when lightly touched the dough springs back halfway.

6. TWENTY MINUTES before the end of final fermentation, preheat the oven to 450°F.

7. PREPARE the buns for the oven by egg washing. Using a sharp razor held perpendicular to the dough, score the top of each bun with 1 lengthwise cut about ¼–½ inch deep and apply egg wash.

8. TRANSFER the buns to the oven and immediately reduce the temperature to 400°F. Bake for 15 minutes, then remove from the oven and garnish the tops with cheese. Place back in the oven and rotate the trays, then bake for 3–5 minutes more, until the cheese has melted and they are light golden brown.

9. REMOVE from the oven and place the baking trays on a cooling rack.

SOFT MULTIGRAIN ROLLS

The multigrain mixture (see Resources, page 332) adds both fiber to your diet and flavor to your meal. The bread is the perfect texture for sandwiches and flavorful enough to accompany your favorite hearty soup.

yield: 24 rolls at 2 oz | FDT: 82°F
soaker: 8 hours to overnight | bulk fermentation: 45–60 minutes
final fermentation: 45–60 minutes | bake: 375°F *and* 16–18 minutes

INGREDIENT	OUNCES	GRAMS	VOLUME	BAKERS %
GRAIN SOAKER				
Water, 80°F	4.5	128	½ cup	16.2%
Multigrain mixture	3.7	105	½ cup	13.4%
FINAL DOUGH				
Milk, whole, 80°F	14.0	397	1⅔ cups	50.5%
Honey	4.0	113	⅓ cup	14.4%
Vegetable oil	2.5	71	¼ cup	9.0%
Malt syrup	0.2	6	¼ tsp	0.7%
Bread flour	15.0	425	3 cups + 2 Tbsp	54.2%
Whole wheat flour	9.0	255	2 cups + 2 Tbsp	32.5%
Yeast, instant dry	0.3	9	2¼ tsp	1.1%
Salt	0.7	20	1 Tbsp	2.5%
Grain soaker	8.2	233	•	29.6%
TOTAL	53.9	1529	•	194.5%
GARNISHES				
Egg wash	as needed			
Sesame seeds	as needed			

1. TO MAKE THE SOAKER, combine the water and multigrain mixture in a bowl, cover with plastic wrap, and allow it to soak overnight or for a minimum of 8 hours at room temperature.

2. TO MAKE THE DOUGH, put the milk, honey, oil and malt in the bowl of a mixer. Combine the flours and yeast and add to the bowl, then add the salt. Put the bowl on a mixer fitted with a dough hook and mix for 4 minutes on low speed, making sure to scrape down and flip the dough over during this process. Increase the speed to medium and mix for another 3 minutes, making sure to scrape down and flip over the dough. Add half of the soaker and mix for 1 minute on low speed. Add the rest of the soaker and mix for 1 additional minute on medium speed. Place the dough in a lightly oiled bowl large enough for it to double in size and cover it with plastic wrap.

3. ALLOW the dough to rest and ferment in a warm place for 45–60 minutes, until when lightly pressed the dough springs back halfway.

4. PLACE the dough on a lightly floured work surface and divide it into 2-oz pieces. Round each piece against the tabletop and place the rounds seam-side down in 4 rows of 3 on 2 baking trays lined with parchment paper. Brush with egg wash and cover lightly with plastic wrap. Allow the dough to rest and ferment in a warm place for 45–60 minutes, until when lightly pressed the dough springs back halfway.

5. TWENTY MINUTES before the end of final fermentation, preheat the oven to 425°F.

6. EGG WASH the rounds again and sprinkle them with sesame seeds.

7. PLACE the trays in the oven and immediately reduce the temperature to 375°F. Bake for 12 minutes, then rotate and bake for another 4–6 minutes until golden brown.

8. REMOVE from the oven and place the trays on a cooling rack.

COTTAGE-DILL ROLLS

Aromatic dill meets spicy horseradish in this herbed and salted dough. Cottage cheese mixed into the dough creates rolls that are soft and moist. For a variation, shape the dough into larger, flattened pieces ideal for baking into hamburger rolls.

yield: 24 rolls at 2 oz or 6 buns at 4.5 oz | FDT: 82°F
bulk fermentation: 45–60 minutes | final fermentation: 30–45 minutes | bake: 400°F *and* 18–20 minutes

INGREDIENT	OUNCES	GRAMS	VOLUME	BAKERS %
Water, 80°F	10.5	298	1¼ cups	39.8%
Cottage cheese, small curd	4.0	113	½ cup	15.2%
Eggs	3.4	96	¼ cup + 2½ Tbsp	12.9%
Butter, soft	1.8	51	¼ cup	6.8%
Malt syrup	0.2	6	⅛ tsp	0.8%
Bread flour	26.4	748	5½ cups	100.0%
Yeast, instant dry	0.2	6	2 tsp	0.8%
Sugar	0.9	26	2 Tbsp	3.4%
Salt	0.6	17	1 Tbsp	2.3%
Fresh dill, chopped	0.6	17	⅓ cup	2.3%
Horseradish, jarred or freshly grated	0.2	6	1 Tbsp	0.8%
TOTAL	48.8	1384	•	185.1%
GARNISHES				
Egg wash	as needed			
Kosher salt	as needed			

1. PUT the water, cheese, eggs, butter and malt in the bowl of a mixer. Combine the flour with the yeast, then add to the bowl. Next add the sugar and salt. Place the bowl on a mixer fitted with a dough hook and mix for 4 minutes on low speed, making sure to scrape down and flip the dough over twice during the mixing process. Increase to medium speed and mix for an additional 4 minutes, making sure to scrape down and flip the dough over. Add the dill and horseradish and mix for another 1 minute on low speed, again making sure to scrape down and flip the dough over once during mixing, and mixing to full gluten development. Place the dough in a lightly oiled bowl large enough for it to double in size and cover it with plastic wrap.

2. ALLOW the dough to rest and ferment in a warm place for 45–60 minutes, until when lightly pressed the dough springs back halfway.

3. PLACE the dough on a lightly floured work surface and divide it into 4.5-oz pieces for hamburger buns or 2-oz pieces for dinner rolls. Round each dough piece against the tabletop, then place the pieces seam-side down on a baking tray lined with parchment paper. For buns, place the pieces in 2 rows of 3; for rolls, place them in 3 rows of 4 on 2 trays.

4. FOR ROLLS, lightly brush the rounds with egg wash.

FOR HAMBURGER BUNS, lightly flatten the pieces with your fingers.

Cover the pieces lightly with lightly oiled plastic wrap. Allow the dough to relax and ferment in a warm place for 30–45 minutes, until when lightly pressed the dough springs back halfway.

FOR HAMBURGER BUNS, uncover after 20 minutes and gently flatten them again with a little egg wash on your fingers.

5. TWENTY MINUTES before the end of final fermentation, preheat the oven to 450°F.

6. PREPARE the dough for the oven by egg washing again and lightly sprinkling the tops with salt.

7. PLACE the trays in the oven and immediately reduce the temperature to 400°F. Bake for 14 minutes, then rotate the trays and bake for an additional 4–6 minutes, until golden brown.

8. REMOVE from the oven and place the baking trays on a cooling rack.

Cinnamon-Raisin Swirl Bread

Cinnamon is a wonderful addition to a dessert, not just for its flavor but also for its medical benefits. It can help control blood sugar levels and protect against heart disease. It is also beneficial as a preservative. Honey and brown sugar–sweetened cinnamon filling is rolled into this warmly spiced, raisin-studded bread. Baked in a loaf pan, the final bread is perfect for slicing and toasting; with a dab of butter, this bread is sure to become a feel-good addition to breakfast.

yield: 2 loaves at 28 oz | FDT: 82°F
bulk fermentation: 55–70 minutes | final fermentation: 75–90 minutes | bake: 375°F *and* 35–40 minutes

INGREDIENT	OUNCES	GRAMS	VOLUME	BAKERS %
Cinnamon Filling (page 90)	4.6	130	•	•
DOUGH				
Milk, whole, 80°F	14.7	417	1¾ cups	54.0%
Eggs	2.5	71	⅓ cup	9.2%
Butter, soft	2.5	71	⅓ cup	9.2%
Malt syrup	0.2	6	⅛ tsp	0.7%
Bread flour	27.2	771	5⅔ cups	100.0%
Yeast, instant dry	0.4	11	1 Tbsp + 1 tsp	1.4%
Sugar	2.5	71	⅓ cup	9.2%
Salt	0.6	16	1 Tbsp	2.1%
Raisins	4.9	139	1 cup (not packed)	18.0%
Cinnamon	0.2	6	1 Tbsp	0.7%
TOTAL	55.7	1577	•	204.5%
GARNISH				
Egg wash	as needed			

1. MAKE the Cinnamon Filling the day prior and store it in the refrigerator. When ready to start mixing the bread, remove the cinnamon filling from the refrigerator and leave it at room temperature for 60 minutes.

2. MAKE THE DOUGH: Put the milk, eggs, butter and malt in the bowl of a mixer. Combine the flour with the yeast and add to the bowl, then add the sugar and salt. Place the bowl on a mixer fitted with a dough hook and mix for 4 minutes on low speed, making sure to scrape down and flip the dough over twice during this process. Mix for another 4 minutes on medium speed, scraping down the bowl and flipping the dough over twice during this process. Add the raisins and mix for 1 minute on low speed. Scrape the bowl down and flip the dough over, then add the cinnamon and continue mixing until the cinnamon is thoroughly swirled into the dough. Place the dough in a lightly oiled bowl large enough for it to double in size and cover it with plastic wrap.

3. ALLOW the dough to rest and ferment in a warm place for 45–60 minutes, until when lightly touched the dough springs back halfway.

4. PLACE the dough on a lightly floured work surface and divide it into two 28-oz pieces. Shape each piece by folding the top and bottom edges over to create a rectangular shape. Cover the dough and let it rest for 10 minutes.

5. ROLL each piece of dough out into a rectangle 12 by 6 inches and spread 2–3 ounces of the cinnamon filling on the surface, leaving a ½-inch border around the outer edge. Roll each end to the middle and keep the outer edges closed. Place in a well-oiled pan, so that the two rolled ends are facing up.

6. EGG WASH each loaf and cover with lightly oiled plastic wrap. Allow the dough to rest and ferment in a warm place for 75–90 minutes, until when lightly pressed the dough springs back halfway.

7. TWENTY MINUTES before the end of final fermentation, preheat the oven to 425°F.

8. UNCOVER the loaves and egg wash a second time.

9. TRANSFER the loaves to the oven and immediately reduce the temperature to 375°F. Bake for 20 minutes. Rotate the loaves and bake for an additional 15–20 minutes, until golden brown.

10. REMOVE the bread from the oven and immediately release it from the pans. Place the loaves on a cooling rack.

Shape the raisin dough into a rectangle. Make sure the width of the rectangle does not exceed the width of the loaf pan. Spread the cinnamon filling onto the dough, allowing for a border with which to handle and shape the dough. Roll each end toward the middle, keeping it tight so as not to form air pockets. Place the dough in the loaf pan so the two rolled ends are facing up.

Cinnamon-Raisin Swirl Bread

CINNAMON FILLING

This filling is fitting for almost any cofee cake or enriched bread. It may
also be used as a filling for other yeasted pastries.

yield: **32 oz**

INGREDIENT	OUNCES	GRAMS	VOLUME	BAKERS %
Butter, melted	11.7	332	1½ cups	100.0%
Brown sugar	11.2	318	1¼ cups + 3 Tbsp	95.7%
Pastry flour	1.5	43	⅓ cup	12.8%
Cinnamon	1.5	43	⅓ cup	12.8%
Honey	1.3	37	2 Tbsp	11.1%
Eggs	4.9	139	½ cup + 1 Tbsp	41.9%
Vanilla extract	dash	dash	dash	dash
TOTAL	32.1	912	•	274.3%

1. PUT the melted butter and brown sugar in the bowl of a mixer fitted with a paddle attachment. Mix for 2 minutes on low speed, making sure to periodically scrape down the bowl.

2. COMBINE the flour, cinnamon and honey, then add to the bowl of the mixer and continue mixing for 2 minutes on low speed, continuing to scrape down the bowl.

3. COMBINE the eggs and vanilla in a separate bowl, then add to the butter mixture and mix for 2 minutes on low speed, continuing to scrape the bowl periodically.

4. TRANSFER to a container to cool at room temperature for 60 minutes. Cover and refrigerate overnight.

CINNAMON ROLLS AND STICKY BUNS

This recipe for sweet dough creates a basic ideal for golden cinnamon rolls as well as for sinfully gooey sticky buns. Either is delicious when scattered with pecans before baking. Warm and glazed, a sweet roll made from this dough is perfect any day for a breakfast or dessert treat with a cup of coffee.

yield: 11–16 rolls | FDT: 80°F

bulk fermentation: 60 minutes | retard: overnight | rest: 30 minutes | final fermentation: 60–75 minutes | bake: 375°F *and* 25–30 minutes

INGREDIENT	OUNCES	GRAMS	VOLUME	BAKERS %
SWEET DOUGH				
Milk, whole, 80°F	7.7	218	¾ cup + 2½ Tbsp	43.3%
Eggs	3.5	99	½ cup	19.7%
Butter, pliable but not melted	1.6	45	3 Tbsp	9.0%
Malt syrup	0.1	2	⅛ tsp	0.6%
Bread flour	17.8	505	4 cups	100.0%
Yeast, instant dry	0.2	6	2 tsp	1.1%
Sugar	2.0	57	¼ cup	11.2%
Salt	0.3	9	½ Tbsp	1.7%
TOTAL	33.2	941	•	186.6%
GARNISHES				
Pan Smear for Sticky Buns (page 94)	6–9	170–255	1 cup	
Pecans for Sticky Buns	3–5	85–141	⅔ cup	
Cinnamon Filling (page 90)	8	227	1 cup	
Flat Glaze (page 94)	as needed			

1. PUT the milk, eggs, butter and malt in the bowl of a mixer. Combine the flour and yeast and add to the bowl, then add the sugar and salt. Put the bowl on a mixer fitted with a dough hook and mix for 4 minutes on low speed, making sure to scrape down and flip the dough twice. Increase the speed to medium and mix for another 5 minutes to full gluten development, making sure to scrape down and flip the dough. Place the dough in a lightly oiled bowl large enough for it to double in size and cover with plastic wrap.

2. ALLOW the dough to rest and ferment in a warm place for 60 minutes, until when lightly pressed the dough springs back halfway.

3. PLACE the dough on a lightly floured work surface. Gently flatten the dough and place it in a baking pan lined with lightly floured parchment paper. Cover the dough and place in the refrigerator overnight.

4. THE NEXT DAY, remove the dough from the refrigerator and allow it to rest at room temperature for 30 minutes. Meanwhile, prepare the pans.

FOR STICKY BUNS, spread 6 oz of pan smear in an 8-inch baking pan to cover the bottom , and sprinkle with 3 oz of pecans. If you want to use a 10-inch baking pan, spread 9 oz of pan smear and sprinkle with 5 oz of pecans. Lightly oil the sides of the pan.

FOR CINNAMON ROLLS, generously oil the pan on the bottom and sides, then cover the bottom with a piece of parchment paper.

5. PLACE the dough on a lightly floured work surface and use a rolling pin to roll it out into a rectangle 9 by 26 inches. Spread the cinnamon filling on the dough, leaving ½ inch of dough exposed at the long top and bottom edges. Starting at one short end, carefully roll the dough up lengthwise and gently press along the final edge to close the seam of the 26-inch-long roll. Place the seam on the bottom and lightly flour the dough, then, using a chef's knife, cut the log into ¾-inch slices. Be careful not to saw through the dough; instead, cut straight down, pressing on the knife. Lay the slices flat in the prepared pans (so that the spiral of filling is visible).

1. Roll the dough out into a large rectangle about ¼ inch thick. Spread the cinnamon filling onto the rectangle, leaving a border of dough. Roll the top border toward you, tucking it in firmly as you go to avoid air pockets.

2. Cut the roll into even ¾-inch sections. Cut straight down so as not to pull or tear the dough. Slightly reshape the dough as you put the rolls in the pan.

3. If you are making cinnamon rolls, bake them with the spiral facing up, in a buttered pan lined with parchment paper. Place them close together so that they run into each other when they bake.

4. If you are making sticky buns, line the bottom of a baking dish with pan smear and nuts and place the rolls on top. Place them close together so that they run into each other when they bake.

FOR STICKY BUNS OR CINNAMON ROLLS USING AN 8-INCH PAN, place 8 buns around the outer edge and 3 in the middle to fill the pan.

FOR STICKY BUNS OR CINNAMON ROLLS USING A 10-INCH PAN, place 11 buns around the outer edge and 5 in the middle to fill the pan.

Cover the pan and allow the dough to rest and ferment in a warm place for 60–75 minutes, until when lightly pressed the dough springs back halfway.

6. TWENTY MINUTES before the end of final fermentation, preheat the oven to 400°F.

7. TRANSFER the buns to the oven and immediately reduce the temperature to 375°F. Bake for 25–30 minutes, until golden brown.

8. REMOVE the pan from the oven and allow it to cool for 5 minutes. Using oven mitts, put a large platter on top of the pan and turn it over quickly to remove the sticky buns from the pan. Place on a tray or large plate with parchment paper. Use a spatula to spread the gooey pan smear all over them. Remove the cinnamon rolls from the pan and brush with glaze while they are still hot.

Sticky Buns

Pan Smear for Sticky Buns

yield: 2 lbs

INGREDIENT	OUNCES	GRAMS	VOLUME	BAKERS %
Butter, soft	6.2	176	¾ cup	100.0%
Brown sugar	12.6	357	1⅔ cups	203.2%
Light corn syrup	11.5	326	1 cup	185.5%
Vanilla extract	0.3	9	2 tsp	4.8%
Salt	0.2	6	1 tsp	3.2%
Bread flour, sifted	1.0	28	¼ cup	16.1%
TOTAL	31.8	902	•	512.8%

CREAM the butter and brown sugar in a mixer with a paddle attachment until light in color and texture, making sure to scrape down the bowl and paddle periodically during the mixing. Add the corn syrup and vanilla and continue mixing, making sure to scrape down the bowl and paddle during the mixing. Add the salt and flour and continue to mix, scraping down the bowl and paddle after the addition. When all ingredients are well combined, put the mixture in a covered container and refrigerate until ready to use.

Flat Glaze

yield: 11 ounces

INGREDIENT	OUNCES	GRAMS	VOLUME	BAKERS %
Powdered sugar, sifted	8.0	227	1½ cups	100.0%
Milk	3.0	85	⅓ cup	37.5%
Vanilla extract	dash	dash	dash	dash
Orange or lemon zest (optional)	1 each	1 each	1 each	•
TOTAL	11.0	312	•	137.5%

COMBINE all of the ingredients in a bowl using a wire whisk. Allow to sit for 10 minutes. Stir before applying.

Cinnamon Rolls

Assorted Coffee Cakes

ALMOND COFFEE CAKE

This classic almond paste–filled cake is as temptingly sweet as ever. It makes an extra-special treat on the weekend. It can also be topped with streusel and finished with a simple glaze.

yield: 2 cakes | FDT: 80°F

retard: overnight | rest: 30 minutes | fermentation: 60 minutes | bake: 375°F and 25–30 minutes

INGREDIENT	OUNCES	GRAMS	VOLUME	BAKERS %
Sweet Dough (page 91)	33.0	936	•	100.0%
Almond Filling (page 99)	18.0	510	2½ cups	54.5%
Almonds, sliced, toasted	6.0	170	1¼ cups	18.2%
TOTAL	57.0	1616	•	172.7%
GARNISHES				
Egg wash	as needed			
Almonds, sliced	4.0	113	½ cup	
Flat Glaze (page 94)	as needed			

1. **MAKE** a recipe of Sweet Dough the day before you want to serve the coffee cake. After mixing, place the dough on a baking tray covered with a piece of floured parchment paper, roll out to 10 by 12 inches, and cover. Refrigerate overnight.

2. **PREPARE** the Almond Filling the day prior also, and refrigerate overnight.

3. **TO SHAPE,** remove the sweet dough and filling from the refrigerator and let them sit at room temperature for 30 minutes. Line 2 baking sheets with parchment paper.

4. **PLACE** the dough on a lightly floured work surface and roll out to a rectangle 12 by 26 inches. Spread the filling on the dough, leaving a ½-inch border at the top and bottom. If the filling is too stiff to spread, warm it slightly in the microwave. Sprinkle the almonds over the filling evenly. Roll the dough up by folding the top edge down halfway and then repeating to the bottom edge. Keep doing this until there is no more dough and close the seam

tightly. Set the roll seam-side down and lightly flour the dough. Cut the dough in half widthwise and place each half lengthwise on a prepared baking tray.

5. **WITH A PAIR OF SCISSORS,** cut each piece of dough to form an epi (see page 178). Open the scissors wide and place into the dough so the tips of the scissors are on the tray at a 45-degree angle and 1 inch from the top end. Cut the dough, but do not cut completely through, making a V-shaped cut, then gently pull the cut dough piece to the left. Cut the dough again 1 inch below where you last cut, and pull the cut piece to the right. Continue this down the whole length of the dough until finished. You should have a loaf that looks sort of like a sheaf of wheat.

6. **BRUSH** the surface with egg wash and cover. Spray a sheet of plastic wrap with oil to prevent it from sticking to the surface of the dough, and loosely cover the loaves. Let the loaves rest and ferment in a warm place for 60 minutes, until when lightly pressed the dough springs back halfway.

7. TWENTY MINUTES before the end of final fermentation, preheat the oven to 400°F.

8. UNCOVER the dough, brush with egg wash again, and sprinkle with almonds. Transfer the baking sheets to the oven and immediately reduce the temperature to 375°F. Bake for 15 minutes, then rotate the pans and bake for an additional 10–15 minutes, until golden brown.

9. PREPARE the glaze while baking the coffee cakes.

10. REMOVE the pans from the oven and brush the hot coffee cakes with hot glaze. Place the trays on a cooling rack and let the cakes cool completely.

STREUSEL

Everyone loves streusel. Change this recipe to suit your liking: Add additional spices, or even nuts for extra crunch.

yield: **2 pounds**

INGREDIENT	OUNCES	GRAMS	VOLUME	BAKERS %
Butter	8.9	252	½ cup	66.0%
All-purpose flour	13.4	380	3⅓ cups	100.0%
Sugar	4.5	128	¼ cup plus 1 Tbsp	33.5%
Brown sugar	4.5	128	¼ cup plus 1 Tbsp	33.5%
Cinnamon	0.5	14	2 Tbsp	6.7%
Salt	0.2	6	¼ tsp	0.1%
TOTAL	32.0	908		239.8%

PUT all the ingredients in the bowl of a mixer fitted with a paddle attachment. Mix until well combined. Refrigerate for 30 minutes to 1 hour, until firm. Break into small chunks and store in an airtight container in the refrigerator.

Almond Filling

This filling is most commonly used in coffee cakes but can be used in cinnamon rolls, sticky buns or babka. It may be stored in the refrigerator in an airtight container for up to 3 weeks.

yield: 1½ lb

INGREDIENT	OUNCES	GRAMS	VOLUME	BAKERS %
Almond paste	12.0	340	1⅓ cups	100.0%
Sugar	1.1	31	2 Tbsp + 1 tsp	9.2%
Butter, soft	6.0	170	¾ cup	50.0%
Eggs	6.0	170	¾ cup	50.0%
Salt	pinch	pinch	pinch	pinch
Vanilla extract	dash	dash	⅛ tsp	dash
Cake flour, sifted	1.1	31	4½ Tbsp	9.2%
TOTAL	26.2	742	•	218.4%

1. **PUT** the almond paste and sugar in a the bowl of a mixer fitted with a paddle attachment and mix for 2 minutes on medium speed. This should break down the almond paste and make the mixture smooth. Make sure to scrape down the bowl and paddle throughout this process.

2. **ADD** the butter and mix for 2 minutes on medium speed, making sure to scrape down the bowl.

3. **COMBINE** the eggs, salt and vanilla in a separate bowl. Add the egg mixture gradually to the mixer on medium speed, making sure to scrape down the bowl.

4. **ADD** the flour on low speed and mix until incorporated.

5. **PLACE** the filling in a container and cover. Refrigerate until needed.

6. **REMOVE** the filling from the refrigerator 30 minutes prior to use to help soften. If it is not soft enough to spread, warm slightly in the microwave.

ALMOND TWISTS

Almond paste can be purchased in a compact tube or can. It clumps up very easily and so it is important to mix it well to remove the lumps before adding other ingredients. After opening, almond paste dries out very quickly, so it is important to keep it tightly wrapped.

yield: **16 twists** | FDT: **80°F**

bulk fermentation: **30 minutes** | retard: **overnight** | rest: **30 minutes** | final fermentation: **45 minutes** | bake: **375°F** *and* **16–18 minutes**

INGREDIENT	OUNCES	GRAMS	VOLUME	BAKERS %
Almond paste	1.3	37	2½ Tbsp	7.3%
Butter, soft	5.0	142	⅔ cup	28.2%
Milk, 60°F	8.4	238	1 cup	47.5%
Honey	0.5	14	2 tsp	2.8%
Malt syrup	0.1	2	⅛ tsp	0.6%
All-purpose flour	17.7	502	4⅓ cups + 1 Tbsp	100.0%
Yeast, instant dry	0.2	6	1½ tsp	1.1%
Salt	0.4	11	2 tsp	2.3%
Almond Filling (page 99)	10.0	283	1¼ cups	•
Almonds, sliced	8.0	227	2 cups	•
TOTAL	51.6	1462	•	189.8%
GARNISHES				
Egg wash	as needed			
Coffee Cake Glaze (page 107)	as needed			
Flat Glaze (page 94) or Cream Cheese Glaze (page 106) (optional)	as needed			

1. MAKE the dough the day before you want to serve the twists. Put the almond paste and half of the butter in the bowl of a mixer fitted with a paddle attachment, and mix to soften and break down the almond paste. Add the rest of the butter and the milk, honey and malt, and blend well. Combine the flour, yeast and salt. Add to the bowl of the mixer and mix for 4 minutes on low speed, making sure to scrape down the bowl and flip the dough over. Mix for 4 minutes on medium speed, making sure to scrape down the bowl and flip the dough over. The dough should have intense gluten development. Place the dough in a lightly oiled bowl large enough for it to double in size and cover it with plastic wrap.

2. ALLOW the dough to rest and ferment in a warm place for 30 minutes, until when lightly pressed the dough springs back halfway.

3. PLACE the dough on a lightly floured work surface, roll out to a rectangle 10 by 12 inches, and place on a baking tray lined with parchment paper. Cover with plastic wrap and refrigerate overnight.

4. PREPARE the Almond Filling a day in advance and store in an airtight container in the refrigerator.

5. REMOVE the dough from the refrigerator and let it sit at room temperature for 30 minutes.

6. PLACE the dough on a lightly floured work surface and roll it into a rectangle 10 by 28 inches. Turn the dough so that a long side is facing you. Spread the almond filling on the bottom half of the dough, then sprinkle half of the almonds over the filling. Fold the top half of the dough down on top of the filling and seal. Cut the dough into 1-inch strips widthwise. Twist each one to a length of 7 inches and place 5 pieces on each tray, pressing the ends down to prevent them from unrolling. Brush with egg wash. Cover the twists lightly with plastic wrap and let rise in a warm place for 45 minutes, until when lightly pressed the dough springs back halfway.

7. TWENTY MINUTES before the end of final fermentation, preheat the oven to 425°F. Prepare the Coffee Cake Glaze for finishing, and prepare the Flat Glaze or Cream Cheese Glaze, if desired.

8. EGG WASH all the twists again and sprinkle with the remaining almonds.

9. TRANSFER the twists to the oven and immediately reduce the temperature to 375°F. Bake for 12 minutes, then rotate the pans and bake for an additional 4–6 minutes, until golden brown.

10. REMOVE from the oven and place the trays on cooling racks, then brush with the Coffee Cake Glaze. Once cooled, the twists can be glazed again with Flat Glaze or Cream Cheese Glaze.

CREAM CHEESE AND PECAN COFFEE CAKE

The name "coffee cake" can cause a misconception because the cake itself does not actually need to contain coffee flavorings. While there are coffee-flavored coffee cakes, the name actually refers to a cake accompanied by a cup of coffee.

yield: **2 cakes** | FDT: **80°F**
retard: **overnight** | rest: **30 minutes** | fermentation: **60 minutes** | bake: **375°F** *and* 25–30 minutes

INGREDIENT	OUNCES	GRAMS	VOLUME	BAKERS %
Sweet Dough (page 91)	33.0	936	•	100.0%
Cream Cheese Filling (page 104)	20.0	567	1½ cups	60.6%
Pecan halves, toasted	4.0	113	1 cup	12.1%
TOTAL	57.0	1616		172.7%
GARNISHES				
Egg wash	as needed			
Pecan halves	4.0	97	1 cup	
Coffe Cake Glaze (page 107)	as needed			

1. MAKE a recipe of Sweet Dough the day before you want to serve the cake. After mixing, place the dough on a baking tray lined with a piece of floured parchment paper, roll out to a rectangle 10 by 12 inches, and cover. Refrigerate overnight.

2. PREPARE the Cream Cheese Filling the day prior also, and refrigerate overnight.

3. TO BAKE, remove the sweet dough and filling from the refrigerator and let them sit at room temperature for 30 minutes. Line 2 baking sheets with parchment paper.

4. PLACE the dough on a lightly floured work surface and roll it out to a rectangle 12 by 26 inches. Spread the filling in an even layer on the dough, leaving a ½-inch border at the top and bottom. If the filling is too stiff to spread, warm it slightly in the microwave. Sprinkle the pecans over the filling evenly. Roll the dough up by the top edge. Keep doing this until there is no more dough and close the seam tightly. Set the roll seam-side down and lightly flour the dough. Cut the dough in half widthwise, then roll each half out to 24 inches long. Connect the 2 ends of each piece to form a ring and place each ring on a separate parchment paper–lined baking tray.

5. WITH A BENCH SCRAPER, cut into the outer edge of each ring ¾ inch. Continue this around the ring every 1½ inches. Go back and gently open the cuts to give them some space between.

6. BRUSH the surface with egg wash. Spray 2 pieces of plastic wrap with spray oil to prevent it from sticking to the surface of the dough and lightly cover the rings. Let the rings rest and ferment in a warm place for 60 minutes, until when lightly pressed the dough springs back halfway.

7. TWENTY MINUTES before the end of final fermentation, preheat the oven to 400°F.

8. UNCOVER the dough, brush it again with egg wash, and sprinkle with pecans.

9. TRANSFER the rings to the oven and immediately reduce the temperature to 375°F. Bake for 15 minutes, then rotate the pans and bake for an additional 10–15 minutes, until golden brown.

10. PREPARE the glaze while baking the coffee cakes.

11. REMOVE the pans from the oven and brush the hot coffee cakes with hot glaze. Place the trays on a cooling rack to cool completely.

CREAM CHEESE FILLING

This filling is used in the Cream Cheese and Pecan Coffee Cake and the Cream Cheese–Apple-Walnut Coffee Cake, but can also be used in cinnamon rolls, sticky buns or babka.

yield: 24 oz

INGREDIENT	OUNCES	GRAMS	VOLUME	BAKERS %
Butter, soft	2.0	57	¼ cup	15.0%
Sugar	4.4	125	⅔ cup	33.1%
Vanilla extract	dash	dash	⅛ tsp	dash
Bread flour	1.3	37	¼ cup + 1 tsp	9.8%
Cornstarch	0.6	17	2 Tbsp	4.5%
Salt	pinch	pinch	pinch	pinch
Eggs	2.3	65	¼ cup	17.3%
Cream cheese, soft	13.3	377	1⅔ cups	100.0%
TOTAL	23.9	678	•	179.7%

1. **PUT** the butter, sugar and vanilla in the bowl of a mixer fitted with a paddle attachment and mix for 2 minutes on low speed. Make sure to scrape down the bowl and paddle throughout this process. Mix for 2 minutes on medium speed, making sure to scrape down the bowl.

2. **SIFT** together the flour, cornstarch and salt, then add to the mixer. Mix on low speed until combined, making sure to scrape down the bowl and paddle.

3. **ADD** the eggs gradually to the mixer on medium speed, making sure to scrape down the bowl and paddle.

4. **ADD** the cream cheese gradually to the mixer on medium speed, making sure to scrape down the bowl and paddle. The mixture will have little lumps and this is acceptable, but large pieces of cream cheese should be blended in.

5. **PLACE** the filling in a container and cover. Refrigerate until needed.

6. **REMOVE** the filling from the refrigerator 30 minutes prior to use to help it soften. If it is not soft enough to spread, warm slightly in the microwave.

CREAM CHEESE–APPLE-WALNUT COFFEE CAKE

The nuts in the filling can be substituted with currants, raisins or any similar dried fruit, or with a mixture of nuts and dried fruit. The filling may also be replaced with any of the other fillings in the book.

yield: **2 cakes** | FDT: **80°F**

retard: **overnight** | rest: **30 minutes** | fermentation: **60 minutes** | bake: **375°F** and **25–30 minutes**

INGREDIENT	OUNCES	GRAMS	VOLUME	BAKERS %
Sweet Dough (page 91)	33.0	936	•	100.0%
Cream Cheese Filling (page 104)	20.0	567	•	60.6%
Apples, diced	9.0	255	1½ cups	27.3%
Walnuts, chopped, toasted	6.0	170	1½ cups	18.2%
TOTAL	68.0	1928	•	206.1%
GARNISHES				
Egg wash	as needed			
Walnuts	as needed			
Streusel (page 98)	6.0	170	1 cup	
Flat Glaze (page 94)	as needed			

1. MAKE a recipe of Sweet Dough the day before you want to serve the cake. After mixing, place the dough on a baking tray lined with a piece of floured parchment paper, roll out to a rectangle 10 by 12 inches, and cover. Refrigerate overnight.

2. PREPARE the Cream Cheese Filling the day prior also, and refrigerate overnight.

3. TO SHAPE, remove the sweet dough and filling from the refrigerator and let them sit at room temperature for 30 minutes. Line 2 baking sheets with parchment paper.

4. PLACE the dough on a lightly floured work surface and roll out to a rectangle 12 by 26 inches. Spread the cream cheese filling on the dough, leaving a ½-inch border at the top and bottom. If the

filling is too stiff to spread, warm it slightly in the microwave. Sprinkle the apples and walnuts over the filling evenly. Roll the dough up by folding the top edge down. Keep doing this until there is no more dough and close the seam tightly. Set the roll seam-side down and lightly flour the dough. Cut the dough in half lengthwise, then cut each piece in half lengthwise, keeping it connected at 1 end. Twist the 2 strips together (see photographs on page 107) and place each one on a separate tray.

5. BRUSH the surface with egg wash. Spray 2 pieces of plastic wrap with spray oil to prevent them from sticking to the surface of the dough and lightly cover the twists. Let the twists rest and ferment in a warm place for 60 minutes, until when lightly pressed the dough springs back halfway.

6. TWENTY MINUTES before the end of fermentation, preheat the oven to 400°F.

7. UNCOVER the dough, brush it again with egg wash, and sprinkle with walnuts and streusel.

8. TRANSFER the twists to the oven and immediately reduce the temperature to 375°F. Bake for 15 minutes, then rotate the pans and bake for an additional 10–15 minutes, until golden brown.

9. PREPARE the glaze while baking the coffee cakes.

10. REMOVE the pans from the oven and brush the hot coffee cakes with hot glaze. Place the trays on a cooling rack to cool completely.

CREAM CHEESE GLAZE

The corn syrup in this glaze gives the baked breads a wonderful shine. It goes well with many sweet doughs and desserts to give them a dramatic final presentation. It can also be brushed on cinnamon rolls and coffee cake, or put into a pastry bag and piped over them. The glaze may be stored in an airtight container for up to 3 weeks in the refrigerator.

yield: 1 lb

INGREDIENT	OUNCES	GRAMS	VOLUME	BAKERS %
Cream cheese, soft	8.0	227	1 cup	100.0%
Powdered sugar, sifted	4.0	113	¾ cup	50.0%
Orange zest	0.2	6	1 Tbsp	2.5%
Vanilla extract	dash	dash	⅛ tsp	dash
Corn syrup	5.0	142	⅔ cup	62.5%
TOTAL	17.2	488	•	215.0%

1. PUT the cream cheese, sugar, zest and vanilla in the bowl of a mixer fitted with a paddle attachment. Mix on medium speed until combined, making sure to scrape down the bowl.

2. ADD the corn syrup gradually on low speed, making sure to scrape down the bowl.

3. PUT the glaze in a covered container in the refrigerator. Cool the bread before coating with this glaze.

COFFEE CAKE GLAZE

This glaze lends several benefits to the final product. It seals in moisture to preserve the bread. It also keeps garnishes in place and, finally, adds a beautiful shine. The glaze may be stored in an airtight container for up to 3 weeks in the refrigerator.

yield: 12 oz

INGREDIENT	OUNCES	GRAMS	VOLUME	BAKERS %
Apple or apricot jelly	8.0	227	¾ cup	100.0%
Water	4.0	113	½ cup	50.0%
TOTAL	12.0	340	1¼ cups	150.0%

COMBINE the jelly and water in a small pot over medium-high heat. Heat the mixture to a boil, stirring constantly, then remove from the heat. Lightly brush the hot glaze onto the product while it is hot (to seal in moisture and prevent having too much glaze).

NOTE: *Leftover glaze can be cooled, placed in an airtight container, and stored in the refrigerator for up to 3 weeks.*

Roll the dough out into a large rectangle. Spread the filling onto the rectangle, leaving a border. Pick up the top edge and roll it toward you, tucking it in firmly as you go to avoid air pockets.

When the dough is all rolled up, rotate it 90 degrees so that the short edge faces you. Using a dough divider, cut each roll in half lengthwise, leaving it connected at the top. This will expose the filling for a nice design element.

Twist the two pieces of dough together, starting at the top and working your way toward you. Secure the top in place to make the dough easier to twist. Pinch the two pieces of dough back together at the bottom to form a single loaf.

SUNFLOWER SEED BREAD

This dough is honey sweetened and wholesomely flavored with wheat bran and sunflower seeds. Bake it into a loaf for summer sandwich bread or shape the dough into rolls for a bread basket.

yield: 2 loaves at 28 oz or about 2 dozen rolls at 2 oz | FDT: 82°F | soaker: overnight | bulk fermentation: 45–60 minutes
final fermentation: 45–60 minutes | bake loaves: 375°F and 40–45 minutes | bake rolls: 400°F and 14–16 minutes

INGREDIENT	OUNCES	GRAMS	VOLUME	BAKERS %
SOAKER				
Milk, whole	22.0	624	2¾ cups	78%
Wheat bran	2.9	82	¾ cup	10.3%
FINAL DOUGH				
Soaker	24.9	706	•	88.3%
Honey	2.5	71	7 Tbsp + 1 tsp	8.9%
Sunflower oil	1.5	43	1½ Tbsp	5.3%
Malt syrup	0.1	2	½ tsp	0.2%
Yeast, instant dry	0.1	2	½ tsp	0.2%
Bread flour	25.3	717	2½ cups	89.7%
Salt	0.6	17	1 Tbsp	2.1%
Sunflower seeds, toasted	2.9	82	5 Tbsp	10.3%
TOTAL	57.9	1640	•	205.0%
GARNISHES				
Egg wash	as needed			
Sunflower seeds	as needed			

1. **TO MAKE THE SOAKER,** combine the milk and wheat bran in a bowl and soak overnight in the refrigerator.

2. **TO MAKE THE DOUGH,** put the soaker, honey, oil, malt, yeast, flour and salt in the bowl of a mixer. Place the bowl on a mixer fitted with a dough hook. Mix for 4 minutes on low speed, making sure to scrape and flip the dough over. Increase the speed to medium and mix for 7 minutes more, making sure to scrape and flip the dough over. The dough should be wet and tacky with full gluten development. Add the sunflower seeds and mix for 1 minute on low speed, then 1 additional minute on medium speed. Place the dough in a lightly oiled bowl large enough for it to double in size and cover with plastic wrap.

3. **PLACE** the dough in a warm place to rest and ferment for 45–60 minutes, until when lightly touched the dough springs back halfway.

4. **PLACE** the dough on a lightly floured work surface and divide it into two 28-oz pieces for pan loaves, or 2-oz pieces for rolls. Round each piece against the tabletop. Cover lightly with plastic

wrap and allow the pieces to rest and ferment for 15 minutes, until when lightly touched the dough springs back halfway.

5. FOR ROLLS, place 3 by 5 on a baking sheet lined with parchment paper. For pan loaves, make the final shaping and roll until the dough pieces are 12 inches long. For loaves, grease 2 loaf pans and place the dough in the pans with the seam sides down. Egg wash the dough, lightly cover with plastic wrap that has been lightly sprayed with oil, and allow to rest and ferment in a warm place for 45–60 minutes, until when lightly touched the dough springs back halfway.

6. TWENTY MINUTES before the end of final fermentation, preheat the oven to 425°F.

7. EGG WASH the dough again and sprinkle with the sunflower seeds. Immediately reduce the oven temperature to 400°F and bake the rolls for 14–16 minutes. To bake the loaves, reduce the oven temperature to 375°F and bake for 40–45 minutes, or until golden brown.

8. REMOVE the pans from the oven and remove the rolls or loaves from the pans immediately.

Sunflower Seed Bread, Mulitgrain Bread and Soft Mulitgrain Rolls

CARAWAY-RYE BREAD

This recipe features the classic pairing of earthy, anise-like caraway seeds with hearty rye. The finished bread is garnished with salt to complete the bold flavor. Two thick slices from a baked loaf of caraway rye make for the start of an excellent sandwich.

yield: 2 loaves at 28 oz or 24 rolls at 2 oz | FDT: 82°F

bulk fermentation: 75 minutes | final fermentation: 60–75 minutes | bake loaves: 400°F *and* 35–40 minutes | bake rolls: 450°F *and* 19–21 minutes

INGREDIENT	OUNCES	GRAMS	VOLUME	BAKERS %
Rye flour, medium	8.3	234	2 cups	25.0%
Bread flour	24.8	703	4½ cups	75.0%
Yeast, instant dry	0.2	6	1½ tsp	0.6%
Sugar	0.6	18	1 Tbsp + 1 tsp	1.9%
Salt	0.8	23	1 Tbsp	2.5%
Vegetable oil	2.6	73	¼ cup	7.8%
Molasses	0.6	18	2 tsp	1.9%
Malt syrup	0.2	6	⅛ tsp	0.6%
Water, 80°F	19.4	551	2 cups + 1½ Tbsp	58.8%
Caraway seeds	0.4	12	1 Tbsp + 2 tsp	1.3%
TOTAL	57.9	1644	•	175.4%
GARNISHES				
Coarse salt	as needed			
Caraway seeds	as needed			

1. MIX together all the ingredients, except for the caraway seeds. In a mixer fitted with a dough hook, mix on low speed for about 4 minutes. The dough will have full gluten development. Increase to medium speed and mix for another 4 minutes. Flip the dough over twice during mixing. Add the caraway seeds and mix for 1 minute on low speed, then 1 minute on medium speed. Flip the dough over twice during mixing.

2. REMOVE the dough from the mixer and place in a lightly oiled bowl covered with a cloth or plastic wrap. Allow the dough to ferment for 45–60 minutes.

3. TWENTY MINUTES before the end of final fermentation, preheat the oven to 475°F.

4. PLACE the dough on a lightly floured work surface and divide into two 28-oz pieces. Preshape the dough into round pieces and place with the seams up. Cover with plastic wrap and allow to rest and ferment for 15 minutes. Preheat the oven to 425°F.

5. ON A CLEAN SURFACE WITH A LITTLE FLOUR, shape each piece of dough into an oblong loaf measuring 12 inches in length. Bring the top edge of each piece over one fourth of the way and tuck it in. Repeat this 3 more times, making sure to close the seam on the one fourth.

6. PLACE in the prepared pans with the seams on the bottom and lightly cover with plastic wrap. Allow to rest and ferment in a warm place for 60–75 minutes.

7. PLACE a baking tray with 3 cups of water under the baking area in the oven 15 minutes before baking.

8. PREPARE the loaves for baking by uncovering and spraying them with water. Allow to sit for 5 minutes, then score the loaves directly down the middle from end to end. Spray each loaf with water and sprinkle the top with salt and caraway seeds.

9. PLACE the loaves in the oven and bake at 400°F for 20 minutes. Then remove the steam tray, rotate the pans, and bake for an additional 15 to 20 minutes.

10. REMOVE from the oven, remove the loaves from the baking pans, and place on a cooling rack.

FOR ROLLS: Divide the dough into 2-oz portions. Form the dough into rounds and place them 4 by 3 on 2 baking trays lined with parchment paper. Cover and allow them to rest and ferment in a warm place for 45 minutes, until when touched lightly the dough springs back halfway. Uncover the rolls and spray with water. Allow them to sit for 5 minutes, then score the tops, making a cut across the center. Spray with water again and sprinkle with salt and caraway seeds. Transfer the trays to the oven and immediately reduce the temperature to 450°F. Bake for 15 minutes, rotate the trays, and bake for another 4–6 minutes, until golden brown. Remove from the oven and place the trays on cooling racks.

Hamburger Buns

Add a touch of gourmet to your summer grilling and make sandwich buns from scratch with this simple recipe. Slightly sweetened with honey, this dough can be shaped into soft hamburger buns or even more simply into small dinner rolls, perfectly topped with a dab of butter.

yield: 12 buns at 4.5 oz or 24 rolls at 2 oz | FDT: 80°F
sponge: 30 minutes | bulk fermentation: 45–60 minutes | final fermentation: 30–45 minutes | bake: 400°F and 18–20 minutes

INGREDIENT	OUNCES	GRAMS	VOLUME	BAKERS %
SPONGE				
Milk, 90°F	10.8	306	1¼ cups	42.2%
Malt syrup	0.1	2	½ tsp	0.4%
Bread flour	12.8	363	2⅔ cups	50.0%
Yeast, instant dry	0.3	9	2¼ tsp	1.2%
FINAL DOUGH				
Sponge	24.0	680	•	93.8%
Milk, 80°F	5.7	162	⅔ cup	22.3%
Honey	2.0	57	2 Tbsp + 2 tsp	7.8%
Butter, soft	2.9	82	⅓ cup	11.3%
Bread flour	12.8	363	2⅔ cups	50.0%
Salt	0.6	17	1 Tbsp	2.3%
TOTAL	48.0	1361	•	187.5%
GARNISH				
Egg wash	as needed			

1. **TO MAKE THE SPONGE,** combine the milk and malt in a bowl. In a separate bowl, combine the flour with the yeast, and then add this mixture to the milk. Mix the sponge together by hand for 2 minutes to develop some gluten structure, making sure all the ingredients are combined into a homogenous mass. Cover the bowl with plastic wrap, and allow the sponge to ferment in a warm place for 30 minutes, until double in size and when lightly touched the dough springs back halfway.

2. **TO MAKE THE FINAL DOUGH,** put the sponge in the bowl of a mixer with the milk, honey and butter. Mix on low speed for 1 min-ute to break up the sponge. Add the flour and salt, then place the bowl on a mixer fitted with a dough hook. Mix for 4 minutes on low speed, making sure to scrape down and flip the dough over twice during this time. Increase the speed to medium and continue to mix for another 4 minutes, making sure to scrape down and flip the dough over twice. The dough should have full gluten development and will feel slightly tacky. Place the dough in a lightly oiled bowl large enough for it to double in size and cover with plastic wrap.

3. **ALLOW** the dough to rest and ferment in a warm place for 45–60 minutes, until when touched lightly it springs back halfway.

4. PLACE the dough on a lightly floured work surface and divide it into 4.5-oz pieces for hamburger buns or 2-oz pieces for dinner rolls. Round each piece against the tabletop, then place the rounds seam-side down on a baking tray lined with parchment paper. For hamburger buns, place them on 2 trays 2 by 3. For rolls, place them 3 by 4 on 2 trays.

5. LIGHTLY brush the rolls with egg wash and, for hamburger buns, lightly flatten the rounds with your fingers (see photograph). Cover the dough lightly with plastic wrap and allow it to rest and ferment for 30–45 minutes, until when touched lightly it springs back half-way. If making hamburger buns, uncover the dough after 20 minutes of rest and gently flatten them again with a little egg wash on your fingertips. Then cover again and continue to let them rest.

6. TWENTY MINUTES before the end of final fermentation, preheat the oven to 450°F. Prepare the dough for the oven by brushing with egg wash again.

7. PLACE the trays in the oven and immediately reduce the temperature to 400°F. Bake for 14 minutes. Rotate the trays and bake for an additional 4–6 minutes, until golden brown.

8. REMOVE the trays from the oven and place them on a cooling rack.

Flatten the rolls to just about ½ inch thick after applying egg wash.

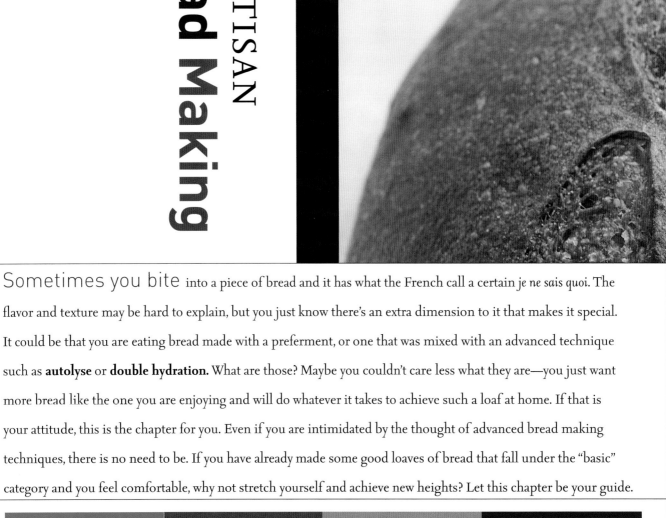

ADVANCED ARTISAN
Bread Making

Sometimes you bite into a piece of bread and it has what the French call a certain *je ne sais quoi*. The flavor and texture may be hard to explain, but you just know there's an extra dimension to it that makes it special. It could be that you are eating bread made with a preferment, or one that was mixed with an advanced technique such as **autolyse** or **double hydration.** What are those? Maybe you couldn't care less what they are—you just want more bread like the one you are enjoying and will do whatever it takes to achieve such a loaf at home. If that is your attitude, this is the chapter for you. Even if you are intimidated by the thought of advanced bread making techniques, there is no need to be. If you have already made some good loaves of bread that fall under the "basic" category and you feel comfortable, why not stretch yourself and achieve new heights? Let this chapter be your guide.

CHAPTER SIX

By now you are already familiar with the twelve steps of bread baking (see page 26). Prepare for a big leap. It's time to try some of the various preferments, including pâte fermentée, sponge, biga, poolish and even sours that you can start on your own. There are also a few advanced mixing techniques. "Autolyse" will help you to improve lean breads and the "blitz" method is the key element in the methods for highly enriched breads such as brioche. Yet another mixing method, called "double hydration," allows you to make better breads that contain a lot of water, such as ciabatta.

If any of this sounds too difficult, don't give up. It just takes a little extra time and extra work, all of which will be worth it when you taste the results. You will get detailed instructions with each recipe in the book, but if you read what follows in this chapter and understand what you need to do, each process will be that much clearer.

Preferments

What is a preferment? It's exactly what it sounds like, with an emphasis on the "PRE." You ferment some of the bread's ingredients ahead of time: a portion of the total flour, water and yeast. Once you've become used to eating bread made with a preferment, it's hard to go back. The dough is stronger and more easily manipulated, the finished bread's flavor and texture have more depth, and even its keeping quality improves. Why is this? When flour, water, yeast (and sometimes salt) ferment over a longer period of time, the dough becomes more acidic and more alcohol is produced, providing more flavor and aroma. More gases develop, allowing for better

leavening. The prolonged fermentation strengthens the gluten, which in turn leads to a more elastic dough with more structure. And because of the aforementioned acidity, the bread will be more tender and last longer on the shelf.

Types of Preferments

Different types of bread lend themselves to different types of preferments, but there are no hard-and-fast rules. French bakers love to use watery poolish in their baguettes. You can, however, make the same bread recipe with a stiffer preferment called a biga, and get a different taste and texture. Experiment and see what you like. Think of preferments as a means to an end: If you want more acidity, a stronger dough, more flavor or more leavening, you have a range of options. One trait all the above preferments share is that they allow for more natural leavening—meaning that you will be able to use less commercial yeast, and in the process, gain a more natural fermented flavor.

Later in the chapter, you'll learn how to make a sour, so you can make sourdough (also known as *pain levain*), which relies upon wild yeast and requires more time. But the good news about the other preferments covered here is that you can use a little commercial yeast to get things started. Here's a look at the various techniques.

SPONGE
A sponge is another classic, but faster, way to strengthen bread dough. Here you take flour, water and yeast; mix them; and allow the mixture to ferment at room temperature for 30–60 minutes.

Sponge. Left to right: after mixing and after fermentation.

PÂTE FERMENTÉE

Pâte fermentée (pronounced "paht fare-men-TAY," or just "paht fur-MENT") is also known as "old dough." It may not sound so appetizing the first time you hear about it, but it's a method that's been used for thousands of years. People learned to simply reserve a small piece of dough from the bread they were making, and use it to help leaven the next day's batch. The recipes in this book (including a lean dough made with pâte fermentée) will instruct you to make a small amount of dough ahead of time for this preferment. You will not actually be taking a piece from a previous batch (unless you frequently make bread and want to do this).

PÂTE FERMENTÉE

100%	Bread flour
69.6%	80° water
1.2%	Dry yeast
2.9%	Salt
1.2%	Malt syrup

To make pâte fermentée, you combine the flour, water, yeast, salt and malt syrup in proportions according to your recipe. It tends to have a doughlike consistency with a flour to water ratio of 1.5:1. It needs to ferment at room temperature for 30 minutes, then is placed in the refrigerator for at least 18 hours. It can stay refrigerated for up to three days. Since you can make pâte fermentée well ahead of time, it can be an easy way to strengthen your dough and add flavor and aroma to the final loaf.

In a pinch, you can make pâte fermentée the same day and let it ferment at room temperature for three hours before using it. If you choose to do this, you will need to make the water in your final recipe colder, because the pâte fermentée will not have been refrigerated.

Pâte Fermentée. Left to right: after mixing and after fermentation.

Then you add the rest of the ingredients when it's time to proceed with your recipe. Why use a sponge? For one thing, it is an especially useful tool for speeding up the fermentation of and strengthening enriched doughs. It allows the yeast in the recipe to get a head start before being added to the final dough.

Consider such holiday breads as challah, stollen, panettone, gugelhopf and gibassier (all of which contain high amounts of fat and sugar). If you were to mix all the ingredients together from the beginning, without making a sponge first, the fat and sugar would hinder the development of gluten and slow the fermentation. It would take a much longer time to make these types of bread. Fermenting a sponge for thirty minutes to an hour moves the process along.

A sponge is also helpful when making bagels and bialys. In this case, the sponge not only helps the yeast along, but, due to the longer fermentation time (one hour), it helps bring flavor to the end product. Once the final dough is mixed and shaped, it is retarded in the refrigerator overnight to provide for a long period of slow fermentation and strengthening. Unlike most other bread doughs, bagel and bialy doughs can be frozen after shaping, then thawed and retarded the night before you plan to bake them. Freezing the dough works in this case because there is a higher amount of yeast in the recipe. In general, though, freezing dough is not recommended because it will not give you the best result. Once frozen, the yeast will never be as active as it might have been otherwise.

BIGA

"Biga" (pronounced BEE-gah) is the word Italians use for a preferment. It is generally a very stiff mixture, with a ratio of flour to water that can be slightly higher than 2:1. To make a biga, you mix the flour, water and a small portion of yeast together in a mixing bowl (you will find the biga hard to mix by hand because it is quite rigid). Make sure to mix this well—fully incorporate all of the flour so you have a homogenous mass. Next, place it in the refrigerator for two hours (to slow down the yeast), then remove it and let it ferment at room temperature for ten to twelve hours. It does require planning ahead, but with a biga you will get a pleasant aroma and a stronger flavor than you would with some of the other preferments. You will also have a dough with a strengthened gluten structure that is more elastic. Biga is often employed with doughs that are soft and wet, such as ciabatta and focaccia. The stiffness of the biga can give these doughs a head start on gluten development.

POOLISH

Poolish (pronounced "poo-LEESH") is the most soupy of the preferments, with a ratio of flour to liquid that is 1:1. It is a technique that originated in Poland, and has been embraced by many French bakers for their baguettes. Like biga, poolish is a mixture of flour, water and a small portion of yeast. And like biga, once the poolish is mixed, it is refrigerated for two hours to slow down the yeast. Next, it is removed

Biga. Left to right: after mixing and after fermentation.

Poolish. Left to right: after mixing and after fermentation.

from the refrigerator and fermented at room temperature for ten to twelve hours. Unlike biga, however, adding poolish to your bread results in a milder flavor and aroma, and more gas production for a lighter loaf. Sometimes if poolish is used in a wet dough, such as ciabatta, you will also use the double hydration mixing technique described later in this chapter for gas production.

WHY RETARD DOUGH?

Some types of bread do better if they are retarded, in other words, if their rate of fermentation is slowed down by refrigeration. The typical refrigerator temperature is 40°F, which works well enough to slow the activity of yeast without stopping it altogether. One good example of retarding is Pizza Dough (page 148). The recipes in this book direct you to mix your pizza dough the night before. Then you let the dough ferment for half an hour and put it in the refrigerator overnight. The next day, when you are ready, let the dough come to room temperature before rolling it out for your crust. Why do this? Retarding the dough allows the crust to become more extensible, meaning that it stretches more easily without ripping. Retarding the dough also helps to enhance its flavor and strength.

Brioche is another type of bread that requires retardation. Because of the high amount of fat and sugar in this type of dough, brioche requires a longer and more involved mixing period called "blitz." Once brioche dough has reached full gluten development during mixing, the rate of fermentation must be slowed down, and the butter in the dough must be prevented from melting. Therefore, brioche dough goes straight from the mixing bowl, covered, into the refrigerator overnight, allowing the fat to chill and making the dough workable so that it can be shaped. Other enriched doughs, such as Sweet Dough (see page 91), are retarded overnight after a brief fermentation period at room temperature. This helps not only with keeping the butter in the dough cold, but also with extensibility, so the rolls are easier to manipulate the next day.

Retardation is also a technique that works well for sourdough breads. Once a sourdough bread has been shaped, refrigerating it overnight will help it to develop more flavor and acidity. Retardation is not required for sourdough, however. The bread can go right into the oven after it is proofed at room temperature for two to three hours. The resulting loaf will have more volume than one that has been retarded, but it will have less flavor and acidity due to the shorter fermentation time.

Sour: In a Category of Its Own

Sour (some people call it sourdough starter) is a preferment that you make yourself without using commercial yeast. You mix the flour and water, and let it capture wild yeast in the air and utilize the yeast present in the flour. This is the way bakers made bread for millennia, all the way back to ancient Egypt. Commercial yeast wasn't invented until the mid-nineteenth century, shortly after Louis Pasteur confirmed that yeast existed. So what does sour mean to you? Why bother if there are so many other preferments you can make using commercial yeast? As good as those preferments are, the flavor and texture of bread made with sour (the French call it *levain*) is incomparable. And like all of the things you have learned about bread up to now, it just takes some extra time and persistence.

Some bread books instruct you to establish a "chef" or a "mother" (a sourdough base that takes a week to ten days) before spending another week or so making a sour to use in your bread. For the recipes in this book, there is really no need to get that complicated. You will need to develop a "base sour" using bread flour a week before you want to use it to bake bread. All this requires is about fifteen minutes of your time each day. You will have to mix flour and water together the first day, stir it the next, then take some of the mixture the third day and feed it with more flour and water, and continue in this fashion until you've reached day seven.

It pays to be consistent in the type of flour you use to build your base sour. Calculate the total amount of flour you will need and make sure you have enough of the flour at the beginning to complete all seven days of feedings while you are establishing the sour. If you change the type of flour during this process, it can alter the results. You will also want to make enough of the sour so you have some left over after you've made your bread. This way, you will have a piece of the sour to feed and keep alive for future batches of bread.

Later in this section, you will learn how to convert your white sour base to another type of sour using other flours. If you want to make a rye sour, for example, you can take your white sour base (after it's been established with seven days of feedings) and turn it into a rye sour by feeding it for two to three more days with rye flour. You can also do this with whole wheat; durum flour; or mixtures of rye and whole wheat, or durum and whole wheat.

Whatever type of sour you are making, you need to pay attention to the ambient temperature. You are looking for a moderate room temperature in the low seventies. If your room temperature is warmer than 80°F, you need to make adjustments to the temperature of the water to compensate. You can either use lower-temperature water, or, after feeding the sour, place it in the refrigerator and take it out after two hours. This will compensate for the higher room temperature.

Now, it's time to make your white sour base.

HOW TO BUILD AND DEVELOP A SOUR

To Establish a White Sour Base:

Day 1

INGREDIENT	OUNCES	GRAMS	VOLUME
Bread flour	4.0	113	1¼ cups
Water, 85°F	4.0	113	½ cup

DAY 1: Mix equal amounts of flour with water (at 85°F) until the mixture is homogenous. Use a bowl big enough for the mixture to double in size. The bowl should be glass or stainless steel, since these, unlike plastic, are less likely to retain odors. (You may use plastic if the vessel is fresh and reserved for this purpose.) Once you have finished mixing and have scraped down the bowl to make it look tidy, cover and let it sit at room temperature for 18 to 24 hours. The goal during this time is for the enzymes to break down the starches in the flour into sugars. Any wild yeast present on the flour or in the air will begin feeding on these sugars.

DAY 2: Uncover your bowl and you will notice that something is happening. You will probably see that your mixture is still wet, but the aroma will have changed from a floury smell to something riper. You will probably see some bubbling. You should not be seeing streaks of mold: If you are, throw it out and start over. If everything looks good, use a clean hand or utensil to mix it together again. (If any foreign bacteria get into the dough, this can change the sour and overtake it.) By mixing the sour, you are moving around the food for the yeast, incorporating air and expelling gas, as well as equalizing the temperature and strengthening the structure. There is no need to feed your starter today. Scrape anything off the sides of your bowl into the mix, cover, and let it sit for another 18 to 24 hours so it has more time to develop acidity and flavor.

Day 3

INGREDIENT	OUNCES	GRAMS	VOLUME
Water, 85°F	4.0	113	½ cup
Mix from Day 2	4.0	113	•
Bread flour	4.0	113	1¼ cups

DAY 3: When you uncover your bowl today, you will notice an even greater change. It should be very bubbly and smell pleasantly fermented. Your wild yeast is ready for a new supply of food. Use a scale to weigh the amount of mixture you need and discard the rest. (Yes, this may seem like a waste, but you don't want your starter to take over your kitchen, so you must throw some out along the way to keep its size in check.) Next, you will place equal parts of fresh water (at 85°F) and your starter mixture from the previous day into a clean mixing bowl. Once you have blended these together, add an equal part of flour to the mix and blend with your hands until it's homogenous. Scrape down the sides of your bowl, cover, and let it sit for another 18 to 24 hours.

Day 4

INGREDIENT	OUNCES	GRAMS	VOLUME
Water, 85°F	3.0	83	⅓ cup
Mix from Day 3	6.0	170	•
Bread flour	3.0	85	⅔ cup

DAY 4: What will you find in the bowl today? The mixture should look different from the one you left the previous day. It should be bubbly, still somewhat soupy, and smell pleasantly fermented, but with a stronger aroma than the previous day. Today when you feed the starter, your proportions will be different: a ratio of water, starter and flour that is 1:2:1. Why? You want to give the wild yeast a chance to take off. Keep the water warm at 85°F. Once you have blended the ingredients, the mixture will be looser than what you saw yesterday. Scrape down the bowl, cover, and let it sit for another 18 to 24 hours.

Days 5–7

INGREDIENT	OUNCES	GRAMS	VOLUME
Water, 55°F	6.0	170	⅔ cup
Mix from Day 4	3.0	85	•
Bread flour	9.0	255	2 cups

DAYS 5–7: When you prepare to feed your starter on Day 5, you will notice it has become very aromatic and bubbly. It is sitting higher in the container than what you saw the previous day. The smell will be very strong.

From here on out, when you feed your starter, you will be using a ratio of 2:1:3. That's two parts water, one part sour and three parts flour.

EXAMPLE	
Water	4 oz
Sour	2 oz
Bread flour	6 oz

You may save as little as 8 oz of the starter, but may refresh as little as you require for the bread you want to make, as seen in the amounts given in the preceding example. The remaining sour would then be discarded. Also, your water should now be at 55°F. The water must be cooler to slow down fermentation in order to build flavor and acidity. You want to level off the starter and let it work itself into the proper balance and range of both acidity and leavening.

Place the water (at 55°F) and the previous day's mix in a bowl and stir it together until dissolved. Add the flour and mix until homogenous. Scrape the bowl down, cover, and let it sit in a place that is at moderate room temperature (68–72°F). After feeding, the sour will be stiffer today, more like a dough. For the next several

Appearance of a developing sour over five days.

CREATING A WHOLE WHEAT SOUR FROM A WHITE SOUR BASE

Feeding your sour with 100 percent whole wheat is not recommended, as this tends to create too much acidity in the sour. Rather, if you substitute 25–30 percent of the bread flour listed in the feeding instructions with whole wheat, you will have a sour that complements your breads nicely. You will not have to adjust the water.

OTHER WAYS TO CHANGE ACIDITY AND FLAVOR

Once you get comfortable with sour starters, you may want to exercise more control over the flavor and acidity of your bread. You can do this by manipulating not only the type of flour you use, but also the amount and temperature of the water, the amount of starter you use, the number of feedings you give your sour, and the environment in which the sour ferments.

Changing Your Sour by Manipulating the Water

More water lends a milder flavor and more leavening power (this is also true of the commercially yeasted preferments—poolish being a good example). Water acts to loosen or open up the structure of the dough, so that the gas produced for leavening will have a greater effect. It will be able to open up the structure more than it would if a dough had less moisture and was therefore more tightly bound together.

Less water leads to a stronger flavor and more acidity, but less leavening power (much like a biga).

Slightly *warmer* water produces a milder flavor, less acidity and more leavening.

Slightly *cooler* water produces a stronger flavor, more acidity and less leavening.

Changing Your Bread by Varying the Amount of Starter

More starter used in the recipe makes for a stronger flavor, more acidity and less leavening.

Less starter in the recipe leads to milder flavor, less acidity and therefore more leavening.

Changing Your Sour by Varying the Feedings

The number of times per day you feed the starter, before baking, can noticeably affect your bread.

Feed it *once* and you get stronger flavor, more acidity and less leavening.

Feed it *twice* and you have milder flavor, less acidity and more leavening.

Changing Your Sour by Modifying the Ambient Temperature

The temperature of the fermentation environment affects the outcome.

A *warmer* environment gives you more flavor and more acidity.

A *cooler* environment provides milder flavoring and more leavening.

All of the elements affect each other. If you change one, you will need to change another to compensate. For example, if you decide to alter your sour by adding more water to it, think about the additional leavening you will achieve through this change. This means you will need to use less starter in your feeding recipe.

Try to have fun while experimenting with your starter. Remember, it's bread, not brain surgery.

HOW TO KEEP YOUR SOUR ALIVE ALL THE TIME AND BAKE BREAD TWICE A WEEK

The first thing to understand is that a sour needs to be fed regularly to be kept alive and active. This keeps the sour balanced in acidity and leavening ability. Feedings do not need to be the regular full feeding, just to maintain the sour; however, if you want to make the bread the next day, a full feeding will give you the correct amount of sour required for baking.

On days when you're not using the sour for baking, you could keep it alive by making only one third of a feeding recipe. The next day, discard the excess of the sour that you don't need to use for the next feeding. This will keep your sour alive and active. The feeding only takes about 10 minutes to do and then you let it sit overnight to do its thing—fermentation. The real beauty of a constantly fed sour is that you could decide that you want to bake bread any day of the week.

Let's take a look at how to structure your week if you want to bake on Wednesday and Sunday, for example. With a sourdough bread, it takes time, planning, understanding and skill. On Monday, you will need to give the sour a full feeding to be ready to mix the bread on Tuesday. This takes about 10 minutes, and then it sits until Tuesday night. On Tuesday, you mix the sour, which will take about 30 minutes. You will have sour left that needs to be fed to keep your base alive, and this feeding only needs to be one-third batch size, since

you won't be baking again until Sunday. While the dough ferments for 2 hours or so, you can have dinner and read the paper or watch the news, and the only thing you have to do is give the dough a 2-minute fold after 1 hour of fermenting. Now, it is time to divide and shape the bread, which takes about 20 minutes. Then the bread will need to rest for 1 hour at room temperature, then be placed in the refrigerator overnight. (So 3 hours and 20 minutes of time total, most of it hands-off.) On Wednesday, you turn the oven on and take the bread out of the refrigerator for about an hour before baking. Now comes the great moment: You have put in a few hours of work over 2 days and you can bake the bread. This takes only 30–40 minutes. You have done it! Have some fresh bread when it cools and don't forget to feed your sour, but only one third of the feeding. How wonderful it is to have fresh-baked sourdough bread. If you have a family, you are sure to finish those two loaves by Sunday.

Next, you'll need to prepare your sour for mixing the bread dough on Saturday, then baking it on Sunday. On Thursday, you feed your sour a one-third batch, then let it sit and ferment until Friday. On Friday, you feed your sour a full feeding, and let it sit and ferment. On Saturday, you are ready to mix the bread dough. After mixing, remember that you need to give the remaining sour base a one-third feeding

and let it sit. Proceed with the sourdough that you mixed and shape later when ready. Refrigerate it, covered, until the next day. On Sunday, you can bake. Now, you have that great moment again that all your work over a few days has come to—baking the bread. You can once again enjoy some wonderful sourdough fresh out of the oven. Remember, though, you need to give your sour base a one-third feeding on Sunday also.

Another suggestion, once you have become comfortable with this, is to make two different breads on the day that you bake with sourdough. You already have the oven on and all it will take is a little more time, planning, understanding and skill. You could mix a bagel, bialy, pizza, pretzel or even sweet dough for cinnamon rolls or sticky buns. You would need to mix this the same day as your other bread on the day before you want to bake it. Then remove it from the refrigerator after the first bread comes out of the oven and prepare whichever dough you have chosen for baking.

The more you bake, the more your timing, planning, organization and skill will improve. You can do it—it just takes time to learn, but a little practice every day will result in wonderful smells in your home and bread that tastes delicious. You will become an even better baker in time, and will learn how to improve and make a greater variety of breads.

Advanced Mixing Techniques

The way in which you mix your bread dough can make a big difference in the outcome. Much of this depends on the type of bread you are making. Some breads that are heavily enriched (such as brioche) require a process called "blitz," where you initially hold back some of the fat and all of the sugar. Other doughs that contain a lot of liquid benefit from a process called "double hydration," where you add the water in stages. Lean breads can be improved with a method called "autolyse." Whether you are making bread at the last minute or have all the time you need, autolyse can give you a lot of bang for the buck, so to speak.

Autolyse

Autolyse (pronounced "auto-LEEZE") is a mixing technique that can quickly and easily improve the flavor and texture of lean bread (that is, bread without added fats or sugars). This method was developed in the 1970s by the French baking expert Professor Raymond Calvel to improve the flour and reduce the use of electricity.

BASIC AUTOLYSE TECHNIQUE FOR THIS BOOK

1. Mix together flour, instant dry yeast (and/or preferment if using) and water until it is homogenous.

2. Let rest for 15 minutes with the dough covered, until the dough appears relaxed, elastic and very smooth.

3. Add salt (and soaker if using). Mix for about 3 minutes, until the dough is homogenous.

How does autolyse work? You may recall that salt is hygroscopic, meaning that it attracts water. Professor Calvel found that if he mixed just the flour and water in the recipe together first, without adding the salt or yeast until about 15 minutes later, the flour could absorb more water and gluten bonds could start forming more effectively. This, as he discovered, turns out a better loaf of bread—he realized that more hydration leads to greater elasticity and greater volume in the finished loaf.

The recipes in this book use the autolyse technique, but, as you may have noticed, with a slight difference. You are directed to add the yeast (or preferment) at the beginning with the flour and liquid. Why? Instant dry yeast (the recommended type in this book) is added to the dry ingredients instead of the liquid and it makes sense to add it there. Since yeast typically doesn't start fermenting until about fifteen minutes after it's activated, the yeast should have no effect one way or the other on your autolyse. The main point is holding back the salt. Again, the advantage to this is that when salt is not present, the flour can absorb 3–5 percent more water. The gluten starts forming without the salt grabbing up its share of the water. After the flour spends fifteen minutes alone with the water, the resultant dough is relaxed, elastic and very smooth in appearance. Now only a short mixing time is required to add in the salt—about three minutes or so. The salt can still do its job to keep the yeast in check and flavor the bread. In addition, the total mixing time is shorter and less air is incorporated so there is less oxidation and the bread has better flavor. When you use this technique, you will accomplish better flavor, better oven-spring and a better overall loaf with less working of the dough.

Autolyse is also useful when you are adding fiber to bread. Whole-grain flour, which has sharp bran pieces that can cut the gluten strands, softens up more when the liquid is added without the salt. After the whole-grain flour and water are mixed, there is no further agitation for fifteen minutes, so the bran does not cause damage while the gluten forms. If, however, you are using a soaker in your bread with large, pointy pieces of grain, you will want to hold that back along with the salt until the rest period is over (see "Soakers," page 63, for more information).

As mentioned, autolyse is a good technique for lean breads. But there is an advanced technique for mixing certain enriched breads, a method known as "blitz."

Blitz

The blitz mixing technique is used for enriched breads with high fat and sugar content, such as brioche, concha, panettone and Day of the Dead bread, also known as *pan de muerto*. Here you mix the dough in stages, initially holding back two thirds of the fat and all of the sugar. Why? So the gluten in the dough will have a chance to develop without the fat coating the gluten strands, and so the sugar won't interfere with water absorption. Remember: Sugar, like salt, is hygroscopic and pulls water away from the other ingredients.

BASIC BLITZ TECHNIQUE

Here, we will use a brioche dough as an example. Before you begin, make sure the butter you are using is pliable—like clay, but no softer than that. It should be cut into pieces. You will be adding the butter in stages, one third at a time.

1. Using a stand mixer with a paddle attachment, mix one third of the butter, plus all of the eggs, milk, flour (blended with instant dry yeast) and lastly salt. Start mixing on slow speed for 4 minutes, flipping the dough and scraping the bowl as you work. Then change to medium speed for 5 minutes, again flipping the dough and scraping the bowl a few times while mixing. You will know it is time to switch to a dough hook when the dough looks homogenous and begins pulling away from the sides of the bowl, but still appears somewhat rough. Work the dough with your hands to check for the gluten window (see page 28) and you will see that it is at partial gluten development.

2. Gradually add half of the remaining butter while mixing on medium speed for about 2 minutes, making sure to scrape the bowl and flip the dough. This is where you need to really watch your mixer. If it is straining, you need to lower the speed a bit.

3. Next, add the sugar gradually, keeping the dough on the hook and not sticking to the sides of the bowl. Mix for 2 minutes on low, to gradually blend in the sugar and avoid causing the gluten structure to separate. If the dough starts sticking to the bowl or sitting on the top, stop adding the butter, scrape and flip the dough, and keep mixing until the dough works back to its gluten structure. Even if you don't have this problem, remind yourself to stop mixing periodically so you can flip the dough and scrape the sides of the bowl.

4. Add the last of the butter while the dough is mixing on medium speed for 3 minutes, keeping the dough on the hook. Scrape the bowl and flip the dough at least twice during this mixing phase. When it is done, the dough should look smooth and have full gluten development. When you gently work a piece of it in your hands to check the gluten window, the dough should form a strong, thin membrane that holds. Once you get to this point, continue on with your recipe as instructed.

Double Hydration

As you just learned in the previous section, brioche is a very strong, enriched dough that requires a specialized mixing technique because of its high fat and sugar content. Another category that requires special handling is that of delicate and viscous doughs, ciabatta being a good example. These doughs benefit from the "double hydration" mixing method—or adding the water in two stages.

Ciabatta—an extremely wet dough—can be mixed by hand and is often made with the preferment poolish. Preferments were discussed earlier in this chapter (see pages 116–19). But to review: You create the preferment (in this case, a poolish) ahead of time, mixing a portion of the recipe's flour, water and a little bit of yeast. Then you let it sit and ferment a while. Poolish has the highest amount of water among the preferments, with a ratio of flour to water that is 1:1. When it's time to mix the bread, you add the rest of the recipe's flour, salt and yeast to the poolish. If, however, you added the entire amount of water in a recipe to the poolish all at once for something like ciabatta—that has a high water content— the dough would end up far too soupy and lacking any gluten structure. How can you develop the gluten in such a bread if the wheat proteins are just floating around? This is where the "double hydration" technique comes into play.

BASIC DOUBLE HYDRATION TECHNIQUE

In this example, we make ciabatta using a poolish:

1. Start mixing your dough with clean hands. Add 80 percent of the recipe's water to the poolish, then add the rest of the ingredients. Holding back 20 percent of the water will help the dough to have more cohesion at first, and will allow the gluten to develop its structure as you mix.

2. Once the dough has reached the improved stage of gluten development (where it holds together well, but is not strong enough to hold a translucent window), you can add the remaining 20 percent of the water in the recipe, but not all at once. Add the remaining water one third at a time, squeezing the dough gently while mixing. Ciabatta is a delicate dough and should not be worked too much. Once you have incorporated all the water, it is time for bulk fermentation, and you proceed along with the rest of your bread-making steps.

Once you know how, it's not a big deal to use some of these fancy mixing techniques. It's all about keeping an open mind. And that's also the mindset you should try to have with the preferments mentioned earlier in the chapter. All of these methods are accessible and worth the extra time you will spend. You just need to plan ahead a little.

You: The Advanced Baker

Keep a few things in mind before you move on to the advanced section of recipes. First, remember to follow all of the steps required. The goal of this book is to make a complicated subject matter more accessible. If a step is included in your recipe, then it is necessary for you to do it—if you want a professional result. You will have successes and failures, but instead of keeping score, try to note with each loaf of bread what you did and how it may have affected the end product.

The best way to learn is to keep baking regularly. With time, you will gain skill and everything you learn will come together in your head. Once you have the knowledge and understanding, you will find passion in your heart and eagerness in your hands. Now, start baking more bread!

Basic Flatbreads

Flat is just that. What defines a flatbread? For one, it is a bread that is relatively flat. It can be lightly leavened with yeast, puffed up with steam, or rolled as thin as parchment. Flatbreads are among the world's oldest types of bread. Before humans knew about fermentation, they were probably forming grains into cakes and baking them. These breads became a staple of nomadic people because they could be made quickly without much equipment and cooked up or baked with very little fuel. Today, flatbreads are among the most commonly eaten breads in the world. The number of regional varieties, even within the same country, can be vast.

CHAPTER SEVEN

IN THIS CHAPTER you will find recipes for some basic international flatbreads. Two of the classics from India are whole wheat *naan*, a bread eaten at every meal in some areas, and flaky *paratha* (or *parantha*), its layers brushed with clarified butter called *ghee*. The versatile Armenian flatbread lavash can be made crisp like a cracker or soft to use as a wrap. Or choose Sardinian flatbread with savory sun-dried tomatoes and cheese. If you have a pasta machine, you can make it paper thin, or just do your best with a rolling pin.

If you are new to baking, a good place to start is with the tortilla, a staple of Mexico. Flour and corn varieties satisfy different tastes and contexts. Corn flour (*masa harina*), with its earthy flavor and coarse texture, mixes up quickly with warm water, and is shaped, relaxed, and flattened with a tortilla press before being browned in a skillet. Flour tortillas, on the other hand, are tenderized with shortening, cut together with your hands like pie dough,

and carefully rolled out with a pin. When cooked in a skillet, the moisture in the dough gently steams up into little pockets here and there. They are soft when bitten into, and shouldn't be rubbery.

Given the number of steps and sheer number of pieces of flatbread, you could involve your friends and family and give everyone a specific task. In fact, you could have a flatbread party with any of the recipes in this section. It is probably easier to make a batch of grissini—the pencil-sized, cheesy Italian breadsticks—if you have a partner helping you roll the dough through a hand-cranked pasta machine. Boil some pasta, toss a salad, and you can build a meal around these breadsticks. Or pick a night for making pizza and create a station with favorite toppings. If you make flatbread into a social affair, then the experience you have will even more so recall how bread was made thousands of years ago: for the community by the community.

Flatbread with Sun-Dried Tomato and Asiago Cheese

These sharp, salty Sardinian crackers are as pleasing to look at as they are packed with flavor. The dough, made with all-purpose and semolina flours, is flavored and tinted red with sun-dried tomato puree; a sprinkling of Asiago cheese in the dough adds a pointedly savory flavor, complementary to the sweetness of the tomato. These thin, crisp crackers are perfect for dipping, or simply snacking on alone.

yield: **80 crackers** | FDT: **80°F**
first rest: **30 minutes** | final rest: **20 minutes** | bake: **375°F** *and* **14–16 minutes**

INGREDIENT	OUNCES	GRAMS	VOLUME	BAKERS %
Sun-dried tomatoes	1.0	28	•	4.7%
Water, 80°F	8.4	238	1 cup + 1 Tbsp	39.8%
Olive oil	2.4	68	⅓ cup	11.4%
Malt syrup	0.1	2	¼ tsp	0.5%
All-purpose flour	9.1	258	2 cups + 2 Tbsp	43.1%
Semolina flour	12.0	340	1¾ cups + 2½ Tbsp	56.9%
Asiago cheese, finely grated	1.0	28	¼ cup	4.7%
Salt	0.2	6	1 tsp	0.9%
TOTAL	34.2	968	•	162.0%
GARNISHES				
Olive oil	as needed			
Salt	as needed			

1. IF USING dehydrated sun-dried tomatoes, they will need to be softened by bringing 1 cup of water to a boil and soaking the tomatoes in the water for 15 minutes. Drain the tomatoes, dry them off, and puree them in a food processor. For oil-packed tomatoes, simply drain them and then puree.

2. PUT the water, oil and malt in the bowl of a mixer. Add the flours, pureed sun-dried tomatoes, cheese and salt. Place the bowl on a mixer fitted with a paddle attachment and mix for 4 minutes on low speed, making sure to scrape down and flip the dough over twice during mixing. The dough will be somewhat dry, but homogenous.

3. REMOVE from the mixer and place the dough on a lightly floured work surface, dividing it into 4-oz pieces, and rounding the pieces against the table into balls. Cover the dough with plastic wrap and allow it to rest at room temperature for 30 minutes.

4. TAKE each dough piece, lightly flour and flatten the dough ball by hand, then put it into a pasta machine, with the machine set on the widest setting. Roll the dough through and, lowering the setting in small increments, continue this process until the dough is as wide as the space between the pasta machine rollers. Remove the dough and turn a quarter turn, lightly dust with flour, then roll the dough through the machine in the opposite direction until the second-to-last setting is reached, or until the dough is as thin as paper. Lay each piece of dough on a parchment paper–lined baking tray and cut off the excess so that the dough fits entirely on the tray. Lightly brush the dough with oil and cover with plastic wrap. Allow the dough to rest at room temperature for 20 minutes.

5. PREHEAT the oven to 425°F.

6. UNCOVER the dough pieces and use a pastry wheel or pizza wheel to cut them into crackers of various shapes. Sprinkle the tops of the crackers lightly with salt.

7. PLACE the baking trays in the oven and immediately reduce the temperature to 375°F. Bake for 10 minutes, then rotate the trays and bake an additional 4–6 minutes, until the bread is light golden brown.

8. REMOVE the baking trays from the oven and place on a cooling rack.

Flatbread with Sun-Dried Tomato and Asiago Cheese

Grissini

GRISSINI

Grissini are thin, crisp breadsticks—long and pencil-like in appearance, and Italian in origin. In this recipe, the dough is flavored with chopped rosemary and boldly accented with Asiago cheese; variations on flavoring are many and may include garlic, other herbs or hard cheeses as your creativity sees fit. Flattened and cut using a pasta machine, these crispy breadsticks are a satisfying snack or appetizer before a meal.

yield: **about 48 pieces** | FDT: **80°F**
first rest: **15 minutes** | *retard:* **8 hours to overnight** | *second rest:* **60 minutes** | *final rest:* **30 minutes** | *bake:* **375°F** *and* **14–16 minutes**

INGREDIENT	OUNCES	GRAMS	VOLUME	BAKERS %
Rosemary leaves, fresh	0.3	7	2 or 3 each	1.7%
Milk, 78°F	6.6	187	¾ cup	45.5%
Olive oil	0.5	14	1 Tbsp	3.4%
Malt syrup	0.5	14	2 tsp	3.4%
High-gluten flour	14.5	411	3 cups	100.0%
Yeast, instant dry	0.2	6	1½ tsp	1.4%
Salt	0.3	9	1¼ tsp	2.1%
Butter, soft	2.2	62	¼ cup	15.2%
Asiago cheese, finely grated	1.0	28	¼ cup	6.9%
TOTAL	26.1	738	•	179.6%
GARNISHES				
Olive oil	as needed			
Salt	as needed			

1. MAKE the dough the day before you want to serve the grissini. Pick the rosemary leaves off the stems and roughly chop them.

2. COMBINE the milk, oil and malt in the bowl of a mixer. Combine the flour with the yeast, and then add them to the milk mixture. Next add the salt and butter. Place the bowl on a mixer fitted with a dough hook and mix for 4 minutes on low speed, making sure to scrape down and flip the dough over twice during the mixing time. Increase the speed to medium and mix for an additional 3 minutes. At this point, the dough will be strong, with good gluten structure. Add the rosemary and cheese, and mix for 1 more minute on medium speed, making sure to scrape down and flip the dough over during this process.

3. REMOVE the dough from the mixer and place it on a lightly floured work surface. Divide it into 6.5-oz pieces and round the pieces against the tabletop. Place each piece in a floured container and cover the container with plastic wrap.

4. LEAVE the dough at room temperature for 15 minutes, and then refrigerate it for a minimum of 8 hours or overnight.

5. REMOVE the dough from the refrigerator and leave it at room temperature for 60 minutes, until it has lost its chill.

6. LIGHTLY flour and flatten each piece and place it in a pasta machine set at its widest setting. Roll the dough through and, lowering the setting in small increments, continue this process until the dough is as wide as the opening on the pasta machine. Then turn the dough a quarter turn and lightly flour and roll the piece through the machine in the opposite direction until it is ¼ inch thick (setting #5). Lightly flour the dough, trim the edges with a pastry wheel to make a straight edge, and pass it through the pasta machine's fettuccini cutter. Lay the pieces of dough on parchment paper–lined baking trays, making sure to lay them out straight and separate (you can cut the ends if the pieces do not fit the tray). Lightly brush the dough pieces with oil, then cover the trays with plastic wrap and allow the dough to rest for 30 minutes at room temperature, to relax.

7. PREHEAT the oven to 400°F.

8. UNCOVER the dough, brush it again with oil, and lightly sprinkle it with salt.

9. PLACE the trays in the oven and immediately reduce the temperature to 375°F. Bake for 10 minutes, then rotate the trays when the pieces start to take on color, and turn the oven down to 350°F. Continue to bake an additional 4–6 minutes, until the bread is a light golden brown and appears dried out.

10. REMOVE the baking trays from the oven and place them on a cooling rack. When completely cool, store in an airtight container.

VARIATIONS: Add finely chopped herbs, roasted garlic or finely grated hard cheeses in the final minute of mixing.

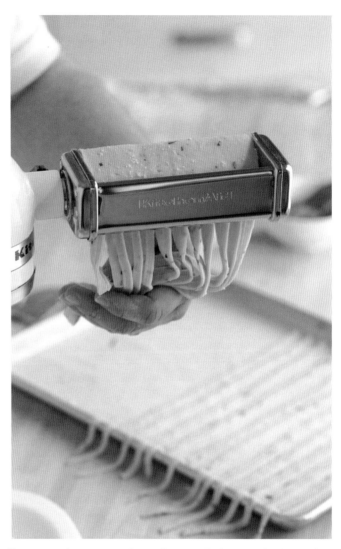

You can use the pasta attachment for a stand mixer to make these thin breadsticks. Gradually roll the dough thinner by changing the width setting each time. When the dough is ¼ inch thick, put the fettuccini attachment on the mixer and run the length of the dough through. Keep the dough strands separated on a baking tray and brush them with olive oil.

LAVASH

Middle Eastern in origin, lavash can be made into various textures ranging from soft and pliable to brittle and golden. In this recipe for crisp, cracker-like lavash, garnish the snack-sized bread with seeds, nuts, salt, pepper or other spices of your choice; sprinkle an uncut, whole round of the thin dough with cinnamon and sugar and chopped nuts for something sweet.

yield: **about 40 crackers** | FDT: **80°F**
retard: **8 hours to overnight** | *rest:* **20 minutes** | *bake:* **375°F** *and* **6–10 minutes**

INGREDIENT	OUNCES	GRAMS	VOLUME	BAKERS %
Water, 84°F	3.9	111	½ cup	29.8%
Milk, whole, 84°F	5.7	162	⅔ cup	43.5%
Molasses	0.4	11	1½ tsp	3.1%
Honey	0.4	11	1⅔ tsp	3.1%
Malt syrup	0.1	2	½ tsp	0.5%
Bread flour	6.1	173	1¼ cups	46.6%
Durum flour	2.6	74	⅓ cup	19.8%
All-purpose flour	2.2	62	½ cup	16.8%
Whole wheat flour	2.2	62	½ cup	16.8%
Yeast, instant dry	0.1	2	½ tsp	0.5%
Salt	0.3	9	1½ tsp	2.3%
TOTAL	24.0	679	•	182.8%
GARNISHES				
Olive oil	as needed			
Spices, nuts, seeds, etc., as desired	as needed			

1. MAKE the dough the day before you want to serve the lavash. Combine the water, milk, molasses, honey and malt. Combine the flours with the yeast, then add to the bowl with the other ingredients. Add the salt and place the bowl on a mixer fitted with a dough hook. Mix for 10 minutes on low, making sure to scrape down and flip over the dough twice during this time. The dough should achieve full gluten development.

2. REMOVE the dough and place it on a lightly floured work surface, then divide it into 4-oz pieces. Place the pieces on a lightly floured baking tray, cover with plastic wrap, and refrigerate for a minimum of 8 hours or overnight.

3. REMOVE the dough from the refrigerator and let it sit at room temperature for 60 minutes, until the dough has lost its chill. Prepare 3 or 4 baking trays with sides by rubbing them with oil and paper towels to remove any dirt, then brush with oil.

4. GENTLY flatten the pieces, then roll them through a pasta machine. Beginning with the rollers at the widest setting, continue to roll the dough through while slowly closing the rollers until you reach the #2 setting, rolling the dough as thin as paper. Lay the flattened dough lengthwise on the trays and spray the surfaces lightly with water to keep them from drying out. Cover the dough with plastic wrap and allow to rest for 20 minutes, until fully relaxed.

5. PREHEAT the oven to 400°F.

6. USING a pastry wheel or pizza wheel, cut the dough into cracker-sized pieces or leave whole, spray them lightly with water, and garnish as desired (see Note).

7. PLACE the trays in the oven and immediately reduce the temperature to 375°F. Bake for 10 minutes, rotate the trays, and continue baking for 3–5 minutes, until the crackers are crisp and golden brown.

8. REMOVE the lavash from the oven and place on a cooling rack. When completely cool, store in an airtight container. It can be kept for up to 3 weeks if kept airtight.

NOTE: *If using cinnamon sugar, do not cut the dough; bake as 1 large piece, because if the sugar falls between the cuts, the dough will get stuck to the tray.*

Lavash

Paratha

Paratha, an Indian flatbread, is traditionally made from wheat flour and pan fried in ghee, an Indian variety of clarified butter. Sometimes stuffed with vegetables or cheese, paratha is soft with a crisp exterior; it is delicious served alongside curries and dishes with thick sauces, or as an accompaniment to yogurt.

yield: **30 pieces at 1 oz** | FDT: **80°F**
first rest: **30 minutes** | *final rest:* **15 minutes** | *cook:* **on stovetop**

INGREDIENT	OUNCES	GRAMS	VOLUME	BAKERS %
Whole wheat flour	13.7	388	3¼ cups	74.9%
Bread flour	4.6	130	1 cup	2.7%
Water, 80°F	11.4	323	1⅓ cups	62.3%
Salt	0.5	14	1 Tbsp	2.7%
Butter, clarified	1.7	48	3 Tbsp	9.3%
TOTAL	31.9	903	•	151.9%

1. COMBINE the flours, water and salt in the bowl of a mixer fitted with a dough hook. Mix on low speed for 6 minutes, or until the mixture becomes a homogenous mass. Put the dough into an oiled bowl, cover with plastic wrap, and let rest for 30 minutes at room temperature, until fully relaxed.

2. PLACE the dough on a lightly floured work surface and divide into 1-oz pieces. Round the pieces against the tabletop. Keep the dough covered with a moist cloth and plastic wrap as you work. Allow the covered dough rounds to rest in a warm place for 15 minutes, until fully relaxed.

3. ROLL each piece of dough out to a circle 5 inches in diameter and brush generously with clarified butter. Fold the circle into thirds and brush the surface with clarified butter again. Turn the piece 90 degrees, fold the dough into thirds again, and pinch together the outer edges to make a round ball. Re-cover the dough and allow it to rest for another 15 minutes, until fully relaxed.

4. ROLL each piece out to a circle 6 inches in diameter. Layer the rounds on a baking pan lined with parchment paper, placing a sheet of parchment paper between each layer to prevent the dough from sticking together. To keep the dough moist, cover the top layer with a lightly moistened towel.

5. HEAT a large skillet over medium heat and cook each piece of dough on both sides for 1 minute, until lighly browned and cooked through. Lightly brush both sides of each paratha with clarified butter, and continue to cook in the skillet again, browning both sides.

6. PLACE the bread in a clean kitchen towel to keep it warm and retain moisture until serving. Tightly wrap and refrigerate if not eating immediately. Reheat in the skillet as needed.

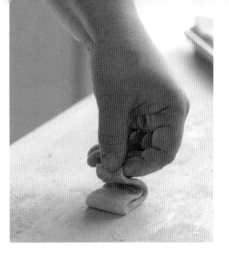

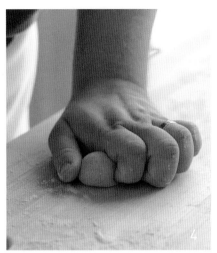

1. Make a very thin circle of dough with your hands and then use a rolling pin to get an even thickness. Brush the round liberally with the clarified butter.

2. Fold the round of dough up by thirds into a strip and brush with butter. Fold the ends of the strip into the center, folding in thirds again.

3. Gather the ends of the dough up into a ball.

4. Place the dough seam-side down and round it up to tighten.

5. After the dough has had time to relax, roll the dough into a thin, flat round and put it into a dry, hot skillet to crisp up each side. While still on the stove, brush butter on both sides of the dough and continue to cook until done.

CLARIFIED BUTTER

Clarified butter is made by heating whole butter until the butterfat and milk solids separate.

The purpose of clarifying butter is to remove its milk solids and water. Using salted butter is not recommended because the concentration of salt in the resulting clarified butter is unpredictable. Unsalted clarified butter can always be salted as it is used.

Heat the butter over low heat until foam rises to the surface and the milk solids drop to the bottom of the pot. The remaining butterfat becomes very clear. Skim the surface foam as the butter clarifies. Pour or ladle off the butterfat into another container, carefully leaving all of the water and milk solids in the pan bottom. After whole butter is clarified, some of its volume is lost due to skimming, decanting, and discarding the water and milk solids; 1 lb/454 g of whole butter yields approximately 12 oz/340 g of clarified butter.

Ghee, which is used in some Asian cuisines, is a type of clarified butter. It has a nutty flavor because the milk solids brown before they are separated from the butterfat.

NAAN

Naan is a traditional bread of India that has a unique texture. The yogurt in the dough adds flavor and serves to create a tender crumb. It is usually topped with sautéed onion or garlic. The addition of cheese is also seen sometimes. Another garnish is sesame seeds or poppy seeds. This bread is traditionally baked on the side wall of a tandoor oven, which is a clay pot oven, but you can use a baking stone in the oven.

yield: 12 pieces at 4 oz | FDT: 78°F
biga: 12–14 hours | first rest: 90–105 minutes | final rest: 60–75 minutes | bake: 475°F and 8–10 minutes

INGREDIENT	OUNCES	GRAMS	VOLUME	BAKERS %
BIGA				
Bread flour	4.3	122	1 cup	17.3%
Yeast, instant dry	0.01	0.3	⅛ tsp	0.04%
Water, 55°F	2.8	79	⅓ cup	11.2%
FINAL DOUGH				
Yogurt	10.3	292	1¼ cups	41.4%
Water, 106°F	8.5	241	1 cup	34.1%
Olive oil	0.8	23	2 Tbsp	3.4%
Malt syrup	0.2	6	½ tsp	0.6%
Biga	7.1	202	1¼ cups	28.6%
Bread flour	19.4	550	4 cups	77.9%
Whole wheat flour	1.2	34	4½ Tbsp	4.8%
Yeast, instant dry	0.2	6	1½ tsp	0.6%
Salt	0.5	14	2 tsp	2.0%
TOTAL	48.2	1368	•	193.4%

1. MIX the biga the day before you want to serve the naan. Combine the flour and yeast in the bowl of a mixer. Add the water and place on a mixer fitted with a dough hook. Mix for 2 minutes on low speed, or until homogenous. The dough should be homogenous, stiff and slightly dry. Place the dough in a lightly oiled bowl large enough for it to double in size. Flip the dough over in the bowl; this will coat the whole dough with oil. Cover the bowl with plastic wrap and refrigerate for 2 hours, then remove and leave at room temperature for 10 to 12 hours. After the fermentation at room temperature, the dough will be less stiff and more like an actual bread dough.

2. TO MAKE THE FINAL DOUGH, put the yogurt, water, oil and malt in the bowl of a mixer. Break up the biga by hand and add it to the other ingredients. Place on a mixer fitted with a dough hook and mix for 2 minutes on low speed to break down the biga. Mix the flours and yeast together, add to the other ingredients, and then add the salt. Mix for 4 minutes on low speed, making sure to scrape down and flip the dough over. Mix for 2 minutes on medium speed, making sure to scrape down and flip the dough over. The dough will be loose and wet and will have a little structure. Place the dough in a lightly oiled bowl large enough for it to double in size and cover with plastic wrap.

3. ALLOW the dough to rest and ferment in a warm place for 60–75 minutes, until when lightly touched the dough springs back halfway.

4. PLACE the dough on a lightly floured work surface and fold in thirds. Cover and allow to ferment in a warm place for 30 minutes, until when lightly touched the dough springs back halfway.

5. PREPARE a baking tray lined with a white cloth napkin or white kitchen towel and flour the liners. Place the dough on a lightly floured work surface and divide it into 3 equal pieces. Roll each piece in flour and stretch it to 12 inches. Place the dough pieces on the floured cloth and bring the cloth up between the pieces

so that they will not touch. Cover and allow the dough to rest and ferment in a warm place for 60–75 minutes, until when lightly touched the dough springs back halfway.

6. PREHEAT the oven to 475°F with a baking stone.

7. PLACE each piece of dough on a lightly floured work surface. Divide it into 4 pieces, then roll the cut sides in flour and stretch each piece out to 8 by 3 inches. Place 4 pieces of dough on a lightly floured oven peel with parchment paper and top as desired. The pieces will need to be baked in batches; allow for 5 minutes in between each batch.

8. TRANSFER each batch to the baking stone and bake for 8–10 minutes, until there is very little color on top.

9. REMOVE from the oven and place on a cooling rack.

Pizza Dough

Personalize your pies with this recipe for pizza dough. Brushed with olive oil and dusted with a semolina-flour mixture, the soft crust makes a delicious canvas upon which to build your creations. Note that the dough can be made ahead of time, frozen, and thawed before later use.

yield: 5 pizzas at 10 oz | FDT: 82°F
bulk fermentation: 30 minutes | retard: 8 hours to overnight | rest: 60 minutes | bake: 450°F *and* 14–16 minutes

INGREDIENT	OUNCES	GRAMS	VOLUME	BAKERS %
Water, 78°F	18.2	516	2 cups + 2 Tbsp	59.1%
Malt syrup	0.2	6	½ tsp	0.6%
Olive oil	1.5	42	3 Tbsp	4.8%
Bread flour	30.8	872	6 cups	100.0%
Yeast, instant dry	0.3	8	2½ tsp	1.0%
Salt	0.7	20	1 Tbsp	2.2%
Sugar	0.4	11	1 Tbsp	1.3%
TOTAL	52.1	1475	•	169.0%
GARNISHES				
Olive oil	2.0	57	¼ cup	
Toppings (see Variations, pages 150–51)	as needed			

1. MAKE the dough the day before you want to serve the pizza. Combine the water, malt and oil. Combine the flour with the yeast, then add to the bowl with the other ingredients. Add the salt and sugar and place the bowl on a mixer fitted with a dough hook. Mix on low speed for 4 minutes, making sure to scrape down and flip the dough over. Mix on medium speed for another 3 minutes, making sure to scrape down and flip the dough over. The dough should feel slightly sticky but have fairly good gluten development. Remove the dough and place it in a lightly oiled bowl large enough for it to double in size and cover with plastic wrap.

2. ALLOW the dough to rest and ferment in a warm place for 30 minutes, until when lightly touched the dough springs back halfway.

3. PLACE the dough on a lightly floured work surface and divide it into 10-oz pieces. Round the pieces against the tabletop. Place each of the dough pieces in a separate oiled container and cover with plastic wrap. Refrigerate for a minimum of 8 hours or overnight for use the next day, or freeze until ready to use (see Note).

4. ONE HOUR BEFORE USE, remove as much dough as you need from the refrigerator and let it rest at room temperature for 60 minutes, until the dough has lost its chill.

5. PLACE the dough on a lightly floured work surface and roll each piece into a circle about 12 inches in diameter.

6. PREHEAT the oven to 500°F with a baking stone. Create a 1:1 mixture of semolina flour and bread flour. Place the rolled dough on a peel lightly floured with the semolina-flour mixture, then lightly brush the dough edges with oil. Apply chosen toppings as desired.

7. TRANSFER the dough to the baking stone and immediately lower the temperature to 450°F. Bake for 14–16 minutes, or until the crust is golden brown on the edges.

NOTE: To freeze dough, oil the outside of the dough and place it in a freezer bag before freezing. When ready to use, remove the dough from the freezer the day prior to baking and place in the refrigerator to thaw. If needed the same day, remove the dough from the freezer and partially thaw it in a microwave set on "thawing mode," then continue to thaw for 2 hours at room temperature.

1. Stretch the pizza dough into a round, working the dough from underneath, using the backside of your hands and knuckles.

2. Add the desired toppings, leaving approximately a ¾-inch border of crust.

3. Load the pizza into a preheated oven on a hot baking stone, using a peel.

4. Top: Pesto Pizza with Cheese, Tomatoes and Peppers; Bottom: White Cheese Pizza with Broccoli

Margherita Pizza

INGREDIENT	OUNCES	GRAMS	VOLUME
Tomato sauce	4.5	128	½ cup
Mozzarella cheese, grated	3.5	99	½ cup

1. SPREAD tomato sauce evenly across the dough, leaving ¾ inch of the edges empty to form a crust.

2. SPRINKLE the mozzarella evenly across the sauce.

Pesto Pizza

INGREDIENT	OUNCES	GRAMS	VOLUME
Pesto	4.0	113	½ cup
Mozzarella cheese, grated	3.5	99	½ cup
Asiago cheese, grated	2.0	57	¼ cup
Yellow peppers, sliced	1.0	28	•
Tomato, small, sliced	1 each	•	•

1. SPREAD pesto over the dough, leaving ½ inch of the edges empty to form a crust.

2. SPRINKLE the mozzarella evenly over the pesto, then sprinkle the asiago evenly over the mozzarella.

3. EVENLY distribute the sliced peppers and tomato over the cheese.

White Pizza

INGREDIENT	OUNCES	GRAMS	VOLUME
Onions, sliced	6.0	170	1 cup
Olive oil	1.0	28	2 Tbsp
Garlic clove, minced	1 each	•	•
Basil, finely chopped	1.0	28	½ cup
Red pepper flakes (optional)	as needed	•	•
Ricotta	7.3	207	1 cup
Salt	as needed	•	•
Pepper	as needed	•	•
Mozzarella cheese, grated	6.0	170	1 cup
Broccoli, roughly chopped, blanched	3.0	85	1 cup

1. **SAUTÉ** the onions lightly in oil until translucent. Set aside.

2. **SAUTÉ** the garlic in the oil until fragrant. Add the basil, and the red pepper flakes if desired. Mix the garlic into the ricotta. Season with salt and pepper to taste.

3. **SPREAD** the ricotta over the dough, leaving ½ inch of the edges empty to form a crust.

4. **EVENLY** distribute the sautéed onions over the ricotta. Sprinkle the mozzarella over the onions. Sprinkle the chopped broccoli over the mozzarella.

RUSTIC DURUM PIZZA

A baking stone is a useful tool for bread baking in general and specifically for pizza. It distributes heat so that even in the most temperamental ovens you can bake an evenly colored pizza. It also improves the overall flavor and texture of the pizza, imparting that professional crispy crust and extra browning on the bottom of the pie.

yield: 5 pizzas at 10 oz | FDT: 82°F

rise: 30 minutes | retard: 8 hours to overnight | rest: 60 minutes | bake: 450°F *and* 14–16 minutes

INGREDIENT	OUNCES	GRAMS	VOLUME	BAKERS %
Water, 80°F	19.2	564	2⅓ cups	63.3%
Malt syrup	0.2	6	1 tsp	0.7%
Olive oil	1.0	31	2 Tbsp	3.6%
Bread flour	17.5	497	3½ cups	57.7%
Durum flour	12.9	365	2¼ cups	42.3%
Yeast, instant dry	0.2	6	1½ tsp	0.7%
Salt	0.9	25	1 Tbsp	2.8%
TOTAL	51.9	1494	•	171.1%

1. MAKE the dough the day before you want to serve the pizza. Combine the water, malt and oil. Combine the flours with the yeast, then add to the bowl with the other ingredients. Add the salt and place the bowl on a mixer fitted with a dough hook. Mix on low speed for 4 minutes, making sure to scrape down and flip the dough over. Mix on medium speed for 3 minutes, making sure to scrape down and flip the dough over. The dough should feel slightly sticky but have fairly good gluten development. Place the dough in a lightly oiled bowl large enough for it to double in size and cover with plastic wrap.

2. ALLOW the dough to rest and ferment in a warm place for 30 minutes, until when lightly touched the dough springs back halfway.

3. PLACE the dough on a lightly floured work surface and divide it into 10-oz pieces. Round the pieces against the tabletop. Tightly wrap the dough in plastic wrap and refrigerate for a minimum of 8 hours or overnight, or freeze until ready to use (see Note).

4. ONE HOUR BEFORE USE, remove as much dough as you need from the refrigerator and let it rest at room temperature until the dough has lost its chill.

5. PLACE the dough on a lightly floured work surface and roll each piece into a circle about 12 inches in diameter.

6. PREHEAT the oven to 500°F with a baking stone. Create a 1:1 mixture of semolina flour and bread flour. Place the rolled dough on a peel lightly floured with the semolina-flour mixture, then lightly brush the dough edges with oil. Apply chosen toppings as desired.

7. TRANSFER the dough to the baking stone and immediately lower the temperature to 450°F. Bake for 14–16 minutes, or until the crust is golden brown on the edges.

NOTE: *To freeze dough, oil the outside of the dough and place it in a freezer bag before freezing. When ready to use, remove the dough from the freezer the day prior to baking and place in the refrigerator to thaw. If needed the same day, remove the dough from the freezer and partially thaw it in a microwave set on "thawing mode," then continue to thaw for 2 hours at room temperature.*

CORN TORTILLAS

A simple mixture of masa harina, water and a bit of salt combine to form a traditional dough for delicious tortillas. Thinned between parchment paper using a tortilla press, the rounds of dough are cooked on a griddle until lightly browned. Start a meal with this simple recipe to satiate your next Mexican food craving.

yield: 32 at 1 oz

first rest: **30 minutes** | second rest: **15 minutes** | cook: **on stovetop**

INGREDIENT	OUNCES	GRAMS	VOLUME	BAKERS %
Water, 100°F	18.0	510	2¼ cups	130.4%
Masa harina, preferably Goya brand	13.8	391	2 cups + 3 Tbsp	100.0%
Salt	0.2	6	1½ tsp	1.4%
TOTAL	32.0	907	•	231.8%

1. IN A MIXING BOWL, combine all the ingredients and mix until they form a homogenous mass. Cover the dough and allow it to rest at room temperature for 30 minutes, until the dough is fully relaxed.

2. PLACE the dough on a lightly floured work surface and divide it into 1-oz portions. Round each piece against the tabletop. Cover the rounded pieces with plastic wrap and allow the dough to rest for 15 minutes at room temperature, until the dough is fully relaxed.

3. SPRAY 2 pieces of parchment paper with oil and place 1 piece of dough between them. Insert into a tortilla press and press the dough, or if you don't have a tortilla press you can flatten the dough using the bottom of a saucepot. Alternatively, roll the dough with a rolling pin until it is 12 inches in diameter.

4. COOK the pressed dough pieces on a flat griddle pan over medium heat until they are lightly browned on both sides. Place the cooked tortillas in a kitchen towel and cover to retain moisture.

NOTE: For rolling in step #3, you can also use a large Ziploc bag with the sides cut open in place of the parchment paper and oil.

FLOUR TORTILLAS

A white-flour version of the classic corn tortilla, this dough makes a thin bread that is easy to make and satisfying to eat. Shape them by hand and thin with a rolling pin, then fill these rustic tortillas to create your own perfect burrito, or to make simple and delicious quesadillas.

yield: **18 pieces at 1.75 oz**

first rest: **20 minutes** | second rest: **15 minutes** | cook: **on stovetop**

INGREDIENT	OUNCES	GRAMS	VOLUME	BAKERS %
All-purpose flour	19.2	544	4¾ cups	100.0%
Shortening	2.7	77	⅓ cup	14.1%
Salt	0.5	14	1 Tbsp	2.6%
Water, 90°F	9.7	275	1 cup + 3½ Tbsp	50.5%
TOTAL	32.1	910	•	167.2%

1. PUT the flour in a mixing bowl and cut in the shortening using 2 butter knives, or rub in using your fingertips to a very fine consistency. Add the salt and water and mix just until they form a homogenous mass. Do not knead or overwork the dough; just bring the ingredients together. Cover the dough and allow it to rest for 20 minutes at room temperature, until the dough has completely relaxed.

2. PLACE the dough on a lightly floured work surface and divide it into 1.75-oz pieces. Round each piece against the tabletop. Cover the rounded pieces with a moist towel and plastic wrap and allow the dough to rest for 15 minutes at room temperature, until fully relaxed.

3. PLACE a dough piece on a floured work surface, lightly flour it, and roll out to a circle 10 inches in diameter. Brush off any excess flour and place the dough on parchment paper. Continue this process until all the pieces are rolled. (The tortillas can be stacked with a piece of parchment paper in between them.)

4. COOK the tortillas on a flat griddle pan over medium heat until they are lightly browned on both sides. Place the cooked tortillas in a kitchen towel and cover to retain moisture. If not eating immediately, tightly wrap and refrigerate. Reheat as needed.

PITA BREAD

This recipe for the well-known Greek bread puffs during baking to create a small round—perfect for filling with hummus, lamb or any sandwich ingredients. Note that the baked bread should have little color and must be covered with a towel following removal from the oven to prevent it from drying out.

yield: 14 pieces at 3 oz | FDT: 82°F

poolish: 12–14 hours | first rest: 75–90 minutes | final rest: 20–25 minutes | bake: 500°F *and* 3–4 minutes

INGREDIENT	OUNCES	GRAMS	VOLUME	BAKERS %
POOLISH				
Water, 55°F	6.3	178	¾ cup	23.0%
Bread flour	6.3	178	1⅓ cups	23.0%
Yeast, instant dry	0.01	0.3	½ tsp	0.04%
FINAL DOUGH				
Poolish	12.6	356	•	46.1%
Water, 95°F	12.6	356	1½ cups	46.2%
Vegetable oil	1.5	43	3 Tbsp	5.5%
Malt syrup	0.2	6	1 tsp	0.6%
Bread flour	20.9	593	4⅓ cups	77.0%
Yeast, instant dry	0.1	3	1 tsp	0.4%
Salt	0.6	17	1 Tbsp	2.2%
TOTAL	48.5	1374	•	178.0%

1. PREPARE the poolish the day before you want to serve the pita. Combine the water, flour and yeast in a bowl and mix together by hand until homogenous. You will still have little lumps and the poolish will be very wet, looser than a dough. Cover the poolish with plastic wrap and refrigerate for 2 hours. Remove and leave at room temperature for 10 to 12 hours. At this point, the poolish will have fermented and will have bubbles visible on its surface.

2. TO MAKE THE FINAL DOUGH, put the poolish in the bowl of a mixer with the water, oil and malt. Combine the flour with the yeast, then add them to the bowl. Add the salt and place the bowl on a mixer fitted with a dough hook. Mix for 4 minutes on low speed, making sure to scrape down the bowl and flip the dough over twice during the mixing time. Then mix for 3 minutes on medium speed, making sure to scrape down the bowl and flip the dough over. At this point, the dough will still feel tacky but will have full gluten development. Place the dough in a lightly oiled bowl large enough for it to double in size and cover with plastic wrap.

3. ALLOW the dough to rest and ferment in a warm place for 60–75 minutes, until when lightly touched the dough springs back halfway.

4. PLACE the dough on a lightly floured work surface and divide it into 3-oz pieces. Cover the dough pieces with plastic wrap and allow them to rest and ferment in a warm place for 15 minutes, until when lightly touched the dough springs back halfway.

5. LIGHTLY flour each dough piece and roll it out to a circle about 5.5 inches in diameter. Place each piece on a tray and cover with a lightly floured cloth. After rolling all the pieces, cover them lightly with plastic wrap. Allow the covered dough to rest and ferment in a warm place for 20–25 minutes, until when lightly touched the dough springs back halfway.

6. PREHEAT the oven to 500°F with a baking stone.

7. USING a piece of stiff cardboard or the back of a cookie sheet, transfer the pieces to a floured peel 1 at a time, then transfer them onto the baking stone. (You will not be able to bake all the pieces at once.) Bake the pieces for 3–4 minutes, until they puff up but brown very little.

8. REMOVE the bread from the oven and place the pieces in a folded kitchen towel to cover them, help retain the moisture, and keep them from drying out.

9. ALLOW the stone to reheat for 10 minutes, then continue baking the remainder of the pitas. Once the pitas are completely cool, they may be tightly wrapped and kept at room temperature, if they are not eaten immediately.

ADVANCED BREADS with Preferments

Preferments are the secret to incomparable bread. It's not overdramatic to say that everything you've been working for, up to now, has led to this moment. If you are comfortable with basic breads, then you are now ready to set regular bread aside and embrace the sublime. You are not, however, being pushed off a cliff. Sour, which involves harnessing wild yeast, is not your only option when it comes to preferments. If you don't feel ready for that, there are lots of methods that work well and involve commercially cultivated yeast. Once you get the lay of the "commercial yeast preferment" land, you can move onto sour—a natural wild yeast culture.

Whole Wheat Pita

For a healthier twist on your favorite pita sandwich, make your own pocket bread using this whole wheat recipe.

yield: 14 pieces at 3 oz | FDT: 82°F
poolish: 12–14 hours | *first rest:* 75 minutes | *final rest:* 20–25 minutes | *bake:* 500°F *and* 3–4 minutes

INGREDIENT	OUNCES	GRAMS	VOLUME	BAKERS %
POOLISH				
Water, 55°F	6.3	177	¾ cup	22.9%
Bread flour	4.2	119	1 cup	15.4%
Whole wheat flour	2.1	60	½ cup	7.7%
Yeast, instant dry	0.01	0.3	1 tsp	0.04%
FINAL DOUGH				
Poolish	12.6	356	•	46.0%
Water, 85°F	12.4	352	1½ cups	45.4%
Vegetable oil	1.5	43	3 Tbsp	5.5%
Malt syrup	0.2	6	1 tsp	0.5%
Bread flour	14.8	418	3 cups + 1 Tbsp	54.0%
Whole wheat flour	6.3	177	1½ cups	22.9%
Yeast, instant dry	0.1	3	1 tsp	0.4%
Salt	0.6	17	1 Tbsp	2.2%
TOTAL	48.5	1372	•	176.9%

1. PREPARE the poolish the day before you want to serve the pita. Place the water in a bowl. Combine the flours with the yeast, then add them to the water. Mix together by hand until homogenous. You will still have little lumps and the poolish will be very wet, looser than a dough. Cover the poolish with plastic wrap and refrigerate for 2 hours. Remove and leave at room temperature for 10 to 12 hours. At this point, the poolish will have fermented and will have bubbles visible on its surface but should not have collapsed in the center.

2. TO MAKE THE FINAL DOUGH, put the poolish in the bowl of a mixer with the water, oil and malt. Combine the flours with the yeast, then add them to the bowl. Add the salt and place the bowl on a mixer fitted with a dough hook. Mix for 4 minutes on low speed, making sure to scrape down the bowl and flip the dough over twice during the mixing time. Then mix for 3 minutes on medium speed, making sure to scrape down the bowl and flip the dough over. At this point, the dough will have full gluten development. Place the dough in a lightly oiled bowl large enough for it to double in size and cover with plastic wrap.

3. **ALLOW** the dough to rest and ferment in a warm place for 60 minutes, until when lightly touched the dough springs back halfway.

4. **PLACE** the dough on a lightly floured work surface and divide into 3-oz pieces. Cover the dough pieces with plastic wrap and allow to ferment in a warm place for 15 minutes, until when lightly touched the dough springs back halfway.

5. **PREHEAT** the oven to 500°F with a baking stone.

6. **LIGHTLY** flour each dough piece and roll it out to a circle about 5.5 inches in diameter. Place each piece on a tray and cover with a lightly floured cloth. After rolling all the pieces, cover them lightly with plastic wrap and allow the covered dough to rest and ferment in a warm place for 20–25 minutes, until when lightly touched the dough springs back halfway.

7. **USING** a piece of stiff cardboard or the back of a cookie sheet, transfer the pieces to a floured peel 1 at a time, then transfer them onto the baking stone. (You will not be able to bake all the pieces at once.) Bake the pieces for 3 to 4 minutes, until they puff up.

8. **REMOVE** the bread from the oven and place the pieces in a folded kitchen towel to cover them, help retain moisture, and keep them from drying out.

9. **ALLOW** the stone to reheat for 10 minutes, then continue baking the remainder of the pitas. Once the pitas are completely cool, they may be tightly wrapped and kept at room temperature, if they are not eaten immediately.

ENGLISH MUFFINS

This recipe brings a classic favorite to the breakfast table. To get the characteristically browned outer crust of the muffins, before baking, the dough is first heated in a skillet for a short time at a low temperature. Slather these muffins with butter and jam, or pile them high with eggs and bacon for a satisfying early-day meal.

yield: **12 muffins at 3½ oz** | FDT: **82°F**
poolish: **12–14 hours** | bulk fermentation: **60–75 minutes** | final fermentation: **15 minutes** | bake: **475°F** *and* **6–8 minutes**

INGREDIENT	OUNCES	GRAMS	VOLUME	BAKERS %
POOLISH				
Water, 55°F	6.8	191	¾ cup	25.0%
Bread flour	6.8	191	1⅓ cups + 1 Tbsp	25.0%
Yeast, instant dry	0.01	0.3	¼ tsp	0.04%
FINAL DOUGH				
Poolish	13.6	383	•	50.1%
Water, 95°F	12.5	354	1½ cups	46.4%
Malt syrup	0.2	6	⅛ tsp	0.6%
Butter	1.0	28	2 Tbsp	3.7%
Bread flour	20.2	573	4¼ cups	75.0%
Yeast, instant dry	0.3	9	1 Tbsp	0.9%
Salt	0.6	18	1 Tbsp	2.3%
Sugar	0.3	9	2 tsp	0.9%
TOTAL	48.6	1380	•	179.9%
GARNISH				
Semolina-flour mixture; ratio 1:1	as needed			

1. PREPARE the poolish the day before you want to serve the muffins. Mix together the water, flour and yeast by hand until homogenous. The poolish will have little lumps and will be wet (unlike a dough). Cover the poolish with plastic wrap and refrigerate for 2 hours. Remove from the refrigerator and leave at room temperature for 10 to 12 hours. At this point, the poolish will have fermented and risen with visible bubbles (it should not have collapsed in the center).

2. TO MAKE THE DOUGH, put the poolish in the bowl of a mixer with the water and malt. In a separate bowl, rub the butter into the flour to make a sandy mixture. Add the yeast to the flour and

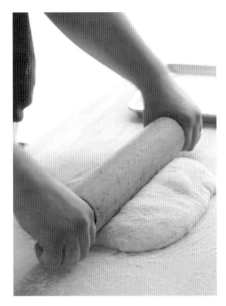

Gently roll out the dough to about ½ inch thick. Try to avoid deflating the dough too much. This will cause it to become tough after baking.

Cut 3-inch strips across the width of the dough. Then cut each strip into 3-inch squares. Put very little pressure on the dough while measuring so that it doesn't deflate.

Brown the top and bottom of the muffins in a medium-hot skillet. Avoid overheating as these need to be baked as well. If the skillet is too hot, the muffins will burn, or dry out or burn in the oven.

butter, then add to the bowl. Add the salt and sugar and place the bowl on a mixer fitted with a dough hook. Mix for 4 minutes on low speed, making sure to scrape down and flip the dough over twice during the mixing process. Then mix for another 2 minutes on medium speed, making sure to scrape down and flip the dough. The dough should be wet and tacky with partial gluten development. Place the dough in a lightly oiled bowl large enough for it to double in size and cover with plastic wrap.

3. PLACE the bowl in a warm place to rest and ferment for 45–60 minutes, until when lightly touched the dough springs back halfway.

4. PLACE the dough on a lightly floured work surface and fold it into thirds. Re-cover the dough with plastic wrap and allow it to rest for another 15 minutes, until when lightly touched the dough springs back halfway.

5. PREHEAT the oven to 475°F.

6. UNCOVER the dough and lightly flour it on all sides with a mixture of semolina flour and bread flour. Then gently roll the dough out into a rectangle (10 by 11 inches) about ½ inch thick. With a pastry wheel or pizza wheel, cut the dough into 3-inch squares (cut in 1 direction to create 3-inch strips, then cut across each strip to create squares). Place the squares on a baking tray lined with parchment paper and lightly cover with plastic wrap. Allow the dough to rest in a warm place for 15 minutes, until when lightly touched the dough springs back halfway.

7. WARM a nonstick skillet over medium heat for 5 minutes. Place a few dough pieces in the skillet, making sure not to overcrowd the pan, and cook until they are brown on each side (if the skillet becomes too hot, quickly lower the heat). Place the cooked dough pieces on a clean tray lined with parchment paper. Repeat with the remaining dough.

8. TRANSFER the muffins to the oven. Bake for 6–8 minutes, until they reach an internal temperature of 205°F.

9. REMOVE the tray from the oven and place on a cooling rack.

VARIATION

MULTIGRAIN ENGLISH MUFFINS

This healthier, heartier version of the English Muffins goes great with all your favorite toppings for a wonderful breakfast.

INGREDIENT	OUNCES	GRAMS	VOLUME	BAKERS %
SOAKER				
Water, 80°F	5.3	149	⅔ cup	21.1%
Multigrain mixture	3.1	88	½ cup	12.5%
Flaxseeds	1.3	35	¼ cup	5.0%
POOLISH				
Bread flour	5.4	153	1 cup + 2 Tbsp	21.7%
Water, 55°F	5.4	153	⅔ cup	21.7%
Yeast, instant dry	0.01	0.3	⅛ tsp	0.04%
FINAL DOUGH				
Poolish	10.8	306	•	43.5%
Water, 95°F	9.8	276	1¼ cups	39.2%
Honey	0.4	11	2 tsp	1.6%
Malt syrup	0.2	6	1 tsp	0.6%
Bread flour	14.6	414	3 cups	58.8%
Whole wheat flour	1.8	50	⅓ cup + 1 Tbsp	7.0%
Butter	0.4	11	1 Tbsp	1.6%
Yeast, instant dry	0.3	9	2 tsp	1.0%
Salt	0.6	17	1 Tbsp	2.4%
Soaker	9.7	272	•	38.6%
TOTAL	48.5	1372	•	194.3%

1. PREPARE the soaker the day before you want to serve the muffins. Add the water to the grains and flaxseeds in a bowl and stir. Cover with plastic wrap and keep at room temperature overnight until needed.

2. PREPARE the poolish the day before you want to serve the muffins, as in step #1 for English Muffins (page 160).

3. TO MAKE THE DOUGH, put the poolish in the bowl of a mixer with the water, honey and malt. In a separate bowl, rub the flours and

butter together to make a sandy mixture. Add the yeast to the flour and butter, then add to the bowl. Add the salt and place the bowl on a mixer fitted with a dough hook. Mix for 4 minutes on low speed, making sure to scrape down and flip the dough over twice during this time. Then mix for 2 minutes on medium speed, making sure to scrape down and flip the dough over. Add one half of the soaker and mix on low speed for 1 minute, making sure to scrape down and flip the dough over during this time. Then mix on medium speed for 1 minute more, making sure to scrape down and flip the dough

over during this time. Add the remaining half of the soaker and mix on low speed for 1 minute, making sure to scrape down and flip the dough over during this time. Then mix on medium speed for 1 minute more, making sure to scrape down and flip the dough over during this time. The dough should be wet and tacky with partial gluten development. Place the dough in a lightly oiled bowl large enough for it to double in size and cover with plastic wrap.

4. PROCEED as for English Muffins.

English Muffins

Pita Bread

IF YOU READ CHAPTER 6, then you know that there are different preferments to meet distinct baking goals. Let's start with the classic baguette, for example. There are seven baguette variations in this section using various preferments, sometimes in combination. (By using a preferment, you are decreasing the amount of actual yeast you use, since the preferment is a form of yeast.) French bakers like to use poolish in their baguettes, which is a preferment that combines equal parts flour and water. It is rather soupy and helps to tenderize the dough, provides a lot of leavening and lends a mild flavor. Then there are variations on the baguette with poolish: one that involves adding pâte fermentée (a.k.a. old dough), and one that combines poolish with sour.

But what if you want more pronounced flavor and less leavening in your baguette? Then choose the recipe made with biga, a preferment with a ratio of a little more than two parts flour to one part water. The biga is stiffer and imparts more acidity to a bread dough than poolish and therefore produces more flavor. It also helps to make the gluten in the final dough recipe stronger. If you want to get creative with your baguette with biga, you may add the biga in combination with pâte fermentée or with sour.

Beyond baguettes, you will also find recipes in this chapter for focaccia made with biga, and ciabatta made with poolish (or with sour). Other yeasted preferment recipes include tantalizing bread varieties such as pesto and cheese pretzels, fig and hazelnut sourdough, currant and pecan sourdough, golden raisin and fennel seed semolina, and apple and cinnamon epi. You can also look forward to pretzels, bialys and a wide range of bagels.

Once you are ready to try sourdough, there is a long list of options—including breads made with white flour, whole wheat, rye and durum. Then there are flavor-enhanced sourdough varieties with such inclusions as roasted onions; chipotle chilies; and apples, walnuts and cranberries.

You will find a lot of recipes in this chapter—attesting to the range of what preferments can do. All of them are flavorful and different in their own right, so get baking!

PEASANT BREAD

The complexity of the flours used in this hearty, rustic bread lends it a unique aroma and flavor. Like traditional European peasant breads, our version combines several flour varieties: whole wheat, rye and bread. The thick, crusty exterior and tender, flavorful crumb make it a simple everyday bread. To extend the shelf life of the whole wheat and rye flours, store them in the freezer.

yield: 2 loaves at 24 oz | FDT: 80°F

biga: 12–14 hours | bulk fermentation: 60–75 minutes | final fermentation: 40–50 minutes | bake: 450°F *and* 30–32 minutes

INGREDIENT	OUNCES	GRAMS	VOLUME	BAKERS %
BIGA				
Water, 55°F	6.0	170	¾ cup	20.8%
Bread flour	6.7	190	1⅓ cups + 1 Tbsp	23.3%
Whole wheat flour	1.9	54	½ cup	6.6%
Rye flour	1.0	28	¼ cup	3.5%
Yeast, instant dry	0.01	0.3	⅛ tsp	0.03%
FINAL DOUGH				
Water, 86°F	15.4	442	2 cups	54.2%
Malt syrup	0.2	4	½ tsp	0.5%
Biga	15.6	442	•	54.2%
Bread flour	9.6	272	2 cups	33.3%
Whole wheat flour	5.8	164	1⅓ cups	20.1%
Rye flour	3.8	108	1 cup	13.2%
Yeast, instant dry	0.2	6	1½ tsp	0.5%
Salt	0.7	20	1 Tbsp + ¼ tsp	2.4%
TOTAL	50.3	1424	•	174.2%
GARNISHES				
Sesame seeds, (optional)	as needed			
Semolina flour, (optional)	as needed			

1. **MIX** the biga the day before you want to serve the bread. Put the water in the bowl of a mixer, combine the flours with the yeast, and then add the flour mixture to the bowl. Place on a mixer fitted with a dough hook and mix for 2 minutes on low speed, or until homogenous. The biga should be stiff and slightly dry. Place it in a lightly oiled bowl large enough for it to double in size. Flip the biga over in the bowl to coat it lightly with oil. Cover the bowl with plastic wrap and refrigerate for 2 hours.

2. **REMOVE** the biga and leave it at room temperature for 10–12 hours before using. After the fermentation, the biga will be less stiff and more like an actual bread dough.

3. **TO MAKE THE FINAL DOUGH,** put the water and malt in the bowl of a mixer. Break the biga up by hand, and then add it to the bowl. Place the bowl on a mixer fitted with a dough hook and mix for 2 minutes on low speed to break down the biga (for autolyse mixing see page 129). Mix the flours with the yeast, then add them to the bowl and incorporate. Mix the dough for 2 minutes on low speed, making sure to scrape down and flip the dough over during this time. Leave the dough in the bowl, cover it, and allow it to rest at room temperature for 15 minutes.

4. **ADD** the salt and mix for 1 minute on low speed, making sure to scrape down and flip the dough over. Increase the speed to medium and mix for 2 minutes, again making sure to scrape down and flip the dough over. The dough should be tacky but have some good gluten structure. Place the dough in a lightly oiled bowl large enough for it to double in size and cover it with plastic wrap.

5. **ALLOW** the dough to rest and ferment in a warm place for 45–60 minutes, until when lightly touched the dough springs back.

6. **PLACE** the dough on a lightly floured work surface and divide it into two 24-oz pieces. Round each dough piece against the table-top, apply sesame seeds and semolina flour for garnish if desired, and cover it, then allow it to rest at room temperature for 15 minutes, until when lightly touched the dough springs back.

7. **LINE** round bowls with cloth napkins or kitchen towels.

8. **SHAPE** each piece of dough into a round. Place each loaf seam-side up in a round bowl with a floured cloth. Cover the dough pieces lightly with plastic wrap and allow them to rest and ferment in a warm place for 40–50 minutes, until when lightly touched the dough springs back.

9. **TWENTY MINUTES** before the end of the final fermentation, preheat the oven to 475°F with a baking stone. Ten minutes before baking the loaves, place a tray filled with 3 cups of warm water below the baking area in the oven to help produce steam.

10. **UNCOVER** the dough and place each piece seam-side down on an oven peel lined with parchment paper. Spray each loaf with water and allow the loaves to sit for 5 minutes to absorb the water, then score each loaf and spray again.

11. **TRANSFER** the loaves and parchment paper to the baking stone and immediately reduce the temperature to 450°F. Bake for 12 minutes. Remove the steam tray and parchment paper and rotate each loaf. Continue baking for another 18–20 minutes, until the crust has a deep color and doesn't give when lightly pressed.

12. **REMOVE** from the oven and place the bread on a cooling rack.

Sesame and Asiago Wheat Bread

This wholesome bread is loaded with flavor from the whole wheat flour, sesame seeds and cubes of Asiago cheese. It is nutty, cheesy and truly satisfying. Although it makes a delicious sliced bread, it's equally tempting divided into individual portions and formed into rolls.

yield: 2 loaves at 24 oz | FDT: 77°F

biga: 12–14 hours | bulk fermentation: 60–75 minutes | final fermentation: 45–60 minutes | bake: 450°F *and* 27–30 minutes

INGREDIENT	OUNCES	GRAMS	VOLUME	BAKERS %
BIGA				
Water, 55°F	3.5	99	½ cup	14.4%
Bread flour	1.8	51	6 Tbsp	7.4%
Whole wheat flour	4.3	120	1 cup	17.5%
Yeast, instant dry	0.01	0.3	pinch	0.04%
FINAL DOUGH				
Water, 88°F	14.1	400	1¾ cups	58.1%
Malt syrup	0.1	3	1 tsp	0.4%
Biga	9.6	271	•	39.4%
Bread flour	5.4	153	1 cup + 2 Tbsp	22.3%
Whole wheat flour	12.8	363	3 cups	52.8%
Yeast, instant dry	0.1	3	1 tsp	0.4%
Salt	0.6	17	1 Tbsp	2.5%
Asiago cheese, cubed	6.5	184	¾ cup	26.8%
Sesame seeds, toasted	1.4	40	1½ Tbsp	5.8%
TOTAL	50.6	1434	•	208.5%
GARNISHES				
Sesame seeds (optional)	as needed			
Asiago cheese, grated	4.0	113	1 cup	•

1. **MIX** the biga the day before you want to serve the bread. Put the water in the bowl of a mixer, combine the flours with the yeast, and add the flour mixture to the bowl. Place on a mixer fitted with a dough hook and mix for 2 minutes on low speed or until homogenous. The biga should be stiff and slightly dry. Place it in a lightly oiled bowl large enough for it to double in size. Flip the biga over in the bowl to coat it lightly with oil. Cover the bowl with plastic wrap and refrigerate for 2 hours.

2. **REMOVE** the biga and leave it at room temperature for 10–12 hours before using. After the fermentation, the biga will be less stiff and more like an actual bread dough.

3. **TO MAKE THE FINAL DOUGH,** put the water and malt in the bowl of a mixer. Break the biga up by hand, and then add it to the bowl. Place the bowl on a mixer fitted with a dough hook and mix for 2 minutes on low speed to break down the biga. Add the flours and yeast (for autolyse mixing, see page 129). Mix for 2 minutes on low speed, making sure to scrape down and flip the dough over. Leave the dough in the bowl, cover it, and allow it to rest at room temperature for 15 minutes.

4. **ADD** the salt and mix for 2 minutes on low speed, making sure to scrape down and flip the dough over. Increase to medium speed and mix for another 2 minutes, making sure to scrape down and flip the dough over. The dough should be a little sticky, but with fairly good gluten development. Add the cubed cheese and sesame seeds and mix for 1 to 2 minutes more on low, making sure to scrape down and flip the dough twice during this mixing. Place the dough in a lightly oiled bowl large enough for it to double in size and cover it with plastic wrap.

5. **ALLOW** the dough to rest and ferment in a warm place for 45–60 minutes, until when lightly touched the dough springs back.

6. **PLACE** the dough on a lightly floured work surface and fold it over in thirds, then place it back in the bowl, re-cover it, and let it rest for 15 minutes at room temperature.

7. **LINE** a baking tray with a white cloth napkin or white kitchen towel. The cloth will need to be floured unless seeds are being applied directly to the loaf.

8. **PLACE** the dough on a lightly floured work surface and divide it into two 24-oz pieces. Round each dough piece against the tabletop. Allow the dough to rest seam-side up and covered for 10 minutes.

9. **SHAPE** each piece into a 10-inch oblong. Spray the dough with water. Roll the top and sides in sesame seeds, if using, then place the loaves seam-side up in the prepared cloth and bring the cloth up between each shaped loaf. Cover the loaves with plastic wrap. Allow the dough to rest and ferment in a warm place for 45–60 minutes, until when lightly touched the dough springs back.

10. **TWENTY MINUTES** before the end of the final fermentation, preheat the oven to 475°F with a baking stone. Ten minutes before baking the loaves, place a tray filled with 3 cups of warm water below the baking area in the oven to help produce steam.

11. **UNCOVER** the loaves and place them seam-side down on an oven peel with parchment paper or baking tray lined with parchment paper, then spray the tops and sides of the loaves with water. Let the dough sit for 5 minutes, score the tops of the loaves ¼–½ inch deep, and then spray the loaves with water again. This will help create steam in the oven and allow the loaves to expand.

12. **TRANSFER** the loaves to the baking stone and immediately reduce the temperature to 450°F. Bake for 12 minutes. Remove the steam tray, rotate the loaves, and sprinkle half of the grated cheese on each loaf. Continue baking for 15–18 minutes. This will allow the loaves to finish baking and form a crust. If at the end of the baking the crust isn't thick enough, turn the oven off and leave the bread in the oven with the door cracked open for 4 to 6 minutes more.

13. **REMOVE** from the oven and place the bread on a cooling rack.

SEMOLINA BREAD

Semolina bread is unique in appearance, aroma and flavor. The semolina and durum flours lend a golden color and nutty taste and scent. To accent the flavor of the bread, use sesame seeds for garnish. If you prefer a more rustic, earthy taste, finish the loaf with a dusting of semolina. Either way, you're sure to enjoy this tender bread.

yield: **3 loaves at 12 oz** | FDT: **82°F**
biga: **12–14 hours** | bulk fermentation: **75–90 minutes** | final fermentation: **40–50 minutes** | bake: **450°F** and **22–24 minutes**

INGREDIENT	OUNCES	GRAMS	VOLUME	BAKERS %
BIGA				
Water, 55°F	4.4	125	½ cup	21.0%
Semolina flour	3.5	99	½ cup	16.7%
Durum flour	3.5	99	¾ cup	16.7%
Yeast, instant dry	0.01	0.3	pinch	0.05%
FINAL DOUGH				
Water, 86°F	11.1	315	1⅓ cups	52.9%
Olive oil	0.9	26	2 Tbsp	4.3%
Malt syrup	0.1	3	½ tsp	0.5%
Biga	11.4	323	•	54.5%
Semolina flour	3.5	99	½ cup	16.7%
Durum flour	3.5	99	½ cup + 2 Tbsp	16.7%
Bread flour	7.0	198	1½ cups	33.3%
Yeast, instant dry	0.1	3	1 tsp	0.5%
Salt	0.5	14	2¼ tsp	2.4%
TOTAL	38.1	1080	•	181.8%
GARNISHES				
Sesame seeds	as needed			
Semolina flour	as needed			

1. MIX the biga the day before you want to serve the bread. Put the water in the bowl of a mixer, combine the flours with the yeast, and add the flour mixture to the bowl. Place on a mixer fitted with a dough hook and mix for 2 minutes on low speed or until homogenous. The biga should be stiff and slightly dry. Place it in a lightly oiled bowl large enough for it to double in size. Flip the biga over in the bowl to coat it lightly with oil. Cover the bowl with plastic wrap and refrigerate for 2 hours.

2. REMOVE the biga and leave it at room temperature for 10–12 hours before using. After the fermentation, the biga will be less stiff and more like an actual bread dough.

3. TO MAKE THE FINAL DOUGH, put the water, oil and malt in the bowl of a mixer. Break the biga up by hand, and then add it to the bowl. Place the bowl on a mixer fitted with a dough hook, and mix for 2 minutes on low speed to break down the biga. Mix the flours with the yeast, then add the mixture to the bowl (for autolyse mixing, see page 129). Mix for 2 minutes on low speed, making sure to scrape down and flip the dough over. Leave the dough in the bowl, cover it, and allow it to rest at room temperature for 15 minutes.

4. ADD the salt and mix for 2 minutes on low speed, making sure to scrape down and flip the dough over. Increase to medium speed and mix for 2 more minutes, making sure to scrape down and flip the dough over. The dough should be a little tacky but have some good gluten structure. Place the dough in a lightly oiled bowl large enough for it to double in size and cover with plastic wrap.

5. ALLOW the dough to rest and ferment in a warm place for 45–60 minutes, until when lightly touched the dough springs back halfway.

6. PLACE the dough on a lightly floured work surface and fold in thirds. Cover, leave on work surface, and allow to ferment at room temperature for 15 minutes.

7. PLACE the dough on a lightly floured work surface and divide it into three 12-oz pieces. Round each piece against the tabletop and cover. Allow the dough to rest seam-side up for 15 minutes.

8. LINE a baking tray or bowls with a cloth napkin or kitchen towels. Also have a spray bottle nearby and some sesame seeds or semolina to garnish.

9. PLACE the dough on a lightly floured work surface and shape it into 10-inch oblongs. Spray with water, then roll the tops and sides in sesame or semolina. Place each shaped loaf seam-side up into the cloth and bring the cloth up between each shaped loaf on the tray. Cover the shaped dough pieces and allow the dough to rest and ferment in a warm place for 40–50 minutes, until when lightly touched the dough springs back halfway.

10. TWENTY MINUTES before the end of the final fermentation, preheat the oven to 475°F with a baking stone. Ten minutes before baking the loaves, place a tray filled with 3 cups of warm water below the baking area in the oven to help produce steam.

11. UNCOVER the dough and place each piece seam-side down on an oven peel lined with parchment paper. Spray each loaf with water and allow it to rest for 5 minutes. Score each loaf and spray each one again.

12. TRANSFER the loaves and parchment paper to the baking stone and immediately reduce the temperature to 450°F. Bake for 12 minutes. Remove the steam tray and parchment paper and rotate each loaf. Continue baking for another 10–12 minutes, until the crust has a deep color and doesn't give when pressed.

13. REMOVE from the oven and place the loaves on a cooling rack.

Semolina with Golden Raisins and Fennel Seeds

Studded with golden raisins and fennel seeds, this flavorful country bread makes an excellent addition to a cheese platter, or can be enjoyed on its own with a little olive oil. Semolina bread is often associated with Italian baking, since the flour is milled from durum wheat—the same high-protein wheat used in pasta making. You can find semolina flour in Italian groceries and natural food stores.

yield: 3 loaves at 12 oz | FDT: 82°F

INGREDIENT	OUNCES	GRAMS	VOLUME	BAKERS %
Golden raisins, plumped	6.2	176	1¼ cups	35.8%
Fennel seeds	0.4	11	1 Tbsp + 2 tsp	2.3%
Cornmeal	0.4	11	1 Tbsp	2.3%
GARNISH				
Cornmeal	as needed			

PREPARE the dough as for Semolina Bread (page 171). Once the dough has reached good gluten development, toss together the raisins, fennel seeds and cornmeal, then add them to the bowl. Mix on low speed for 2 minutes, making sure to scrape down and flip the dough twice. Place the dough in a lightly oiled bowl large enough for it to double in size and cover with plastic wrap. Proceed as for Semolina Bread.

TO MAKE OLIVE AND CHEESE BREAD: Replace the raisins and fennel seeds with 4 oz olives, rinsed and coarsely chopped, and 4 oz cheese, diced (Asiago, Manchego, piavé, provolone). Omit the cornmeal.

Pecan and Raisin Bread and Sesame and Asiago Wheat Bread

PECAN AND RAISIN BREAD

Laced throughout with plump raisins and buttery pecans, this subtly sweet loaf makes a nice sandwich or toasting bread. If you prefer, exchange the raisins for currants and use your favorite type of nut. You can also prepare this bread with a sour rather than pâte fermentée, substituting the same amount of sour and using the same method. This will yield a more flavorful bread, as the acidity of the sour will help to tenderize and accent the other ingredients.

yield: **2 loaves at 24 oz** | FDT: **82°F**
pâte fermentée: **1 day** | bulk fermentation: **80–95 minutes** | final fermentation: **75–90 minutes** | bake: **450°F** *and* **30–32 minutes**

INGREDIENT	OUNCES	GRAMS	VOLUME	BAKERS %
PÂTE FERMENTÉE				
Water, 80°F	2.4	68	¼ cup	69.6%
Flour	3.5	98	¾ cup	100.0%
Yeast, instant dry	0.05	1	pinch	1.4%
Salt	0.05	1	pinch	1.4%
FINAL DOUGH				
Water, 90°F	14.6	414	1¾ cups	76.0%
Malt syrup	0.1	3	½ tsp	0.5%
Pâte fermentée	6.0	168	•	31.3%
Bread flour	15.4	437	3¼ cups	80.2%
Whole wheat flour	3.8	108	¾ cup + 2 Tbsp	19.8%
Yeast, instant dry	0.1	3	1 tsp	0.5%
Salt	0.5	14	2¼ tsp	2.6%
Raisins	6.0	170	1 cup	31.3%
Pecan pieces, toasted	5.0	142	1¼ cups	26.0%
TOTAL	51.5	1459	•	268.2%

1. MAKE the pâte fermentée the day before you want to serve the bread. Put the water in the bowl of a mixer, combine the flour with the yeast and salt, and add the flour mixture to the bowl. Place on a mixer fitted with a dough hook and mix for 4 minutes on low speed or until homogenous. Place in a lightly oiled bowl large enough for it to double in size. Cover the bowl with plastic wrap.

2. ALLOW the pâte fermentée to ferment at room temperature for 30 minutes, then refrigerate for at least 18 hours or up to 3 days.

3. TO MAKE THE FINAL DOUGH, put the water and malt in the bowl of a mixer, then break up the pâte fermentée by hand and add to the bowl. Place the bowl on a mixer fitted with a dough hook and mix for 2 minutes on low speed to break up the pâte fermentée (for autolyse mixing, see page 129). Mix the flours and the yeast together, then add them to the bowl and mix for 4 minutes, making sure to scrape down and flip the dough over twice during this process. Leave the dough in the bowl, cover it, and let it rest at room temperature for 15 minutes.

4. ADD the salt and mix for 2 minutes on low speed, making sure to scrape down and flip the dough over. Then increase the speed to medium and mix for 2 more minutes, making sure to scrape down and flip the dough over. Add the raisins and pecans and mix for 1 minute on low speed, making sure to scrape down and flip the dough over. The dough should be a little sticky, but will have fairly good gluten development. Place the dough in a lightly oiled bowl large enough for it to double in size and cover with plastic wrap.

5. ALLOW the dough to rest and ferment in a warm place for 45–60 minutes, until when lightly touched the dough springs back.

6. PLACE the dough on a lightly floured work surface and fold it over in thirds, then leave it on the work surface, cover, and let rest for 15 minutes.

7. UNCOVER the dough and divide it into two 24-oz pieces. Shape each dough piece into a round, place it on a lightly floured surface, and cover. Allow the dough to rest and ferment at room temperature for 20 minutes.

8. LINE a baking tray or bowls with cloth napkins or kitchen towels. The cloth will need to be floured.

9. SHAPE each dough piece into a 10-inch oblong. Place each shaped loaf seam-side up into the cloth and bring the cloth up between each loaf on the tray. Cover the shaped dough pieces and allow them to rest and ferment in a warm place for 75–90 minutes, until when lightly touched the dough springs back halfway.

10. TWENTY MINUTES before the end of the final fermentation, preheat the oven to 475°F with a baking stone. Ten minutes before baking the loaves, place a tray filled with 3 cups of warm water below the baking area in the oven to help produce steam.

11. UNCOVER the dough and place each piece seam-side down on an oven peel lined with parchment paper. Spray the loaves with water and allow them to rest for 5 minutes, then score each loaf down the middle and spray the loaves again. This will help create steam in the oven and allow the loaf to expand.

12. TRANSFER the loaves and parchment to the baking stone and immediately reduce the temperature to 450°F. Bake for 12 minutes. Remove the steam tray and paper, and rotate each piece. Continue baking for another 18–20 minutes, until the crust has a deep color and does not give when lightly pressed.

13. REMOVE from the oven and place the loaves on a cooling rack.

Apple-Cinnamon Epi

The whole wheat flour in this fruit bread lends a deeper, more rustic flavor. It also gives the bread a slightly darker color that will set off the color of the apples.

yield: 4 loaves at 12 oz | FDT: 82°F

pâte fermentée: **1 day** | *bulk fermentation:* **70–85 minutes** | *final fermentation:* **35–45 minutes** | *bake:* **450°F** *and* **23–25 minutes**

INGREDIENT	OUNCES	GRAMS	VOLUME	BAKERS %
Pâte Fermentée (page 175)				
FINAL DOUGH				
Water, 90°F	15.2	431	2 cups	71.5%
Malt syrup	0.2	5	1 tsp	0.8%
Pâte fermentée	4.3	123	•	20.4%
Bread flour	21.3	603	4½ cups	100.0%
Whole wheat flour	0.9	26	3 Tbsp	4.2%
Yeast, instant dry	0.1	3	1 tsp	0.6%
Salt	0.5	14	2½ tsp	2.3%
Gala apples, diced	4.2	119	⅔ cup	19.8%
Cinnamon, ground	0.1	3	1½ tsp	0.5%
TOTAL	46.8	1327	•	220.1%

1. MAKE the pâte fermentée the day before you want to serve the bread.

2. TO MAKE THE FINAL DOUGH, put the water and malt in the bowl of a mixer, then break up the pâte fermentée by hand and add to the bowl. Mix the flours and yeast together and add to the bowl. Add the salt, place the bowl on a mixer fitted with a dough hook, and mix for 8 minutes on low speed. Make sure to scrape down and flip the dough over twice during this process. Add the apples and cinnamon and mix for 1 minute on low speed, making sure to scrape down and flip the dough over. The dough should be a little sticky, but with fairly good gluten development. Place the dough in a lightly oiled bowl large enough for it to double in size and cover with plastic wrap.

3. ALLOW the dough to rest and ferment in warm place for 45–60 minutes, until when lightly touched the dough springs back halfway.

4. PLACE the dough on a lightly floured work surface and fold it over in thirds, then place back in the bowl, cover, and let rest for 15 minutes.

5. LINE a baking tray with white cloth napkins or kitchen towels. The cloth will need to be floured unless seeds are being applied to the loaf.

6. PLACE the dough on a lightly floured work surface and divide it into four 12-oz pieces. Shape each piece into a 6-inch oblong. Leave the loaves seam-side up on the work surface Cover lightly with plastic wrap, and let rest at room temperature for 10 minutes.

7. SHAPE each dough piece into an oblong. Place each oblong seam-side down on a lightly floured work surface. Roll the loaf back and forth just slightly about 1 inch in each direction, working the dough out to 12 inches. With your hands at a 45-degree angle to the center, place downward pressure to close the ends with a tapered look. Place the loaf on a lightly floured tray with the seam up and bring the cloth up to place the other loaves on the tray. Place the loaves on the cloth-covered tray with the seams up. Cover the loaves lightly with additional cloth or plastic wrap.

8. LET the loaves rest and ferment in a warm place for 35–45 minutes, until when lightly touched the dough springs back halfway.

9. TWENTY MINUTES before the end of the final fermentation, preheat the oven to 475°F with a baking stone. Ten minutes before baking the loaves, place a tray filled with 3 cups of warm water below the baking area in the oven to help produce steam.

10. UNCOVER the dough and place each piece on an oven peel with parchment paper or baking tray with parchment paper and spray the tops and sides of each loaf with water. Cut the top of each loaf by cutting at a 45-degree angle with a pair of sharp kitchen shears. Spray the loaves with water again. This will help create steam in the oven and allow the loaf to expand.

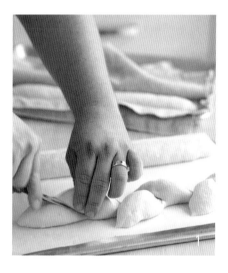

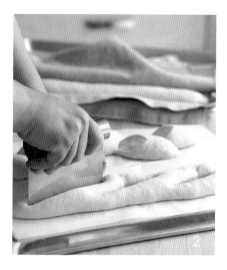

1. To make an epi, use very clean scissors to cut evenly spaced segments of dough. Cut at a 45-degree angle and make sure not to cut completely through the dough. After cutting each segment, pull it to the side, alternating sides each time.

2. To make a fougasse variation, an alternative design is to use a bench scraper or dough cutter and slice segments into the cylinder of dough. Place each cut at an angle and space the cuts evenly down the center of the cylinder.

3. To make an alternative fougasse variation, you can also cut vertically down the length of the cylinder to create an oval shape. Leave a section at the top and bottom uncut so that the dough remains a single piece. Once cut, gently pull apart the two sides until you have the desired shape.

4. To make a double epi, use very clean scissors to cut evenly spaced segments of dough. Cut at a 45-degree angle and make sure not to go completely through the dough. After cutting each segment, pull it to the side, alternating sides each time.

11. TRANSFER the loaves to the baking stone and immediately reduce the temperature to 450°F. Bake for 15 minutes. Remove the steam tray and parchment paper, rotate the loaves, and bake for 8–10 minutes more. This will allow the loaves to finish baking and a crust to form. If at the end of the baking the crust isn't thick enough, turn the oven off and leave the bread in the oven with the door cracked open for 4–6 minutes.

12. REMOVE from the oven and place the loaves on a cooling rack.

NOTE: If you don't have enough room to bake all 4 loaves at once, then place 2 of them in the refrigerator for 15 minutes. This is called retarding and the cooler temperature of the refrigerator slows down the yeast's rate of fermentation. You will then bake the loaves you had at room temperature the whole time first and the ones from the refrigerator after these.

Each variation has its own unique qualities and beauty to present; double epi, epi, and fougasse variation.

Bagels and Bialys

BAGELS

Cooked first in boiling water to give them a shiny crust, bagels are then finished off in the oven to attain their characteristic chewy interior and golden color. This dense classic is at home eaten plain, toasted and slathered with butter or cream cheese, or smeared with a flavored spread and topped with sandwich fixings.

yield: **6 at 5.2 oz** | FDT: **80°F**

sponge: **60 minutes** | retard: **overnight** | rest: **10 minutes** | initial bake: **500°F** *and* **10 minutes** | final bake: **475°F** *and* **4–6 minutes**

INGREDIENT	OUNCES	GRAMS	VOLUME	BAKERS %
SPONGE				
Water, 90°F	6.2	176	¾ cup	29.7%
Malt syrup	0.1	3	⅛ tsp	0.5%
High-gluten flour	6.2	176	1¼ cups	29.7%
Yeast, instant dry	0.1	3	⅛ tsp	0.5%
FINAL DOUGH				
Sponge	12.6	358	•	60.4%
Water, 75°F	5.8	164	¾ cup	27.8%
Malt syrup	0.2	6	⅛ tsp	1.0%
High-gluten flour	14.7	417	3 cups	70.3%
Yeast, instant dry	0.1	3	⅛ tsp	0.5%
Salt	0.5	14	¼ tsp	2.4%
TOTAL	33.9	962	•	162.4%
GARNISHES				
Semolina flour	as needed			
Vegetable oil spray	as needed			
Malt syrup (step #8)	1	28	3 Tbsp	
Seeds, minced garlic, dried onions, etc.	as needed			

1. MAKE and shape the dough the day before you want to serve the bagels. To make the sponge, combine the water and malt in a bowl. In a separate bowl, combine the flour with the yeast, and then add this mixture to the water. Mix the sponge together by hand for 2 minutes to develop some gluten structure, making sure all the ingredients are combined into a homogenous mass. Cover the bowl with plastic wrap, and allow the sponge to ferment in a warm place for 60 minutes, until double in size.

2. TO MAKE THE DOUGH, put the sponge, water and malt in the bowl of a mixer fitted with a dough hook. Mix the ingredients for 1 minute on low speed to break up the sponge (it can be broken up a little by hand if needed, also). Combine the flour and yeast and add them to the bowl, then add the salt. Mix the ingredients for 10 minutes on low speed, making sure to scrape down and flip the dough over in the bowl 3 times during this process. Mix to full gluten development.

3. PLACE the dough on a lightly floured work surface. Divide the dough into six 5.2-oz pieces, then tightly preshape them into 5-inch oblongs. Place the dough pieces on the work surface seam-side up. Cover and allow to rest for 5 minutes.

4. SHAPE each piece into a bagel. Flatten out a piece of dough and bring the top edge down a third of the way and tuck it in. Repeat this step 2 more times, then tightly roll the piece out to 10 inches and moisten about 1 inch of the end. Join the 2 ends, overlapping the dough about 1 inch. Place the fingers of 1 hand in the hole, with the other hand on the outside, and roll the dough with your fingers to connect the 2 ends and make the thickness even throughout. Then gently pull and rotate to create an even hole in the bagel.

5. PREPARE a baking tray with a moderate dusting of semolina flour. Place the bagels on the tray, seam-side down, and cover them with plastic wrap. Refrigerate the bagels overnight.

6. TO FINISH THE BAGELS, preheat the oven to 500°F and bring 3 quarts of water to a boil on the stove.

7. REMOVE the bagels from the refrigerator and let stand at room temperature for 10 minutes. Meanwhile, prepare 2 baking trays, 1 lined with a cooling rack and 1 lined with parchment paper that has been sprayed with vegetable oil spray.

8. MIX the malt into the boiling water. Add 3 bagels to the water and stir them, allowing them to sit in the water for 20 seconds. Remove from the water and place on the cooling rack. Let sit dripping for 30 seconds, then place them on the parchment paper–lined tray, making sure that the flat side of the dough is placed down. If desired, they can be dipped in seeds or other garnishes before placing them on the parchment paper. Repeat this process with all of the bagels.

9. TRANSFER the tray to the oven and bake for 10 minutes, then rotate and bake for an additional 4–6 minutes at 475°F. Remove the bagels from the oven when they are partially brown (you do not want to bake to full color as this will make a dry bagel).

10. REMOVE the bagels from the tray and place on a cooling rack.

NOTE: *These can also be baked directly on a baking stone with the parchment paper.*

1. Lay a piece of preshaped dough in front of you. Pull the top end toward you and fold it a third of the way down. Repeat this twice more until you have a cylindrical shape.

2. Once you have rolled the dough to 10 inches, wet 1 inch of an end and overlap it with the other end, creating a circle. Gently press to secure the edges together without flattening one section of the bagel.

3. Roll the bagel out to an even thickness by placing 3 to 4 fingers in the hole and the other hand outside as a guide. Move slowly around the bagel so as not to twist or disfigure the dough.

4. Place only a few bagels at a time into the boiling water. This will ensure proper cooking. Remove after 20 seconds and place them on a cooling rack to allow them to dry slightly.

5. Dip the bagels into the topping of your choice, then place on a lightly oiled parchment paper–lined baking sheet. A good way to use up leftover toppings is to combine them to make "everything" bagels.

Honey-Wheat Bagels

Subtly sweet and irresistibly chewy, these nourishing bagels are the perfect way to start the day. For a yummy treat and a quick pick-me-up in the morning, try one sliced in half, toasted warm, and topped with peanut butter and banana.

yield: 6 bagels at 5 oz | FDT: 80°F

INGREDIENT	OUNCES	GRAMS	VOLUME	BAKERS %
SPONGE				
Water, 90°F	6.2	176	¾ cup	29.7%
Malt syrup	0.1	3	⅛ tsp	0.5%
High-gluten flour	4.2	119	¾ cup + 1½ Tbsp	20.1%
Whole wheat flour	2.0	57	½ cup	9.6%
Yeast, instant dry	0.1	3	⅛ tsp	0.5%
FINAL DOUGH				
Sponge	12.6	358	•	60.4%
Water, 75°F	4.2	119	½ cup	20.1%
Malt syrup	0.2	6	⅛ tsp	1.0%
Honey	1.2	34	3 Tbsp	5.7%
High-gluten flour	8.3	235	1⅔ cups	39.7%
Whole wheat flour	6.4	181	1½ cups	30.6%
Yeast, instant dry	0.1	3	⅛ tsp	0.5%
Salt	0.5	14	¼ tsp	2.4%
TOTAL	33.5	949	•	160.4%

PREPARE and bake the dough as for basic Bagel recipe (page 181).

Sun-Dried Tomato and Basil Bagels

Sun-dried tomato and basil are a classic flavor duo that will go well with a variety of cream cheese flavors.

yield: **6 bagels at 5.5 oz** | FDT: **80°F**

INGREDIENT	OUNCES	GRAMS	VOLUME	BAKERS %
Sun-dried tomatoes	2.7	77	•	14.1%
Basil, finely sliced	0.3	9	2 Tbsp	1.6%
Bread flour	0.6	17	2 Tbsp	3.1%

1. THE SUN-DRIED TOMATOES need to be plumped in hot water for 10 minutes if dried, then drained and pureed. If they are packed in oil, just drain and puree.

2. PREPARE the dough as for Bagels (page 181) until step #3.

3. COMBINE the pureed tomatoes, basil and bread flour in a bowl. Add to the dough in the mixer and mix for 1–2 minutes, making sure to scrape down and flip the dough over in the bowl 2 times. If it is not incorporating, take the dough out of the mixer and chop it up with a scraper, then return to the mixer to mix more. Proceed as for basic Bagel recipe.

Trail Mix Bagels

This bagel makes a great on-the-go lunch. It contains a great balance of food groups for a satisfying and filling meal.

yield: **6 bagels at 5.5 oz** | FDT: **80°F**

INGREDIENT	OUNCES	GRAMS	VOLUME	BAKERS %
Almonds, slivered, toasted	1.0	28	¼ cup	5.2%
Raisins	1.0	28	3 Tbsp	5.2%
Chocolate M & M's	1.0	28	2 Tbsp	5.2%
Sunflower seeds, toasted	1.0	28	3 Tbsp	5.2%

1. PREPARE the dough as for Bagels (page 181) until step #3.

2. COMBINE the almonds, raisins, M & M's and sunflower seeds in a bowl. Add the trail mix to the mixer with the dough, and mix for 1–2 minutes, making sure to scrape down and flip the dough over in the bowl 2 times. If not incorporating, take the dough out of the mixer and chop it up with a scraper, then mix some more. Proceed as for basic Bagel recipe.

Blueberry Bagels

You can't beat these distinctive treats. They're naturally low-fat, uniquely delicious, and full of flavor thanks to the dried blueberries studded throughout. Young and old alike are sure to love this bagel!

yield: **6 at 5.5 oz** | FDT: **80°F** | sponge: **60 minutes** | freeze: **2 hours** | retard: **overnight** | rest: **10 minutes** |
initial bake: **500°F** *and* **10 minutes** | final bake: **475°F** *and* **4–6 minutes**

INGREDIENT	OUNCES	GRAMS	VOLUME	BAKERS %
SPONGE				
Water, 90°F	5.8	164	¾ cup	30.4%
Malt syrup	0.1	3	⅛ tsp	0.5%
High-gluten flour	5.8	164	1 cup + 2 tsp	30.4%
Yeast, instant dry	0.1	3	1 tsp	0.5%
FINAL DOUGH				
Sponge	11.8	335	•	61.8%
Water, 75°F	5.2	147	⅔ cup	27.2%
Malt syrup	0.2	6	⅛ tsp	1.0%
High-gluten flour	13.3	377	2⅔ cups	69.6%
Yeast, instant dry	0.1	3	⅛ tsp	0.5%
Salt	0.5	14	¼ tsp	2.6%
Dried blueberries, plumped	3.5	99	¾ cup	18.3%
Bread flour	0.6	17	1¼ tsp	3.1%
TOTAL	35.2	997	•	184.1%
GARNISHES				
Semolina flour	as needed			
Vegetable oil spray	as needed			
Malt syrup	1	28		

1. **MAKE** and shape the dough the day before you want to serve the bagels. To make the sponge, combine the water and malt in a bowl. In a separate bowl, combine the flour with the yeast, and then add this mixture to the water. Mix the sponge together by hand for 2 minutes to develop some gluten structure, making sure all the ingredients are combined into a homogenous mass. Cover the bowl with plastic wrap and allow the sponge to ferment in a warm place for 60 minutes.

2. **TO MAKE THE DOUGH,** put the sponge, water and malt in the bowl of a mixer fitted with a dough hook. Mix the ingredients for 1 minute on low speed to break up the sponge (it can be broken up a little by hand if needed, also). Combine the high-gluten flour and yeast and add them to the bowl, then add the salt. Mix the ingredients for 10 minutes on low speed, making sure to scrape down and flip the dough over in the bowl 3 times during this process. Mix to full gluten development.

3. **IN A SEPARATE BOWL,** toss the blueberries with the bread flour. Add the blueberry mixture to the dough in the mixer and mix for 1–2 minutes, making sure to scrape down and flip the dough over in the bowl 2 times during this process. If the berries are not mixed in well, take the dough out of the mixer and chop it up with a scraper, then mix some more.

4. **PLACE** the dough on a lightly floured work surface. Divide the dough into six 5.5-oz pieces, then tightly preshape them into 5-inch oblongs. Place the dough pieces on the work surface seam-side up. Cover and allow to rest for 5 minutes.

5. **NOW SHAPE** each piece into a bagel. Flatten out a piece of dough and bring the top edge down a third of the way and tuck it in. Repeat this step 2 more times, then tightly roll the piece out to 10 inches and moisten about 1 inch of the end. Join the 2 ends, overlapping the dough about 1 inch. Place the fingers of 1 hand in the hole, with the other hand on the outside, and roll the dough with your fingers to connect the 2 ends and make the thickness even throughout. Then gently pull and rotate to create an even hole in the bagel.

6. **PREPARE** a baking tray with a moderate dusting of semolina flour. Place the bagels on the tray, seam-side down, and cover them with plastic wrap. Place the bagels in the freezer for 2 hours, then transfer them to the refrigerator and refrigerate overnight.

7. **TO FINISH THE BAGELS,** preheat the oven to 500°F and bring 3 quarts of water to a boil on the stove.

8. **REMOVE** the bagels from the refrigerator and let stand at room temperature for 10 minutes. Meanwhile, prepare 2 baking trays, 1 lined with a cooling rack and 1 lined with parchment paper that has been sprayed with vegetable oil spray.

9. **MIX** the malt into the boiling water. Add 3 bagels to the water and stir them, allowing them to sit in the water for 20 seconds. Remove from the water and place on the cooling rack. Let sit dripping for 30 seconds, then place them on the parchment paper–lined tray, making sure that the flat side of the dough is placed down. If desired, they can be dipped in crystal sugar before being placed on the parchment. Repeat this process with all of the bagels.

10. **TRANSFER** the tray to the oven and bake for 10 minutes, then rotate and bake for an additional 4–6 minutes at 475°F. Remove the bagels from the oven when they are partially brown (you do not want to bake to full color as this will make a dry bagel).

11. **REMOVE** the bagels from the tray and place on a cooling rack.

NOTE: *These can also be baked directly on a baking stone covered with parchment paper.*

Bialys

BIALYS

Similar in texture to the ever-popular bagel, bialys are unique single-serving breads brought to the United States by immigrants from Bialystok, a city in Poland. The dimpled bun is sprinkled with a filling of onions and poppy seeds, making it the perfect accompaniment to a bowl of soup or a hearty salad.

yield: **8 pieces at 4 oz** | FDT: **80°F**

sponge: **60 minutes** | bulk fermentation: **10 minutes** | retard: **overnight** | rest: **10 minutes** | bake: **475°F** and **14–16 minutes**

INGREDIENT	OUNCES	GRAMS	VOLUME	BAKERS %
SPONGE				
Water, 90°F	6.1	173	¾ cup	29.6%
High-gluten flour	6.1	173	1¼ cups	29.6%
Yeast, instant dry	0.1	3	⅛ tsp	0.5%
FINAL DOUGH				
Sponge	12.3	349	•	59.7%
Water, 75°F	6.5	184	¾ cup + 1 Tbsp	31.6%
Malt syrup	0.1	3	⅛ tsp	0.5%
High-gluten flour	14.5	411	3 cups	70.4%
Yeast, instant dry	0.1	3	⅛ tsp	0.5%
Salt	0.4	11	2 tsp	1.9%
TOTAL	33.9	961	•	164.6%
GARNISHES				
Semolina flour	as needed			
Bialy Filling (page 191)	as needed			
Olive oil	as needed			

1. MAKE the dough the day before you want to serve the bialys. To make the sponge, put the water in a bowl, then combine the flour and yeast in another bowl and add the mixture to the water. Mix the sponge by hand for 2 minutes to develop some gluten structure, making sure the ingredients are combined into a homogenous mass. Cover the bowl with plastic wrap and allow the sponge to ferment in a warm place for 60 minutes, until doubled in size.

2. TO MAKE THE DOUGH, put the sponge, water and malt in the bowl of a mixer fitted with a dough hook. Mix for 2 minutes on low speed, to break up the sponge. The sponge can also be broken up by hand a little first. Combine the flour and yeast, and add them to the mixture, then add the salt. Mix for 10 minutes on low speed, making sure to scrape down and flip the dough over in the bowl 3 times during the process.

3. REMOVE the dough and place it on a lightly floured work surface. Divide it into 4-oz pieces, and then preshape the pieces into round pieces. Allow the pieces to rest for 10 minutes, covered, at room temperature.

4. LIGHTLY dust a sheet tray with semolina flour. Shape each dough piece into a bialy. Flatten out a piece of dough and lightly flour both sides so that it will not stick to the table or the cup. Using a plastic cup or ceramic coffee cup with a bottom diameter of about 3 inches, make a deep depression in the center of the piece of dough. Remove the cup and gently stretch the center with your fingers to make it thinner, about ½-inch thick. Place the bialys on the prepared tray, cover with plastic wrap, and refrigerate overnight.

5. TO BAKE THE BIALYS, preheat the oven to 500°F. Ten minutes before baking the loaves, place a tray filled with 3 cups of warm water below the baking area in the oven to help produce steam.

6. REMOVE the bialys from the refrigerator and allow them to rest at room temperature for 10 minutes. In the meantime, prepare the Bialy Filling.

7. BRUSH the dough pieces lightly with oil. Stretch each piece out to about a 6-inch oblong, then place it on a baking tray lined with parchment paper. Make sure to depress the center to a thin layer, about ¼ inch thick, so that it will not burst in the oven and push out the filling. Place 2 tablespoons of filling in the center of each bialy.

8. PLACE the tray in the oven and immediately reduce the heat to 475°F. Bake for 10 minutes, then rotate and bake for an additional 4–6 minutes. Remove the bialys from the oven when they are just beginning to brown (you don't want to bake to full color, as this will make a dry bialy).

9. REMOVE the bialys from the tray and place on a cooling rack.

TRADITIONAL BIALY FILLING

yield 12 oz

INGREDIENT	OUNCES	GRAMS	VOLUME
Onions, medium dice	11.0	312	2¾ cups
Olive oil	0.6	17	1 Tbsp + 1 tsp
Poppy seeds	0.2	6	2 tsp
Salt	0.1	3	½ tsp
TOTAL	11.9	338	•

COMBINE all the ingredients in a bowl. Cover until needed.

ROASTED ONION BIALY FILLING

Asiago cheese is similar in flavor and texture to Parmesan and Romano cheeses. It gives the filling a slight sharpness that enhances the flavor of the sweet roasted onions.

yield 14.8 oz

INGREDIENT	OUNCES	GRAMS	VOLUME
Onions, sliced ½ inch thick (see Note)	12.0	340	4 cups
Olive oil	1.0	28	2 Tbsp
Asiago cheese, grated	2.8	79	¾ cup
TOTAL	15.8	447	•

1. PREHEAT the oven to 450°F.

2. TOSS the onions with the oil and spread out on a baking tray. Roast them for 10–20 minutes, stirring occasionally, until they have a golden brown color. Allow to cool.

3. COMBINE the cooled onions and cheese in a bowl. Cover until needed.

NOTE: Use a mixture of onions (for example, shallots, green onions, Spanish onions and red onions).

Baguettes, Double Epi, Epi and
Fougasse Variation

BAGUETTE WITH POOLISH

Using a preferment will develop a more open structure in this baguette, along with providing more flavor. Try the various preferments to see which combination works best for you. Spraying the dough with water and adding steam to the oven are important for developing a crispy crust. The steam helps the dough expand without cracking, while venting the steam later allows the surface to caramelize into a beautiful crust.

yield: 3 loaves at 12 oz | FDT: 82°F
poolish: 12–14 hours | bulk fermentation: 85–100 minutes | final fermentation: 40–50 minutes | bake: 475°F *and* 20–22 minutes

INGREDIENT	OUNCES	GRAMS	VOLUME	BAKERS %
POOLISH				
Water, 55°F	5.5	156	⅔ cup	24.7%
Bread flour	5.5	156	1 cup + 2 Tbsp	24.7%
Yeast, instant dry	0.01	0.3	⅛ tsp	0.04%
FINAL DOUGH				
Water, 85°F	9.5	269	1 cup + 3 Tbsp	42.6%
Malt syrup	0.2	6	⅛ tsp	0.9%
Poolish	11.0	312	•	49.4%
Bread flour	16.8	476	3½ cups	75.3%
Yeast, instant dry	0.1	3	1 tsp	0.4%
Salt	0.5	14	2½ tsp	2.2%
TOTAL	38.1	1080	•	170.8%
GARNISH				
Seeds	as needed			

1. PREPARE the poolish the day before you want to serve the baguette. Put the water in a bowl. Mix the flour and yeast together, add to the water, and mix by hand until homogenous. You will have little lumps, and the poolish will be wet and will not resemble a dough. Cover with plastic wrap and refrigerate for 2 hours. Then remove and place at room temperature for 10–12 hours before using. After this the poolish will have fermented and risen, and there will be bubbles on it. It should not have collapsed in the center.

2. TO MAKE THE DOUGH, put the water and malt in the bowl of a mixer, then add the poolish. Place the bowl on a mixer fitted with a dough hook and mix for 2 minutes on low speed to break down the poolish. Combine the flour and yeast and add to the poolish, then add the salt. Mix the dough for 4 minutes, making sure to scrape down and flip over the dough. Then mix for 2 minutes on medium speed, making sure to scrape down and flip over the dough. The dough should be a little sticky, but with fairly good (improved) gluten development. Place the dough in a lightly oiled bowl large enough for it to double in size and cover with plastic wrap.

3. ALLOW the dough to rest and ferment in a warm place for 45–60 minutes, until when lightly touched the dough springs back halfway.

4. PLACE the dough on a lightly floured work surface and fold it over in thirds, then place it back in the bowl, covered, for 30 minutes.

5. LINE a baking tray with a white cloth napkin or kitchen towel. The cloth will need to be floured unless seeds are being applied to the loaf.

6. PLACE the dough on a lightly floured work surface and divide it into three 12-oz pieces. Preshape each piece into a 6-inch oblong.

7. THE DOUGH PIECES need a final shaping into 6-inch oblongs. This can be done by taking the ends on the left and right of each piece and bringing them together so they just meet in the center of the loaf. Then bring the top of each loaf over halfway and tuck in. Then bring the top of the loaf over all the way to the bottom and close the seam tightly. Place the loaves seam-side up on the work surface, cover lightly with plastic wrap, and let rest for 10 minutes.

8. PLACE each oblong seam-side down with a little flour, and roll the loaf back and forth just slightly, about 1 inch in each direction. Try to keep the seam on the bottom and work each loaf out to 12 inches long. With your hands at a 45-degree angle to the center, place downward pressure on the ends of each loaf to close them with a tapered look. Place the loaves seam-side up on the prepared tray and bring the cloth up between each loaf on the tray. To apply seeds, brush or spray each loaf with water and then roll the top and sides in seeds. Place the loaves seam-side up on the tray with the cloth. Cover the loaves with any additional cloth, then lightly cover with plastic wrap. Allow the dough to rest and ferment in a warm place for 40–50 minutes, until when lightly touched the dough springs back.

9. TWENTY MINUTES before the end of the final fermentation, preheat the oven to 500°F with a baking stone. Ten minutes before baking the loaves, place a tray filled with 3 cups of warm water below the baking area in the oven to help produce steam.

10. PLACE the loaves lengthwise on the back of a baking tray lined with parchment paper by flipping them onto a piece of thick cardboard, then sliding them onto the tray. Keeping the seam on the bottom, spray the top and sides of each loaf with water. Let sit for 5 minutes, then score the top of each loaf with a sharp razor, cutting ¼–½ inch deep. Spray the loaves with water again. This will help add steam in the oven and will allow the loaves to expand.

11. TRANSFER the loaves to the baking stone with parchment paper or keep on the tray, score, and immediately reduce the temperature to 475°F. Bake for 12 minutes. Remove the parchment paper and steam tray, rotate the loaves, and bake for 8–10 minutes more. This will allow the loaves to finish baking and a crust to form. If at the end of the baking the crust isn't thick enough, turn the oven off and leave the bread in the oven with the door cracked open for 4-6 minutes.

12. REMOVE from the oven and place the loaves on a cooling rack.

NOTE: If you don't have enough room to bake all 3 loaves at once, place 1 of the loaves in the refrigerator for 15 minutes. This is called retarding and the cooler temperature of the refrigerator slows down the yeast's rate of fermentation. You will then bake the loaves you had at room temperature first, and the one from the refrigerator after the first loaves are finished.

Baguette with Biga

Baguettes made with a preferment will have a more open structure and more flavor.

yield: 3 loaves at 12 oz | FDT: 82°F | biga: 12–14 hours

INGREDIENT	OUNCES	GRAMS	VOLUME	BAKERS %
BIGA				
Water, 55°F	4.5	128	½ cup	19.7%
Bread flour	7.2	204	1½ cups	31.4%
Yeast, instant dry	0.01	0.3	pinch	0.04%
FINAL DOUGH				
Water, 85°F	9.7	275	1¼ cups	42.4%
Malt syrup	0.2	5	⅛ tsp	0.8%
Biga	11.7	332	2 cups	51.1%
Bread flour	15.7	445	3¼ cups	68.6%
Yeast, instant dry	0.1	3	1 tsp	0.6%
Salt	0.5	14	2½ tsp	2.3%
TOTAL	37.9	1074	•	165.8%

1. MIX the biga the day before you want to serve the dough. Put the water in the bowl of a mixer. Combine the flour and yeast, add to the water, and mix on low speed for 2 minutes, or until homogenous. The biga should be stiff and slightly dry, but it is correct. Place it in a lightly oiled bowl that is large enough for it to double in size. Flip the biga over in the bowl to coat it lightly with oil. Cover the bowl with plastic wrap and refrigerate for 2 hours.

2. REMOVE the biga and leave it at room temperature for 10–12 hours before using. After the fermentation, the biga will be less stiff and more like an actual bread dough.

3. PROCEED as directed in Baguette with Poolish (page 193), substituting the biga for the poolish.

Baguette with Biga and Pâte Fermentée

yield: 3 loaves at 12 oz | FDT: 82°F | pâte fermentée: 1 day | biga: 12–14 hours | final fermentation: 40–50 minutes |
bake: 475°F *and* 20–22 minutes

INGREDIENT	OUNCES	GRAMS	VOLUME	BAKERS %
Pâte Fermentée (page 175)				
BIGA				
Water, 55°F	4.5	128	½ cup	22.5%
Bread flour	6.3	179	1⅓ cups	31.5%
Yeast, instant dry	pinch	0.3	pinch	0.05%
FINAL DOUGH				
Water, 90°F	9.6	272	1¼ cups	48.0%
Malt syrup	0.2	6	¾ tsp	0.9%
Biga	10.8	307	•	54.1%
Pâte fermentée	3.5	99	•	17.5%
Bread flour	13.7	388	2¾ cups	68.5%
Yeast, instant dry	0.1	3	1 tsp	0.7%
Salt	0.5	14	2½ tsp	2.5%
TOTAL	38.4	1089	•	192.2%

1. MAKE the pâte fermentée the day before you want to serve the bread.

2. MIX the biga the day before as well. Put the water in the bowl of a mixer. Combine the flour and yeast, add to the water, and mix on low speed for 2 minutes, or until homogenous. The dough will be stiff and slightly dry, but it is correct. Place it in a lightly oiled bowl that is large enough for the biga to double in size. Flip the biga over in the bowl to coat it lightly with oil. Cover the bowl with plastic wrap and refrigerate for 2 hours, then remove and leave at room temperature for 10–12 hours before using. After the fermentation, the biga will be less stiff and more like an actual bread dough.

3. PROCEED as directed in Baguette with Poolish (page 193), substituting the pâte fermentée and biga for the poolish.

Baguette with Pâte Fermentée

yield: **3 loaves at 12 oz** | FDT: **82°F** | *pâte fermentée:* **1 day** | *final fermentation:* **40–50 minutes** | *bake:* **475°F** *and* **20–22 minutes**

INGREDIENT	OUNCES	GRAMS	VOLUME	BAKERS %
Pâte Fermentée (page 175)				
FINAL DOUGH				
Water, 90°F	14.1	400	1¾ cups	73.4%
Malt syrup	0.2	6	⅛ tsp	1.0%
Pâte fermentée	3.9	111	•	20.3%
Bread flour	19.2	544	4 cups	100.0%
Yeast, instant dry	0.1	3	1 tsp	0.7%
Salt	0.4	11	2 tsp	2.1%
TOTAL	37.9	1075	•	197.5%

1. MAKE the pâte fermentée the day before you want to serve the bread.

2. PROCEED as directed in Baguette with Poolish (page 193), substituting the pâte fermentée for the poolish.

Baguette with Poolish and Pâte Fermentée

yield: 3 loaves at 12 oz | FDT: 82°F | poolish: 12–14 hours | pâte fermentée: 1 day | final fermentation: 40–50 minutes |
bake: 475°F *and* 20–22 minutes

INGREDIENT	OUNCES	GRAMS	VOLUME	BAKERS %
POOLISH				
Water, 55°F	4.0	113	½ cup	20.0%
Bread flour	4.0	113	¾ cup	20.0%
Yeast, instant dry	0.01	0.3	pinch	0.05%
Pâte Fermentée (page 175)				
FINAL DOUGH				
Water, 90°F	10.0	284	1¼ cups	50.0%
Malt syrup	0.2	6	1 tsp	1.0%
Pâte fermentée	3.5	99	•	17.5%
Poolish	8.0	227	•	40.1%
Bread flour	16.0	454	3⅓ cups	80.0%
Yeast, instant dry	0.1	3	1 tsp	0.5%
Salt	0.5	14	2½ tsp	2.5%
TOTAL	38.3	1087	•	191.6%

1. PREPARE the poolish the day before you want to serve the baguette. Put the water in a bowl. Mix the flour and yeast together, add to the water, and mix by hand until homogenous. You will have little lumps, and the poolish will be wet and will not resemble a dough. Cover with plastic wrap and refrigerate for 2 hours. Then remove and place at room temperature for 10–12 hours before using. After this the poolish will have fermented and risen, and will have bubbles on it. It should not have collapsed in the center.

2. MAKE the pâte fermentée the day before you want to serve the bread.

3. PROCEED as directed in Baguette with Poolish (page 193), adding the pâte fermentée with the poolish.

BAGUETTE WITH POOLISH AND SOUR

yield: **3 loaves at 12 oz** | FDT: **82°F** | poolish: **12–14 hours** | final fermentation: **40–50 minutes** | bake: **475°F** and **20–22 minutes**

INGREDIENT	OUNCES	GRAMS	VOLUME	BAKERS %
POOLISH				
Water, 55°F	4.2	119	½ cup	20.1%
Bread flour	4.2	119	1 cup	20.1%
Yeast, instant dry	0.01	0.3	pinch	0.05%
FINAL DOUGH				
Water, 85°F	10.2	289	1¼ cups	48.8%
Malt syrup	0.2	6	1 tsp	1.0%
Sour of your choice (see pages 214–19)	2.0	57	•	9.6%
Poolish	8.4	238	•	40.2%
Bread flour	16.7	473	3½ cups	79.9%
Yeast, instant dry	0.1	3	1 tsp	0.5%
Salt	0.5	14	2½ tsp	2.4%
TOTAL	38.1	1080	•	182.4%

1. MAKE sure your sour is fully developed for the day of mixing. Prepare the poolish the day before you want to serve the baguette. Put the water in a bowl. Mix the flour and yeast together, add to the water, and mix by hand until homogenous. You will have little lumps, and the poolish will be wet and will not resemble a dough. Cover with plastic wrap and refrigerate for 2 hours. Then remove and place at room temperature for 10–12 hours before using. After this the poolish will have fermented and risen, and will have bubbles on it. It should not have collapsed in the center.

2. PROCEED as directed in Baguette with Poolish (page 193), adding the sour with the poolish.

CIABATTA

A classic of Italy's Lake Como region, ciabatta is known for its texture—soft and airy on the inside, crisp and crusty on the outside. Its wet dough creates a characteristic interior of big, irregular holes ideal for sopping up pasta sauce. This is an easy bread to make at home. It can also be made into smaller loaves for individual sandwiches or rolls. For the best results, bake ciabatta on a baking stone.

yield: 3 loaves at 16 oz | FDT: 80°F
poolish: 12–14 hours | bulk fermentation: 60–70 minutes | final fermentation: 20–30 minutes | bake: 475°F *and* 28–30 minutes

INGREDIENT	OUNCES	GRAMS	VOLUME	BAKERS %
POOLISH				
Water, 55°F	6.9	196	¾ cup + 2 Tbsp	25.7%
Bread flour	6.9	196	1½ cups	25.7%
Yeast, instant dry	0.01	0.3	⅛ tsp	0.04%
FINAL DOUGH				
Water, 86°F	14.9	422	1¾ cups + 2 Tbsp	55.4%
Malt syrup	0.2	6	⅛ tsp	0.7%
Poolish	13.8	392	•	51.4%
Bread flour	20.0	567	4 cups + 3 Tbsp	74.3%
Yeast, instant dry	0.2	4	1 tsp	0.6%
Salt	0.6	17	1 Tbsp	2.2%
TOTAL	49.7	1408	•	184.6%
GARNISH				
Semolina-flour mixture; ratio: 1:1	as needed			

1. PREPARE the poolish the day before you want to serve the ciabatta. Put the water in a bowl. Mix the flour and yeast together, add to the water, and mix by hand until homogenous. You will have little lumps and the poolish will be wet and will not resemble a dough. Cover with plastic wrap and refrigerate for 2 hours. Then remove and place at room temperature for 10–12 hours before using. After

this the poolish will have fermented and risen, and there will be bubbles on it. It should not have collapsed in the center.

2. TO MAKE THE DOUGH, use a bowl large enough for the final dough. Add 1½ cups of the water to the bowl, reserving the rest for later (see "Basic Double Hydration Technique," page 130).

1. Ciabatta dough is very wet and therefore requires a lot of flour while handling. Fold the dough, working quickly, but handle the dough gently to maintain its airy texture.

2. Portion the dough into 3 pieces so that each piece is roughly the same size. This bread is not carefully shaped in order to give it a rustic look.

3. Dust both sides of the dough in a pile of semolina and flour mixture. This is a very traditional look and helps identify it as ciabatta bread.

4. Lightly stretch the dough as you place it on the cloth-lined tray that has been dusted with semolina flour. Try not to move it once you have placed it on the tray so that it ferments properly.

Add the malt and poolish, then break the poolish up by hand into little pieces for 1 minute. Combine the flour and the yeast and add to the bowl while stirring. Add the salt and work the mixture with your hands for about 4 minutes, making sure to scrape and squeeze the dough with your fingers to help break it down. The dough should have some structure at this point. Start adding the remaining water in thirds until it is all incorporated, making sure the dough has absorbed the water before adding more. At the end, the dough will be weak and lacking in structure, but this is okay because of the previous structure development. Cover the dough in a lightly oiled bowl and allow it to rest and ferment in a warm place for 20–30 minutes, until doubled in size.

3. CAREFULLY transfer the dough to a lightly floured work surface using a dough scraper and fold it over in thirds, then leave it on the work surface and cover. Let the dough rest and ferment for 30 minutes, until when lightly touched the dough springs back halfway.

4. FOLD the dough over in thirds again, then leave it on the work surface and cover it again. Let the dough rest and ferment for another 10 minutes, until when lightly touched the dough springs back halfway.

5. LINE a baking tray with a white cloth napkin or kitchen towel and dust it with some of the semolina-flour mixture.

6. UNCOVER the dough and divide it into 3 equal pieces by eye. Roll each dough piece in a pile of the semolina-flour mixture, then gently stretch it lengthwise, being careful not to pull it too hard. Place it upside-down on the baking tray. Continue this process with the remaining dough pieces, and then cover the tray lightly with plastic wrap. Allow the dough to rest and ferment at room temperature for 20–30 minutes, until when lightly touched the dough springs back halfway.

7. TWENTY MINUTES before the end of the final fermentation, preheat the oven to 500°F with a baking stone. Ten minutes before baking the loaves, place a tray filled with 3 cups of warm water below the baking area in the oven to help produce steam.

8. UNCOVER the dough and flip all the pieces onto a stiff piece of cardboard dusted with semolina. Spray the tops with water, then slide the dough onto an oven peel lined with parchment paper. Spray the loaves with water and allow them to sit for 5 minutes.

9. TRANSFER the loaves and parchment paper to the baking stone and immediately reduce the oven temperature to 475°F. Bake for 12 minutes, then remove the steam tray and parchment paper and rotate each piece. Continue baking for another 16–18 minutes, until the crust has a deep color and doesn't give when lightly pressed.

10. REMOVE from the oven and place the loaves on a cooling rack.

Fig and Hazelnut Bread

The fig, whose abundance on the tree represents fertility, is very healthy for you. It is a good source of fiber and calcium.

yield: **2 loaves at 24 oz** | FDT: **80°F**
bulk fermentation: **80–95 minutes** | final fermentation: **65–75 minutes** | bake: **450°F** *and* **28–30 minutes**

INGREDIENT	OUNCES	GRAMS	VOLUME	BAKERS %
Water, 85°F	13.8	391	1¾ cups	76.2%
White sour (page 214)	6.6	187	•	36.5%
Bread flour	14.5	411	3 cups	80.1%
Whole wheat flour	3.6	102	¾ cup + 1½ Tbsp	19.9%
Yeast, instant dry	0.1	3	1 tsp	0.6%
Salt	0.5	14	2½ tsp	2.8%
Dried figs, large dice	5.7	162	¾ cup + 1 Tbsp	31.5%
Hazelnuts, whole, toasted	5.7	162	1¼ cups	31.5%
TOTAL	50.6	1435	•	279.7%

1. PLACE the water and malt in the bowl of a mixer, then break up the sour by hand and add. Place the bowl on a mixer fitted with a dough hook and mix for 2 minutes on low speed in order to break up the sour. Mix the flours and yeast together, then add both to the mixer (for autolyse mixing, see page 129). Mix on low speed for 2 minutes, making sure to scrape down the sides and flip the dough over twice during this time. Cover the bowl and let rest for 15 minutes.

2. ADD the salt and mix for 2 minutes on low speed, making sure to scrape and flip over once, then increase the speed to medium and mix for 2 minutes, again making sure to scrape and flip the dough over once. Add the figs and hazelnuts, then mix for 1 minute on low speed, making sure to scrape and flip the dough over once. The dough should be a little sticky, but with fairly good gluten development. Place the dough in a lightly oiled bowl large enough for the dough to double in size and cover with plastic wrap.

3. ALLOW the dough to rest and ferment in a warm place for 45–60 minutes, until when lightly touched the dough springs back halfway.

4. PLACE the dough on a lightly floured work surface and fold it over in thirds, then leave it on the work surface, covered. Let the dough rest and ferment for 15 minutes, until when lightly touched the dough springs back halfway.

5. DIVIDE the dough into two 24-oz pieces. Round each dough piece against the tabletop, place it on a lightly floured surface, and cover. Allow to rest and ferment for 20 minutes, until when lightly touched the dough springs back halfway.

6. LINE a baking tray or bowls with white cloth napkins or kitchen towels. Flour the cloth lightly.

7. SHAPE each round piece into a 10-inch oblong. Place each shaped loaf seam-side up on the prepared tray or in bowls, bringing the cloth up between each shaped loaf on the tray. Cover the shaped dough pieces and allow them to rest and ferment in a warm place for 65–75 minutes, until when lightly touched the dough springs back halfway.

8. TWENTY MINUTES before the end of the final fermentation, preheat the oven to 475°F with a baking stone. Ten minutes before baking the loaves, place a tray filled with 3 cups of warm water below the baking area in the oven to help produce steam.

9. UNCOVER the dough and place each piece seam-side down on an oven peel lined with parchment paper. Spray each loaf with water and allow the bread to rest for 5 minutes. Then score each loaf ¼–½ inch deep and spray each loaf again. Transfer the loaves and parchment paper to the baking stone, then immediately reduce the temperature to 450°F. Bake for 12 minutes, then remove the steam tray and parchment paper and rotate each piece. Continue baking for another 16–18 minutes, until the crust is deep in color and doesn't give when pressed.

10. REMOVE from the oven and place the loaves on a cooling rack.

Fougasse

For those who love crusty bread, this distinctive loaf from Provence fits the bill. Fougasse gets its unique shape from cutting slashes through the dough and stretching the sections apart to form a rough ladder shape. The special design gives the loaf more crust per piece. Serve with cheese and dips, or simply pull apart and enjoy as is.

yield: 2 loaves at 12 oz | FDT: 82°F

pâte fermentée: 1 day | bulk fermentation: 65–80 minutes | final fermentation: 75–90 minutes | bake: 450°F *and* 15 minutes

INGREDIENT	OUNCES	GRAMS	VOLUME	BAKERS %
Pâte Fermentée (page 175)				
FINAL DOUGH				
Water, 90°F	9.6	272	1¼ cups	73.3%
Malt syrup	0.1	3	⅛ tsp	0.8%
Pâte fermentée	2.7	77	•	20.6%
Bread flour	11.2	318	2⅓ cups	85.5%
Whole wheat flour	1.9	54	¼ cup + 3 Tbsp	14.5%
Yeast, instant dry	0.1	3	⅛ tsp	0.8%
Salt	0.3	9	⅛ tsp	2.3%
TOTAL	25.9	736	•	197.8%
GARNISHES				
Semolina flour	as needed			
Olive oil (optional)	as needed			
Kosher salt (optional)	as needed			
Sesame seeds (optional)	as needed			
Herbs and cheese (optional)	as needed			

1. MAKE the pâte fermentée the day before you want to serve the bread.

2. TO MAKE THE DOUGH, put the water and malt in the bowl of a mixer, then break up the pâte fermentée by hand and add. Place on a mixer fitted with a dough hook and mix for 2 minutes on low speed to break up the pâte fermentée. Combine the flours and the yeast and add (for autolyse mixing, see page 129). Mix for 2 minutes, making sure to scrape down and flip the dough over twice during this time. Cover the bowl and let it sit at room temperature for 15 minutes.

3. ADD the salt and mix for 3 minutes, making sure to scrape down and flip the dough over. The dough should be a little sticky, but with fairly good gluten development. Place the dough in a lightly oiled bowl large enough for it to double in size and cover with plastic wrap.

4. ALLOW the dough to rest and ferment in a warm place for 45–60 minutes, until when lightly touched the dough springs back halfway.

5. PLACE the dough on a lightly floured work surface and divide it into two 12-oz pieces. Round each dough piece against the tabletop. Place them on a lightly floured surface and cover. Allow to rest and ferment for 20 minutes, until when lightly touched the dough springs back halfway.

6. LINE two baking trays with a white napkin or kitchen towel. Flour the cloth.

7. ROLL each dough piece into an elongated triangle about ¼ inch thick (see photograph, page 207). Place them on the prepared tray and cover with a cloth. Allow to rest and ferment in a warm place for 75–90 minutes, until when lightly touched the dough springs back halfway.

8. TWENTY MINUTES before the end of the final fermentation, preheat the oven to 475°F with a baking stone. Ten minutes before baking the loaves, place a tray filled with 3 cups of warm water below the baking area in the oven to help produce steam.

9. UNCOVER the dough, lightly flour it with semolina, and place an oven peel with parchment paper on top. Carefully flip the dough onto the peel, or flip it onto a piece of stiff cardboard and then transfer it to the oven peel with parchment paper. Cut through the dough with a metal scraper in a design resembling a leaf or ladder (see photograph, page 207). After cutting, pull the dough outward to open each cut section. The dough can be brushed with oil and lightly salted if desired. If not using oil, spray the loaves with water, let sit for 5 minutes, and spray again. The dough could also be garnished with sesame seeds or herbs and cheese at this point, if desired.

10. TRANSFER the loaves to the baking stone and immediately reduce the temperature to 450°F. Bake for 10 minutes, then remove the steam tray and parchment paper and rotate each piece.

Fougasse

Continue baking for another 5 minutes, until the crust has a deep color and doesn't give when pressed.

11. REMOVE from the oven and place the loaves on a cooling rack.

Roll the dough into an elongated triangle ¼ inch thick. Use a bench scraper or dough cutter to form a ladder design. This creates a larger surface area to become crunchy during baking.

Pull the dough gently at the edges to widen the holes.

VARIATION

FOUGASSE WITH GARLIC AND ROSEMARY

This dense, crusty bread gets added flavor from roasted garlic and fresh rosemary. Fougasse is quite versatile and easy to work with, so if you feel like experimenting, try adding different garnishes to the dough. Everything from nuts and seeds to herbs, spices and cheese make tasty additions. Simply add the desired garnishes to the dough at the same stage you would add the garlic and rosemary.

INGREDIENT	OUNCES	GRAMS	VOLUME	BAKERS %
Rosemary, fresh, chopped	0.1	3	1 Tbsp	0.8%
Garlic, roasted	0.1	3	1 tsp	0.8%

PREPARE the pâte fermentée and dough as for Fougasse (page 205). Add the salt and mix as in step #3, then add the rosemary and roasted garlic and mix on low speed for 2 minutes, making sure to scrape down and flip the dough over. Proceed as directed for Fougasse.

Pretzels

PRETZELS

Pretzels began in Europe when a monk shaped extra bread dough into a shape that looked like hands crossed over a chest in the sign of prayer. These soft pretzels were valued highly throughout Europe for hundreds of years. The use of lye gives the pretzel its characteristic flavor, sheen and color. You'll need to begin this recipe two days before you plan to serve the pretzels.

yield: **6 pieces at 5 oz** | FDT: **78°F**

pâte fermentée: **1 day** | rest: **5 minutes** | retard: **8 hours to overnight** | bake: **450°F** *and* **15–17 minutes**

INGREDIENT	OUNCES	GRAMS	VOLUME	BAKERS %
Pâte Fermentée (page 175)				
FINAL DOUGH				
Water, 75°F	9.9	281	1¼ cups	51.3%
Pâte fermentée	4.0	113	•	20.7%
Malt syrup	0.4	11	¼ tsp	2.1%
High-gluten flour	19.3	547	3¾ cups	100.0%
Yeast, instant dry	0.3	9	2½ tsp	1.6%
Salt	0.4	11	2 tsp	2.1%
Butter	1.0	28	2 Tbsp	5.2%
TOTAL	35.3	1000	•	183.0%
LYE SOLUTION				
Water, boiling	24	680	3 cups	
Sodium hydroxide (lye)	1.25			
Water, 60°F	8	227	1 cup	
GARNISH				
Coarse salt	2			

1. MAKE the pâte fermentée 2 days before you want to serve the pretzels.

2. PUT the water, pâte fermentée and malt in the bowl of a mixer fitted with a dough hook. Mix for 1 minute on low speed to break up the pâte fermentée. You can also first break the pâte fermentée up with a scraper first. Combine the flour and yeast and add to the pâte fermentée, then add the salt and butter. Mix for 10 minutes on low speed, making sure to scrape down and flip the dough over in the bowl 3 times. Test the gluten window (see page 28); the dough should have full gluten development and should be very strong and stiff.

3. PLACE the dough on a lightly floured work surface. Divide it into six 5-oz pieces. Preshape the pieces tightly into 5-inch oblongs. Place the pieces on the work surface seam-side up and cover. Allow the dough to rest for 5 minutes.

4. PUT a piece of dough on a clean, dry surface with no flour and flatten it. Fold the dough over in thirds, making sure to tighten well. Roll each piece out to 30 inches. If the dough becomes too elastic to roll to the full length, stop rolling to allow the dough to rest and shape the other portions part of the way, then go back to the first one you started to roll and finish them all in consecutive order. Put a 30-inch rope on a work surface and form it into an upside-down U. Take each end piece and cross them over in the middle twice. Then take each end and bring it to the top inside of the U. Make sure to press the ends in well; if needed you can moisten the ends with water. Place the shaped pretzel on a baking tray lined with parchment paper that is sprayed with oil. Finish shaping all the pieces and place them on the tray.

5. REFRIGERATE the pretzels, uncovered, overnight (a minimum of 8 hours) so they can form a skin.

6. TO BAKE THE PRETZELS, preheat the oven to 475°F. Remove the pretzels from the refrigerator 15 minutes before baking. Line a baking tray with oiled parchment paper.

7. PREPARE the lye solution. Cover your work surface with newspapers. Pour the boiling water into a stainless steel bowl on your work surface. Wearing gloves, measure the sodium hydroxide into another stainless steel bowl. Add to the bowl of water, then stir with a metal whisk until the lye is dissolved. Add the cold water and stir. Let this sit for 10 minutes. Wearing gloves, dip 2 pretzels in the solution for 15 seconds, then take each one out with both hands, let the solution drip off, and place the pretzels on the prepared tray. Repeat this process with the rest of the pretzels. Sprinkle the pretzels with coarse salt.

8. PUT the tray in the oven and immediately reduce the temperature to 450°F. Bake for 12 minutes, then rotate and bake for an additional 3–5 minutes, until the pretzels are dark brown.

9. REMOVE from the oven, let cool for 5 minutes, then remove the pretzels from the tray to a cooling rack.

NOTE: To make different shapes, scale and shape the dough accordingly. Follow dipping and baking instructions as above.

For rolls: 2 oz each
For stuffed sticks (see pages 212–13): 4 oz each (5 inches long)
For subs: 5 oz each (5 inches long)

1. Flatten a portion of dough and fold it over into thirds. Roll it out until it reaches 30 inches in length. Do not use flour on the surface of the table or the pretzel. If it becomes difficult to roll out to the full length, let it rest for a bit and then try rolling it out again. This will allow the gluten to relax and make the dough easier to stretch.

2. Make an upside-down U shape with the dough, holding each end firmly in each hand.

3. Cross your right hand over your left while still holding the ends of the pretzel. The pretzel should be able to flip twice, causing a twist in the center. Or keep the pretzel on the table, cross your hands over once, release and pick up the ends on their new sides, and cross your hands again. This will give you the same shape. Take the ends and press each into the top sides of the U to make a pretzel. Make sure they are firmly pressed in so that they do not come apart while baking.

4. Each step of shaping a pretzel is important for the overall quality of the final product.

5. Dip the pretzel in a lye solution.

Garlic, Herb and Cheese Pretzel Stuffing

The log shape of these pretzels allows them to be sliced down the center and filled with almost anything your culinary imagination can contrive.

yield: enough for 7 stuffed pretzel sticks

INGREDIENT	OUNCES	GRAMS	VOLUME
Cheddar cheese, grated	7.0	198	1¾ cups
Garlic, minced	0.6	17	1 Tbsp
Rosemary, fresh, chopped	0.4	11	2 Tbsp
TOTAL	8.0	226	•

1. IN A BOWL, combine the ingredients.

2. IMMEDIATELY after dipping the pretzels in the lye solution, while still wearing protective gloves, cut a long slit down the center from end to end of each pretzel while it is on the tray. Spread open the center cut and spoon in the filling in an even layer and bake as directed on page 209 for Pretzels.

NOTE: *The rosemary can be replaced with your favorite herb, or a mixture. The cheese can be replaced with mozzarella, Colby or jalapeño Jack.*

Pesto and Cheese Pretzel Stuffing

yield: enough for 7 stuffed pretzel sticks

INGREDIENT	OUNCES	GRAMS	VOLUME
Pesto	5.0	142	1 cup
Mozzarella cheese, grated	8.0	227	2 cups
TOTAL	13.0	369	•

1. IN A BOWL, combine the ingredients.

2. IMMEDIATELY after dipping the pretzels in the lye solution, while still wearing protective gloves, cut a long slit down the center from end to end of each pretzel while it is on the tray. Spread open the center cut and spoon in the filling in an even layer and bake as directed on page 209 for Pretzels.

NOTE: *The mozzarella can be replaced with Jack, Manchego, Asiago, Parmesan or Romano cheeses.*

Sun-Dried Tomato and Cheese Pretzel Stuffing

yield: enough for 7 stuffed pretzel sticks

INGREDIENT	OUNCES	GRAMS	VOLUME
Mozzarella cheese, grated	7.0	198	1¾ cups
Sun-dried tomatoes, oil-packed, diced (see Note)	2.0	57	•
Basil, thinly sliced	0.2	6	2 Tbsp
Garlic, minced	0.5	14	1 Tbsp
TOTAL	9.7	275	•

1. IN A BOWL, combine the ingredients.

2. IMMEDIATELY after dipping the pretzels in the lye solution, while still wearing protective gloves, cut a long slit down the center from end to end of each pretzel while it is on the tray. Spread open the center cut and spoon in the filling in an even layer and bake as directed on page 209 for Pretzels.

NOTE: Use sun-dried tomatoes packed in oil for better flavor. If using dried, though, rehydrate them in hot water, then drain and slice.

Sourdough Feeding

Each sour feeding is unique. They will each provide a distinct flavor and aroma. Your sour needs to be nurtured along the way to perform optimally on a regular basis.

WHITE SOUR BASE FEEDING

This sour will help to produce a mild flavor and aroma and give your bread the best volume or most leavening.

yield: **18 oz**

INGREDIENT	OUNCES	GRAMS	VOLUME	BAKERS %
Water, 60°F	5.9	167	¾ cup	64.8%
White sour starter (page 120)	3.0	85	•	33.0%
Bread flour	8.4	238	1¾ cups	92.3%
Whole wheat flour	0.7	20	2 Tbsp + 2 tsp	7.7%
TOTAL	18.0	510	•	197.8%

1. PUT the water and sour starter in the bowl of a mixer fitted with a dough hook and mix on low speed for 1 minute to break up the sour. Add the flours and mix for 3 minutes on low speed, making sure to scrape down and flip the sour over. The sour should be a little sticky with fairly good gluten development. Place the sour in a lightly oiled bowl large enough for it to double in size and cover.

2. LEAVE the sour at room temperature for 18–20 hours to ferment. It is then ready to be used.

NOTES: Make sure never to use all of your sour for baking or you will have to start over.

The sour feeding can also be mixed by hand until totally homogenous. Place the sour in an oiled container and cover.

WHEAT SOUR BASE FEEDING

This sour will give your bread more flavor and aroma with an earthy taste and will have less volume than the white sour. Have a sour base ready at all times, and develop a baking schedule to utilize and help maintain your sour.

yield: **18 oz**

INGREDIENT	OUNCES	GRAMS	VOLUME	BAKERS %
Water, 60°F	5.9	167	¾ cup	64.8%
White sour starter (page 120)	3.0	85	•	33.0%
Bread flour	6.4	181	1⅓ cups	70.3%
Whole wheat flour	2.7	77	⅔ cup	29.7%
TOTAL	18.0	510	•	197.8%

1. PUT the water and sour starter in the bowl of a mixer fitted with a dough hook and mix on low speed for 1 minute to break up the sour. Add the flours and mix for 3 minutes on low speed, making sure to scrape down the bowl and flip the sour over. The sour should be a little sticky with fairly good gluten development. Place the sour in a lightly oiled bowl large enough for it to double in size and cover.

2. LEAVE the sour at room temperature for 18–20 hours to ferment. It is then ready to be used.

Durum Sour Base Feeding

Breads produced with this sour will have a mild "sour" flavor with the overriding flavor of sweet durum.

yield: **18 oz**

INGREDIENT	OUNCES	GRAMS	VOLUME	BAKERS %
Water, 60°F	5.9	167	¾ cup	64.8%
White sour starter (page 120)	3.0	85	•	33.0%
Bread flour	6.4	181	1⅓ cups	70.3%
Durum flour	2.7	77	½ cup	29.7%
TOTAL	18.0	510	•	197.8%

1. PUT the water and sour starter in the bowl of a mixer fitted with a dough hook and mix on low speed for 1 minute to break up the sour. Add the flours and mix for 3 minutes on low speed, making sure to scrape down and flip the sour over. The sour should be a little sticky with fairly good gluten development. Place the sour in a lightly oiled bowl large enough for it to double in size and cover.

2. LEAVE the sour at room temperature for 18–20 hours to ferment. It is then ready to be used.

Durum and Whole Wheat Sour Base Feeding

This sour will produce a stronger "sour" flavor than a starter that does not contain whole wheat, but will have sweet overtones characteristic of durum.

yield: **18 oz**

INGREDIENT	OUNCES	GRAMS	VOLUME	BAKERS %
Water, 60°F	5.9	167	¾ cup	64.8%
White sour starter (page 120)	3.0	85	•	33.0%
Bread flour	6.3	179	1⅓ cups	69.2%
Durum flour	1.4	40	¼ cup	15.4%
Whole wheat flour	1.4	40	5 Tbsp + 2 tsp	15.4%
TOTAL	18.0	511	•	197.8%

1. **PUT** the water and sour starter in the bowl of a mixer fitted with a dough hook and mix on low speed for 1 minute to break up the sour. Add the flours and mix for 3 minutes on low speed, making sure to scrape down and flip the sour over. The sour should be a little sticky with fairly good gluten development. Place the sour in a lightly oiled bowl large enough for it to double in size and cover.

2. **LEAVE** the sour at room temperature for 18–20 hours to ferment. It is then ready to be used.

Rye Sour Base Feeding

This sour will produce the strongest flavor and aroma of any sour. It will, however, produce the least amount of volume.

yield: 24.1 oz

INGREDIENT	OUNCES	GRAMS	VOLUME	BAKERS %
Water, 60°F	10.2	289	1¼ cups	100.0%
Rye sour starter (page 126)	3.5	99	•	34.3%
Rye flour, medium	10.2	289	2¾ cups	100.0%
Salt	0.2	6	1 tsp	2.0%
TOTAL	24.1	683	•	236.3%

1. PUT the water and sour starter in the bowl of a mixer fitted with a dough hook and mix on low speed for 1 minute to break up the sour. Add the flour and mix for 3 minutes on low speed, making sure to scrape down and flip the sour over. The sour should be a little sticky with fairly good gluten development. Place the sour in a lightly oiled bowl large enough for it to double in size and cover.

2. LEAVE the sour at room temperature for 18–20 hours to ferment. It is then ready to be used.

Rye and Whole Wheat Sour Base Feeding

This sour will have the robust flavor of rye along with earthy tones from the
whole wheat, giving it the most complex flavor and aroma.

yield: **18 oz**

INGREDIENT	OUNCES	GRAMS	VOLUME	BAKERS %
Water, 60°F	5.9	167	¾ cup	64.8%
White sour starter (page 120)	3.0	85	•	33.0%
Bread flour	6.3	179	1⅓ cups	69.2%
Rye flour, medium	1.4	40	⅓ cup	15.4%
Whole wheat flour	1.4	40	⅓ cup	15.4%
TOTAL	18.0	511	•	197.8%

1. PUT the water and sour starter in the bowl of a mixer fitted with a dough hook and mix on low speed for 1 minute to break up the sour. Add the flours and mix for 3 minutes on low speed, making sure to scrape down and flip the sour over. The sour should be a little sticky with fairly good gluten development. Place the sour in a lightly oiled bowl large enough for it to double in size and cover.

2. LEAVE the sour at room temperature for 18–20 hours to ferment. It is then ready to be used.

Sourdough Bread

SOURDOUGH BREAD

Crafting sourdough bread, given the proper time and care, is a truly rewarding experience. No other bread has the character and depth of this naturally fermented loaf. From the creation of the leavener to the development of the dough's complex flavor, everything about the way this bread is made contributes to its exceptional taste and texture.

yield: **2 loaves at 24 oz** | FDT: **78°F**

bulk fermentation: **130 minutes** | *final fermentation:* **60 minutes** | *retard:* **overnight** | *rest:* **60–75 minutes** | *bake:* **450°F** *and* **30–32 minutes**

INGREDIENT	OUNCES	GRAMS	VOLUME	BAKERS %
Water, 80°F	16.3	462	2 cups	66.5%
White sour (page 214)	9.6	272	•	39.2%
Malt syrup	0.2	6	½ tsp	0.8%
Bread flour	22.8	646	4¾ cups	93.1%
Whole wheat flour	1.7	48	⅓ cup + 1 Tbsp	6.9%
Salt	0.7	20	1 Tbsp	2.9%
TOTAL	51.3	1454	•	209.4%

1. MAKE the dough the day before you want to serve the bread. Put the water, sour and malt in the bowl of a mixer fitted with a dough hook. Mix for 1 minute on low speed, to break up the sour (for autolyse mixing, see page 129). Add the flours and mix on low speed for 2 minutes, making sure to scrape down and flip the dough over. Cover the dough in the bowl and let it sit for 15 minutes.

2. ADD the salt and mix for 2 minutes on low speed, making sure to scrape down and flip the dough over. Mix for 2 minutes on medium speed, making sure to scrape down and flip the dough over. The dough should be a little sticky, but with fairly good gluten development. Place the dough in a lightly oiled bowl large enough for it to double in size and cover it with plastic wrap.

3. ALLOW the dough to rest and ferment in a warm place for 60 minutes, until when lightly touched the dough springs back halfway.

4. PLACE the dough on a lightly floured work surface and fold it over in thirds, then leave it on the work surface, covered. Let the dough rest and ferment for 60 minutes, until when lightly touched the dough springs back halfway.

5. DIVIDE the dough into two 24-oz pieces. Round each dough piece against the tabletop. Place them on a lightly floured surface and cover. Allow to rest and ferment for 10 minutes.

6. LINE a baking tray or oblong baskets with white cloth napkins or kitchen towels. Dust the cloth with flour.

7. SHAPE each piece of dough into a 10-inch oblong. Place each shaped loaf seam-side up on the cloth and then bring the cloth up between each loaf on the tray. Cover the shaped dough pieces and allow the dough to rest and ferment at room temperature for 60 minutes, then refrigerate the dough overnight. (This is called retarding the bread, to help slow down fermentation and develop more flavor and acidity.)

8. REMOVE the dough from the refrigerator and leave it at room temperature for 60–75 minutes before baking.

9. TWENTY MINUTES before baking, preheat the oven to 475°F with a baking stone. Ten minutes before baking the loaves, place a tray filled with 3 cups of warm water below the baking area in the oven to help produce steam.

10. UNCOVER the dough and place each piece seam-side down on an oven peel lined with parchment paper. Spray each loaf with water and allow it to sit for 5 minutes. Then score each loaf ¼–½ inch deep and spray each loaf again.

11. TRANSFER the loaves and parchment paper to the baking stone and immediately reduce the temperature to 450°F. Bake for 12 minutes. Remove the steam tray and parchment paper and rotate each piece, then continue baking for another 18–20 minutes, until the crust has a deep color and doesn't give when pressed.

12. REMOVE the bread from the oven and place on a cooling rack.

APPLE, CRANBERRY AND WALNUT SOURDOUGH

Typically thought of as indigenous American flavors, the apple, cranberry and
walnut make this the perfect selection for every Thanksgiving table.

yield: **2 loaves at 24 oz** | FDT: **78°F**

bulk fermentation: **130 minutes** | final fermentation: **60 minutes** | retard: **overnight** | rest: **75–90 minutes** | bake: **450°F** *and* **30–32 minutes**

INGREDIENT	OUNCES	GRAMS	VOLUME	BAKERS %
Water, 80°F	9.9	281	1¼ cups	66.4%
White sour (page 214)	5.8	164	•	38.9%
Malt syrup	0.1	3	⅛ tsp	0.7%
Bread flour	13.9	394	3 cups	93.3%
Whole wheat flour	1.0	28	1½ Tbsp	6.7%
Salt	0.4	11	2 tsp	2.7%
Apple, medium dice, Fuji, Gala or Granny Smith	6.7	190	2 cups	45.0%
Cranberries, dried	4.5	128	⅓ cup	30.2%
Walnuts, toasted	6.7	190	2 cups	45.0%
Cinnamon, ground	0.2	6	1 Tbsp	1.3%
Whole wheat flour	1.2	34	¼ cup	8.1%
TOTAL	50.4	1429	•	338.3%

1. MAKE the dough the day before you want to serve the bread. Put the water, sour and malt in the bowl of a mixer fitted with a dough hook. Mix for 1 minute on low speed, to break up the sour (for autolyse mixing, see page 129). Add the flours and mix on low speed for 2 minutes, making sure to scrape down and flip the dough over. Cover the dough in the bowl and let it sit for 15 minutes.

2. ADD the salt and mix for 2 minutes on low speed, making sure to scrape down and flip the dough over. Mix for 2 minutes on medium speed, making sure to scrape down and flip the dough over. The dough should be a little sticky, but with fairly good gluten development.

3. IN A SEPARATE BOWL, toss together the apples, cranberries, walnuts, cinnamon and ¼ cup whole wheat flour. Add the mixture to the dough in the mixer. Mix for 1 to 2 minutes on low speed, making sure to scrape down and flip the dough over. If the inclusions are not mixed in well, place the dough on a lightly floured work surface and knead it the rest of the way by hand. Place the dough in a lightly oiled bowl large enough for it to double in size and cover it with plastic wrap.

4. ALLOW the dough to rest and ferment in a warm place for 60 minutes, until when lightly touched the dough springs back halfway.

5. PLACE the dough on a lightly floured work surface and fold it over in thirds, then leave it on the work surface, covered. Let the dough rest and ferment for 60 minutes, until when lightly touched the dough springs back halfway.

6. DIVIDE the dough into two 24-oz pieces. Round each dough piece against the tabletop. Place them on a lightly floured surface and cover. Allow to rest and ferment for 10 minutes.

7. LINE a baking tray or oblong baskets with white cloth napkins or kitchen towels. Dust the cloth with flour.

8. SHAPE each piece of dough into a 10-inch oblong. Place each shaped loaf seam-side up on the cloth and then bring the cloth up between each loaf on the tray. Cover the shaped dough pieces and allow the dough to rest and ferment at room temperature for 60 minutes, then refrigerate the dough overnight. (This is called retarding the bread, to help slow down fermentation and develop more flavor and acidity.)

9. REMOVE the dough from the refrigerator and leave at room temperature for 75–90 minutes before baking.

10. TWENTY MINUTES before baking, preheat the oven to 475°F with a baking stone. Ten minutes before baking the loaves, place a tray filled with 3 cups of warm water below the baking area in the oven to help produce steam.

11. UNCOVER the dough and place each piece seam-side down on an oven peel lined with parchment paper. Spray each loaf with water and allow it to sit for 5 minutes. Then score each loaf ¼–½ inch deep and spray each loaf again.

12. TRANSFER the loaves and parchment paper to the baking stone and immediately reduce the temperature to 450°F. Bake for 12 minutes. Remove the steam tray and parchment paper and rotate each piece, then continue baking for another 18–20 minutes, until the crust has a deep color and doesn't give when pressed.

13. REMOVE the bread from the oven and place on a cooling rack.

CLOCKWISE: **Apple, Cranberry and Walnut Sourdough; Currant and Pecan Sourdough**

Almond, Currant and Orange Sourdough

Fresh-cut or toasted with butter, this bread's sweet marriage of almonds, currants and oranges brings the essence of the Mediterranean to you in every bite.

yield: 2 loaves at 24 oz | FDT: 78°F

bulk fermentation: 130 minutes | final fermentation: 60 minutes | retard: overnight | rest: 60–75 minutes | bake: 450°F *and* 30–32 minutes

INGREDIENT	OUNCES	GRAMS	VOLUME	BAKERS %
Water, 80°F	12.3	349	1½ cups	67.2%
Wheat sour (page 215)	7.2	204	•	39.3%
Malt syrup	0.1	3	⅛ tsp	0.5%
Bread flour	12.7	360	1½ cups	69.4%
Whole wheat flour	5.6	159	1⅓ cups	30.6%
Salt	0.5	14	1½ tsp	2.7%
Almond slivers, toasted	4.0	113	1 cup	21.9%
Currants	2.4	68	½ cup	13.1%
Orange peel, candied, diced	5.0	142	¾ cup	27.3%
Whole wheat flour	0.8	23	3 Tbsp	4.4%
TOTAL	50.6	1435	•	276.4%

1. MAKE the dough the day before you want to serve the bread. Put the water, sour and malt in the bowl of a mixer fitted with a dough hook. Mix for 1 minute on low speed, to break up the sour (for autolyse mixing, see page 129). Add the flours and mix on low speed for 2 minutes, making sure to scrape and flip the dough over. Cover the dough in the bowl and let sit for 15 minutes.

2. ADD the salt and mix for 2 minutes on low speed, making sure to scrape down and flip the dough over. Then mix for 2 minutes on medium speed, making sure to scrape down and flip the dough over. The dough should be a little sticky, but with fairly good gluten development.

3. IN A SEPARATE BOWL, toss the almonds, currants, orange peel and 3 Tbsp whole wheat flour. Add the mixture to the dough in the mixer. Mix for 1 minute on low speed, making sure to scrape down and flip the dough over. If the inclusions are not mixed in well, place the dough on a lightly floured work surface and knead it the rest of the way by hand. Place the dough in a lightly oiled bowl large enough for it to double in size and cover it with plastic wrap.

4. ALLOW the dough to rest and ferment in a warm place for 60 minutes, until when lightly touched the dough springs back halfway.

5. PLACE the dough on a lightly floured work surface and fold it over in thirds, then leave it on the work surface, covered. Let the dough rest and ferment for 60 minutes, until when lightly touched the dough springs back halfway.

6. DIVIDE the dough into two 24-oz pieces. Round each dough piece against the tabletop. Place them on a lightly floured surface and cover. Allow to rest and ferment for 10 minutes.

7. LINE a baking tray or oblong baskets with white cloth napkins or kitchen towels. Dust the cloth with flour.

8. SHAPE each piece of dough into a 10-inch oblong. Place each shaped loaf seam-side up on the cloth and then bring the cloth up between each loaf on the tray. Cover the shaped dough pieces and allow the dough to rest and ferment at room temperature for 60 minutes, then refrigerate the dough overnight. (This is called retarding the bread, to help slow down fermentation and develop more flavor and acidity.)

9. REMOVE the dough from the refrigerator and leave at room temperature for 60–75 minutes before baking.

10. TWENTY MINUTES before baking, preheat the oven to 475°F with a baking stone. Ten minutes before baking the loaves, place a tray filled with 3 cups of warm water below the baking area in the oven to help produce steam.

11. UNCOVER the dough and place each piece seam-side down on an oven peel lined with parchment paper. Spray each loaf with water and allow it to sit for 5 minutes. Then score each loaf ¼–½ inch deep and spray each loaf again.

12. TRANSFER the loaves and parchment paper to the baking stone and immediately reduce the temperature to 450°F. Bake for 12 minutes. Remove the steam tray and parchment paper and rotate each piece, then continue baking for another 18–20 minutes, until the crust has a deep color and doesn't give when pressed.

13. REMOVE the bread from the oven and place on a cooling rack.

CHIPOTLE SOURDOUGH

If heat is what you're after, the ingredients in this bread will deliver. Use it
to create your most memorable grilled cheese sandwich.

yield: 2 loaves at 24 oz | FDT: 78°F

bulk fermentation: 130 minutes | final fermentation: 60 minutes | retard: overnight | rest: 60–75 minutes | bake: 450°F and 30–32 minutes

INGREDIENT	OUNCES	GRAMS	VOLUME	BAKERS %
Water, 80°F	14.7	417	1¼ cups	66.5%
White sour (page 214)	8.7	247	•	39.4%
Malt syrup	0.2	6	⅛ tsp	0.9%
Bread flour	20.6	584	4.29	93.2%
Whole wheat flour	1.5	43	⅓ cup	6.8%
Salt	0.6	17	3 tsp	2.7%
Chipotles, pureed (see Note)	2.6	74	¼ cup	11.8%
Whole wheat flour	1.3	37	¼ cup	5.9%
TOTAL	50.2	1425	•	227.2%

1. MAKE the dough the day before you want to serve the bread. Put the water, sour and malt in the bowl of a mixer fitted with a dough hook. Mix for 1 minute on low speed, to break up the sour (for autolyse mixing, see page 129). Add the flours and mix on low speed for 2 minutes, making sure to scrape down and flip the dough over. Cover the dough in the bowl and let it sit for 15 minutes.

2. ADD the salt and mix for 2 minutes on low speed, making sure to scrape down and flip the dough over. Mix for 2 minutes on medium speed, making sure to scrape down and flip the dough over. The dough should be a little sticky, but with fairly good gluten development.

3. IN A SEPARATE BOWL, toss together the chipotles and ¼ cup whole wheat flour. Add the mixture to the dough in the mixer. Mix for 1 minute on low speed, making sure to scrape down and flip the dough over. If the inclusions are not mixed in well, place the dough on a lightly floured work surface and knead it the rest of the way by hand. Place the dough in a lightly oiled bowl large enough for it to double in size and cover it with plastic wrap.

4. ALLOW the dough to rest and ferment in a warm place for 60 minutes, until when lightly touched the dough springs back halfway.

5. PLACE the dough on a lightly floured work surface and fold it over in thirds, then leave it on the work surface, covered. Let the dough rest and ferment for 60 minutes, until when lightly touched the dough springs back halfway.

6. DIVIDE the dough into two 24-oz pieces. Round each dough piece against the tabletop. Place them on a lightly floured surface and cover. Allow to rest and ferment for 10 minutes.

7. LINE a baking tray or oblong baskets with white cloth napkins or kitchen towels. Dust the cloth with flour.

8. SHAPE each piece of dough into a 10-inch oblong. Place each shaped loaf seam-side up on the cloth and then bring the cloth up between each loaf on the tray. Cover the shaped dough pieces and allow the dough to rest and ferment at room temperature for 60 minutes, then refrigerate the dough overnight. (This is called retarding the bread, to help slow down fermentation and develop more flavor and acidity.)

9. REMOVE the dough from the refrigerator and leave at room temperature for 60–75 minutes before baking.

10. TWENTY MINUTES before baking, preheat the oven to 475°F with a baking stone. Ten minutes before baking the loaves, place a tray filled with 3 cups of warm water below the baking area in the oven to help produce steam.

11. UNCOVER the dough and place each piece seam-side down on an oven peel lined with parchment paper. Spray each loaf with water and allow it to sit for 5 minutes. Then score each loaf ¼–½ inch deep and spray each loaf again.

12. TRANSFER the loaves and parchment paper to the baking stone and immediately reduce the temperature to 450°F. Bake for 12 minutes. Remove the steam tray and parchment paper and rotate each piece, then continue baking for another 18–20 minutes, until the crust has a deep color and doesn't give when pressed.

13. REMOVE the bread from the oven and place on a cooling rack.

NOTE: *Chipotles packed in adobo sauce will provide the most uniform flavor.*

CURRANT AND PECAN SOURDOUGH

Currants add a complex flavor that perfectly blends with the pecans. This bread is
sublime toasted, with butter and a sprinkling of cinnamon sugar.

yield: 2 loaves at 24 oz | FDT: 78°F

bulk fermentation: 130 minutes | *final fermentation:* 60 minutes | *retard:* overnight | *rest:* 60–75 minutes | *bake:* 450°F *and* 30–32 minutes

INGREDIENT	OUNCES	GRAMS	VOLUME	BAKERS %
Water, 80°F	12.5	354	1½ cups	68.3%
Wheat sour (page 215)	7.2	204	•	39.3%
Malt syrup	0.1	3	⅛ tsp	0.5%
Bread flour	12.7	360	1⅔ cups	69.4%
Whole wheat flour	5.6	159	1⅓ cups	30.6%
Salt	0.5	14	2½ tsp	2.7%
Currants	3.6	102	½ cup	19.7%
Pecan halves, toasted	7.6	215	2 cups	41.5%
TOTAL	49.8	1411	•	272.0%

1. MAKE the dough the day before you want to serve the bread.
Put the water, sour and malt in the bowl of a mixer fitted with
a dough hook. Mix for 1 minute on low speed, to break up the
sour (for autolyse mixing, see page 129). Add the flours and mix
on low speed for 2 minutes, making sure to scrape down and flip
the dough over. Cover the dough in the bowl and let it sit for 15
minutes.

2. ADD the salt and mix for 2 minutes on low speed, making sure
to scrape down and flip the dough over. Mix for 2 minutes on
medium speed, making sure to scrape down and flip the dough
over. The dough should be a little sticky, but with fairly good gluten development.

3. IN A SEPARATE BOWL, toss together the currants and pecans.
Add the mixture to the dough in the mixer. Mix for 1 minute
on low speed, making sure to scrape down and flip the dough
over. If the inclusions are not mixed in well, place the dough on

a lightly floured work surface and knead it the rest of the way by
hand. Place the dough in a lightly oiled bowl large enough for it to
double in size and cover it with plastic wrap.

4. ALLOW the dough to rest and ferment in a warm place for 60 minutes, until when lightly touched the dough springs back halfway.

5. PLACE the dough on a lightly floured work surface and fold it
over in thirds, then leave it on the work surface, covered. Let the
dough rest and ferment for 60 minutes, until when lightly touched
the dough springs back halfway.

6. DIVIDE the dough into two 24-oz pieces. Round each dough
piece against the tabletop. Place them on a lightly floured surface
and cover. Allow to rest and ferment for 10 minutes.

7. LINE a baking tray or oblong baskets with white cloth napkins
or kitchen towels. Dust the cloth with flour.

8. SHAPE each piece of dough into a 10-inch oblong. Place each shaped loaf seam-side up on the cloth and then bring the cloth up between each loaf on the tray. Cover the shaped dough pieces and allow the dough to rest and ferment at room temperature for 60 minutes, then refrigerate the dough overnight. (This is called retarding the bread, to help slow down fermentation and develop more flavor and acidity.)

9. REMOVE the dough from the refrigerator and leave at room temperature for 60–75 minutes.

10. TWENTY MINUTES before baking, preheat the oven to 475°F with a baking stone. Ten minutes before baking the loaves, place a tray filled with 3 cups of warm water below the baking area in the oven to help produce steam.

11. UNCOVER the dough and place each piece seam-side down on an oven peel lined with parchment paper. Spray each loaf with water and allow it to sit for 5 minutes. Then score each loaf ¼–½ inch deep and spray each loaf again.

12. TRANSFER the loaves and parchment paper to the baking stone and immediately reduce the temperature to 450°F. Bake for 12 minutes. Remove the steam tray and parchment paper and rotate each piece, then continue baking for another 18–20 minutes, until the crust has a deep color and doesn't give when pressed.

13. REMOVE the bread from the oven and place on a cooling rack.

Everything Sourdough

Who doesn't like an everything bagel? Here, it is transformed into a sourdough bread, making it even more flavorful.

yield: **2 loaves at 24 oz** | FDT: **78°F**

bulk fermentation: **130 minutes** | final fermentation: **60 minutes** | retard: **overnight** | rest: **60–75 minutes** | bake: **450°F** *and* **30–32 minutes**

INGREDIENT	OUNCES	GRAMS	VOLUME	BAKERS %
Olive oil	1.0	28	2 Tbsp	•
Onions, medium dice	6.2	176	½ cup	32.6%
Garlic, thinly sliced	1.0	28	3 Tbsp	5.3%
Water, 80°F	12.8	363	1½ cups	67.4%
Wheat sour (page 215)	7.5	213	•	39.5%
Malt syrup	0.2	6	⅛ tsp	1.1%
Bread flour	13.2	374	2¾ cups	69.5%
Whole wheat flour	5.8	164	1⅓ cups	30.5%
Salt	0.5	14	1½ tsp	2.6%
Sesame seeds, toasted	1.0	28	2 Tbsp	5.3%
Poppy seeds	0.8	23	2 Tbsp	4.2%
Black pepper, cracked	0.1	3	1½ tsp	0.5%
Whole wheat flour	1.0	28	¼ cup	5.3%
TOTAL	51.1	1448	•	263.8%
GARNISHES				
Sesame seeds	as needed			
Poppy seeds	as needed			
Salt	as needed			
Semolina flour	as needed			

1. MAKE the dough the day before you want to serve the bread. Heat the oil in a large sauté pan. Add the onions and sauté over medium heat until translucent. Add the garlic and sauté over medium heat until fragrant. Reserve.

2. PUT the water, sour and malt in the bowl of a mixer fitted with a dough hook. Mix for 1 minute on low speed, to break up the sour (for autolyse mixing, see page 129). Add the flours and mix on low speed for 2 minutes, making sure to scrape down and flip the dough over. Cover the dough in the bowl and let it sit for 15 minutes.

3. ADD the salt and mix for 2 minutes on low speed, making sure to scrape down and flip the dough over. Mix for 2 minutes on medium speed, making sure to scrape down and flip the dough over. The dough should be a little sticky, but with fairly good gluten development.

4. IN A SEPARATE BOWL, toss together the onions, garlic, sesame seeds, poppy seeds, pepper and ¼ cup whole wheat flour. Add the mixture to the dough in the mixer. Mix for 1 minute on low speed, making sure to scrape down and flip the dough over. If the inclusions are not mixed in well, place the dough on a lightly floured work surface and knead it the rest of the way by hand. Place the dough in a lightly oiled bowl large enough for it to double in size and cover it with plastic wrap.

5. ALLOW the dough to rest and ferment in a warm place for 60 minutes, until when lightly touched the dough springs back halfway.

6. PLACE the dough on a lightly floured work surface and fold it over in thirds, then leave it on the work surface, covered. Let the dough rest and ferment for 60 minutes, until when lightly touched the dough springs back halfway.

7. DIVIDE the dough into two 24-oz pieces. Round each dough piece against the tabletop. Place them on a lightly floured surface and cover. Allow to rest and ferment for 10 minutes.

8. LINE a baking tray or oblong baskets with white cloth napkins or kitchen towels. Dust the cloth with flour.

9. SHAPE each piece of dough into a 10-inch oblong. Place each shaped loaf seam-side up on the cloth and then bring the cloth up between each loaf on the tray. Cover all of the shaped dough pieces and allow the dough to rest and ferment at room temperature for 60 minutes, then refrigerate the dough overnight. (This is called retarding the bread, to help slow down fermentation and develop more flavor and acidity.)

10. REMOVE the dough from the refrigerator and leave at room temperature for 60–75 minutes.

11. PREHEAT the oven to 475°F with a baking stone. Ten minutes before baking the loaves, place a tray filled with 3 cups of warm water below the baking area in the oven to help produce steam.

12. UNCOVER the dough and place each piece seam-side down on an oven peel lined with parchment paper. Spray each loaf with water and allow it to sit for 5 minutes. Then score each loaf ¼–½ inch deep and spray each loaf again. Sprinkle a mixture of sesame seeds, poppy seeds and salt on each loaf.

13. TRANSFER the loaves and parchment paper to the baking stone and immediately reduce the temperature to 450°F. Bake for 12 minutes. Remove the steam tray and parchment paper and rotate each piece, then continue baking for another 18–20 minutes, until the crust has a deep color and doesn't give when pressed.

14. REMOVE the bread from the oven and place on a cooling rack.

GARLIC AND CHEESE SOURDOUGH

The best choices of cheese for this bread are soft, such as a mozzarella, Jack or young Asiago.

yield: 2 loaves at 24 oz | FDT: 78°F

bulk fermentation: 130 minutes | final fermentation: 60 minutes | retard: overnight | rest: 60–75 minutes | bake: 450°F *and* 30–32 minutes

INGREDIENT	OUNCES	GRAMS	VOLUME	BAKERS %
Water, 80°F	12.0	340	2½ cups	67.0%
Wheat sour (page 215)	7.0	198	•	39.1%
Malt syrup	0.1	3	⅛ tsp	0.6%
Bread flour	12.4	352	1⅓ cups	69.3%
Whole wheat flour	5.5	156	1⅔ cups	30.7%
Salt	0.5	14	2½ tsp	2.8%
Garlic, roasted	1.8	51	•	10.1%
Cheese, cubed	10.5	298	1 cup	58.7%
Whole wheat flour	1.0	28	¼ cup	5.6%
TOTAL	50.8	1440	•	283.9%
GARNISH				
Cheese, grated	3	85	½ cup	

1. MAKE the dough the day before you want to serve the bread. Put the water, sour and malt in the bowl of a mixer fitted with a dough hook. Mix for 1 minute on low speed, to break up the sour (for autolyse mixing, see page 129). Add the flours and mix on low speed for 2 minutes, making sure to scrape down and flip the dough over. Cover the dough in the bowl and let it sit for 15 minutes.

2. ADD the salt and mix for 2 minutes on low speed, making sure to scrape down and flip the dough over. Mix for 2 minutes on medium speed, making sure to scrape down and flip the dough over. The dough should be a little sticky, but with fairly good gluten development.

3. IN A SEPARATE BOWL, toss together the garlic, cubed cheese and ¼ cup whole wheat flour. Add the mixture to the dough in the mixer. Mix for 1 minute on low speed, making sure to scrape down and flip the dough over. If the inclusions are not mixed in well, place the dough on a lightly floured work surface and knead it the rest of the way by hand. Place the dough in a lightly oiled bowl large enough for it to double in size and cover it with plastic wrap.

4. ALLOW the dough to rest and ferment in a warm place for 60 minutes, until when lightly touched the dough springs back halfway.

5 PLACE the dough on a lightly floured work surface and fold it over in thirds, then leave it on the work surface, covered. Let the dough rest and ferment for 60 minutes, until when lightly touched the dough springs back halfway.

6. DIVIDE the dough into two 24-oz pieces. Round each dough piece against the tabletop. Place them on a lightly floured surface and cover. Allow to rest and ferment for 10 minutes.

7. LINE a baking tray or oblong baskets with white cloth napkins or kitchen towels. Dust the cloth with flour.

8. SHAPE each piece of dough into a 10-inch oblong. Place each shaped loaf seam-side up on the cloth and then bring the cloth up between each loaf on the tray. Cover the shaped dough pieces and allow the dough to rest and ferment at room temperature for 60 minutes, then refrigerate overnight. (This is called retarding the bread, to help slow down fermentation and develop more flavor and acidity.)

9. REMOVE the dough from the refrigerator and leave at room temperature for 60–75 minutes.

10. TWENTY MINUTES before baking, preheat the oven to 475°F with a baking stone. Ten minutes before baking the loaves, place a tray filled with 3 cups of warm water below the baking area in the oven to help produce steam.

11. UNCOVER the dough and place each piece seam-side down on an oven peel lined with parchment paper. Spray each loaf with water and allow it to sit for 5 minutes. Then score each loaf ¼–½ inch deep and spray each loaf again.

12. TRANSFER the loaves and parchment paper to the baking stone and immediately reduce the temperature to 450°F. Bake for 12 minutes. Remove the steam tray and rotate each piece, then continue baking for another 10 minutes. Remove the loaves from the oven and sprinkle half the grated cheese on each loaf. Return the loaves to the oven and bake for an additional 8–10 minutes, until the crust and cheese are a deep golden brown and the crust doesn't give when pressed.

13. REMOVE the bread from the oven and place on a cooling rack.

JALAPEÑO AND CHEDDAR SOURDOUGH

For a milder-flavor cheese you can choose a Jack, which works equally well with
the peppers. Served with a hot cup of chili, this bread is unparalleled.

yield: 2 loaves at 24 oz | FDT: 78°F

bulk fermentation: 130 minutes | final fermentation: 60 minutes | retard: overnight | rest: 60–75 minutes | bake: 450°F *and* 30–32 minutes

INGREDIENT	OUNCES	GRAMS	VOLUME	BAKERS %
Water, 80°F	11.8	335	1½ cups	67.0%
White sour (page 214)	6.9	196	•	39.2%
Malt syrup	0.1	3	pinch	0.6%
Bread flour	16.4	465	3½ cups	93.2%
Whole wheat flour	1.2	34	4½ Tbsp	6.8%
Salt	0.5	14	2¼ tsp	2.8%
Canned diced jalapeños, drained	3.6	102	⅓ cup	20.5%
Cheddar cheese, cubed	10.5	298	⅔ cup	59.7%
Whole wheat flour	1.0	28	¼ cup	5.7%
TOTAL	52.0	1474	•	295.5%
GARNISH				
Cheddar cheese, grated	3.0			

1. MAKE the dough the day before you want to serve the bread. Put the water, sour and malt in the bowl of a mixer fitted with a dough hook. Mix for 1 minute on low speed, to break up the sour (for autolyse mixing, see page 129). Add the flours and mix on low speed for 2 minutes, making sure to scrape down and flip the dough over. Cover the dough in the bowl and let it sit for 15 minutes.

2. ADD the salt and mix for 2 minutes on low speed, making sure to scrape down and flip the dough over. Mix for 2 minutes on medium speed, making sure to scrape down and flip the dough over. The dough should be a little sticky, but with fairly good gluten development.

3. IN A SEPARATE BOWL, toss together the jalapeños, cubed cheese and ¼ cup whole wheat flour. Add the mixture to the dough in the mixer. Mix for 1 minute on low speed, making sure to scrape down and flip the dough over. If the inclusions are not mixed in well, place the dough on a lightly floured work surface and knead it the rest of the way by hand. Place the dough in a lightly oiled bowl large enough for it to double in size and cover it with plastic wrap.

4. ALLOW the dough to rest and ferment in a warm place for 60 minutes, until when lightly touched the dough springs back halfway.

5. PLACE the dough on a lightly floured work surface and fold it over in thirds, then leave it on the work surface, covered. Let the dough rest and ferment for 60 minutes, until when lightly touched the dough springs back halfway.

6. DIVIDE the dough into two 24-oz pieces. Round each dough piece against the tabletop. Place them on a lightly floured surface and cover. Allow to rest and ferment for 10 minutes.

7. LINE a baking tray or oblong baskets with white cloth napkins or kitchen towels. Dust the cloth with flour.

8. SHAPE each piece of dough into a 10-inch oblong. Place each shaped loaf seam-side up on the cloth and then bring the cloth up between each loaf on the tray. Cover the shaped dough pieces and allow the dough to rest and ferment at room temperature for 60 minutes, then refrigerate overnight. (This is called retarding the bread, to help slow down fermentation and develop more flavor and acidity.)

9. REMOVE the dough from the refrigerator and leave at room temperature for 60–75 minutes.

10. TWENTY MINUTES before baking, preheat the oven to 475°F with a baking stone. Ten minutes before baking the loaves, place a tray filled with 3 cups of warm water below the baking area in the oven to help produce steam.

11. UNCOVER the dough and place each piece seam-side down on an oven peel lined with parchment paper. Spray each loaf with water and allow it to sit for 5 minutes. Then score each loaf ¼–½ inch deep and spray each loaf again.

12. TRANSFER the loaves and parchment paper to the baking stone and immediately reduce the temperature to 450°F. Bake for 12 minutes. Remove the steam tray and rotate each piece, then continue baking for another 10 minutes. Remove the loaves from the oven and sprinkle half the grated cheese on each loaf. Return the loaves to the oven and bake for an additional 8–10 minutes, until the crust and cheese are a deep golden brown and the crust doesn't give when pressed.

13. REMOVE the bread from the oven and place on a cooling rack.

Onion Sourdough

If you like, you can add cheese to this bread (use 6 oz grated Asiago, Parmesan or Gruyère) with the onions. If using cheese, make sure to bake the bread with parchment paper under it for the entire baking time. For the onions called for in the ingredient list, you can use a mixture of shallots, scallions, and Spanish and red onions. This mixture works well and has a wonderful flavor.

yield: 2 loaves at 27 oz | FDT: 78°F

bulk fermentation: 130 minutes | final fermentation: 60 minutes | retard: overnight | rest: 60–75 minutes | bake: 450°F *and* 32 minutes

INGREDIENT	OUNCES	GRAMS	VOLUME	BAKERS %
Onions, sliced ½ inch thick	14.0	397	1½ cups	47.1%
Water, 80°F	12.7	360	1½ cups	66.5%
White sour (page 214)	7.5	213	•	39.3%
Malt syrup	0.2	6	⅛ tsp	1.0%
Bread flour	17.8	505	3¾ cups	93.2%
Whole wheat flour	1.3	37	⅓ cup	6.8%
Salt	0.5	14	2½ tsp	2.6%
Black pepper, cracked	0.1	3	1½ tsp	0.5%
Whole wheat flour	1.7	48	⅓ cup	8.9%
TOTAL	55.8	1583	•	265.9%

1. MAKE the dough the day before you want to serve the bread. Place the onions on a baking sheet with a little olive oil. Roast at 400°F until soft, golden brown and aromatic.

2. PUT the water, sour and malt in the bowl of a mixer fitted with a dough hook. Mix for 1 minute on low speed, to break up the sour (for autolyse mixing, see page 129). Add the flours and mix on low speed for 2 minutes, making sure to scrape down and flip the dough over. Cover the dough in the bowl and let it sit for 15 minutes.

3. ADD the salt and mix for 2 minutes on low speed, making sure to scrape down and flip the dough over. Mix for 2 minutes on medium speed, making sure to scrape down and flip the dough over. The dough should be a little sticky, but with fairly good gluten development.

4. IN A SEPARATE BOWL, toss together the onions, pepper and ⅓ cup whole wheat flour. Add the mixture to the dough in the mixer. Mix for 1 minute on low speed, making sure to scrape down and flip the dough over. If the inclusions are not mixed in well, place the dough on a lightly floured work surface and knead it the rest of the way by hand. Place the dough in a lightly oiled bowl large enough for it to double in size and cover it with plastic wrap.

5. ALLOW the dough to rest and ferment in a warm place for 60 minutes, until when lightly touched the dough springs back halfway.

6. PLACE the dough on a lightly floured work surface and fold it over in thirds, then leave it on the work surface, covered. Let the dough rest and ferment for 60 minutes, until when lightly touched the dough springs back halfway.

7. DIVIDE the dough into two 24-oz pieces. Round each dough piece against the tabletop. Place them on a lightly floured surface and cover. Allow the dough to rest and ferment for 10 minutes.

8. LINE a baking tray or oblong baskets with white cloth napkins or kitchen towels. Dust the cloth with flour.

9. SHAPE each piece of dough into a 10-inch oblong. Place each shaped loaf seam-side up on the cloth and then bring the cloth up between each loaf on the tray. Cover the shaped dough pieces and allow the dough to rest and ferment at room temperature for 60 minutes, then refrigerate overnight. (This is called retarding the bread, to help slow down fermentation and develop more flavor and acidity.)

10. REMOVE the dough from the refrigerator and leave at room temperature for 60–75 minutes.

11. TWENTY MINUTES before baking, preheat the oven to 475°F with a baking stone. Ten minutes before baking the loaves, place a tray filled with 3 cups of warm water below the baking area in the oven to help produce steam.

12. UNCOVER the dough and place each piece seam-side down on an oven peel lined with parchment paper. Spray each loaf with water and allow it to sit for 5 minutes. Then score each loaf ¼–½ inch deep and spray each loaf again.

13. TRANSFER the loaves and parchment paper to the baking stone and immediately reduce the temperature to 450°F. Bake for 12 minutes. Remove the steam tray and parchment paper and rotate each piece, then continue baking for another 20 minutes, until the crust has a deep color and doesn't give when pressed.

14. REMOVE the bread from the oven and place on a cooling rack.

Sun-Dried Tomato and Asiago Cheese Sourdough

The sweetness of the tomatoes and cheese balances the complex sour flavors of the sourdough. Serve with a fresh tossed salad or some grilled vegetables in summer for a hearty addition to a light meal.

yield: **2 loaves at 24 oz** | FDT: **78°F**

bulk fermentation: **130 minutes** | final fermentation: **60 minutes** | retard: **overnight** | rest: **60–75 minutes** | bake: **450°F** *and* **30–32 minutes**

INGREDIENT	OUNCES	GRAMS	VOLUME	BAKERS %
Sun-dried tomatoes	6.6	187	⅓ cup	35.3%
Water, 80°F	12.5	354	1½ cups	66.8%
White sour (page 214)	7.3	207	•	39.0%
Malt syrup	0.2	6	⅛ tsp	1.1%
Bread flour	17.4	493	3⅔ cups	93.0%
Whole wheat flour	1.3	37	⅓ cup	7.0%
Salt	0.5	14	2½ tsp	2.7%
Asiago cheese, grated (see Note)	3.2	91	½ cup	17.1%
Whole wheat flour	1.3	37	⅓ cup	7.0%
TOTAL	50.3	1426	•	269.0%
GARNISH				
Asiago cheese, grated (see Note)	3	85	¾ cup	

1. MAKE the dough the day before you want to serve the bread. The sun-dried tomatoes need to be plumped in hot water for 10 minutes if dried, then drained and roughly chopped. If they are packed in oil, just drain and chop.

2. PUT the water, sour and malt in the bowl of a mixer fitted with a dough hook. Mix for 1 minute on low speed, to break up the

sour (for autolyse mixing, see page 129). Add the bread flour and mix on low speed for 2 minutes, making sure to scrape down and flip the dough over. Cover the dough in the bowl and let sit for 15 minutes.

3. ADD the salt and mix for 2 minutes on low speed, making sure to scrape down and flip the dough over. Mix for 2 minutes on medium speed, making sure to scrape down and flip the dough over. The dough should be a little sticky, but with fairly good gluten development.

4. IN A SEPARATE BOWL, toss together the tomatoes, grated cheese and ⅓ cup whole wheat flour. Add the mixture to the dough in the mixer. Mix for 1 minute on low speed, making sure to scrape down and flip the dough over. If the inclusions are not mixed in well, place the dough on a lightly floured work surface and knead it the rest of the way by hand. Place the dough in a lightly oiled bowl large enough for it to double in size and cover it with plastic wrap.

5. ALLOW the dough to rest and ferment in a warm place for 60 minutes, until when lightly touched the dough springs back halfway.

6. PLACE the dough on a lightly floured work surface and fold it over in thirds, then leave it on the work surface, covered. Let the dough rest and ferment for 60 minutes, until when lightly touched the dough springs back halfway.

7. DIVIDE the dough into two 24-oz pieces. Round each dough piece against the tabletop. Place them on a lightly floured surface and cover. Allow the dough to rest and ferment for 10 minutes.

8. LINE a baking tray or oblong baskets with white cloth napkins or kitchen towels. Dust the cloth with flour.

9. SHAPE each piece of dough into a 10-inch oblong. Place each shaped loaf seam-side up on the cloth and then bring the cloth up between each shaped loaf on the tray. Cover the shaped dough pieces and allow the dough to rest and ferment at room tempera-

ture for 60 minutes, then refrigerate overnight. (This is called retarding the bread, to help slow down fermentation and develop more flavor and acidity.)

10. REMOVE the dough from the refrigerator and leave at room temperature for 60–75 minutes.

11. TWENTY MINUTES before baking, preheat the oven to 475°F with a baking stone. Ten minutes before baking the loaves, place a tray filled with 3 cups of warm water below the baking area in the oven to help produce steam.

12. UNCOVER the dough and place each piece seam-side down on an oven peel lined with parchment paper. Spray each loaf with water and allow it to sit for 5 minutes. Then score each loaf ¼–½ inch deep and spray each loaf again.

13. TRANSFER the loaves and parchment paper to the baking stone and immediately reduce the temperature to 450°F. Bake for 12 minutes. Remove the steam tray and rotate each piece, then continue baking for another 10 minutes. Remove the loaves from the oven and sprinkle half the grated cheese on each loaf. Return the loaves to the oven and bake for an additional 8–10 minutes, until the crust and cheese are a deep golden brown and the crust doesn't give when pressed.

14. REMOVE the bread from the oven and place on a cooling rack.

NOTE: You can replace the Asiago cheese with Manchego or Parmesan cheese.

SOURDOUGH CIABATTA

This dough will be very wet, as are all ciabatta doughs. The use of a sour will give this bread
a slightly denser structure and more pronounced flavor than regular ciabatta.

yield: **2 loaves at 24 oz** | FDT: **78°F**

bulk fermentation: **75 minutes** | final fermentation: **60–70 minutes** | bake: **475°F** *and* **28–30 minutes**

INGREDIENT	OUNCES	GRAMS	VOLUME	BAKERS %
Water, 80°F	13.0	369	1⅔ cups	58.0%
White sour (page 214)	8.4	238	•	37.5%
Malt syrup	0.2	6	⅛ tsp	0.9%
Bread flour	20.3	576	4¼ cups	90.6%
Whole wheat flour	2.1	60	½ cup	9.4%
Yeast, instant dry	0.1	3	1 tsp	0.4%
Salt	0.6	17	1 Tbsp	2.7%
Water, 80°F	3.3	94	⅓ cup + 1 Tbsp	14.7%
TOTAL	48.0	1363	•	214.2%
GARNISH				
Semolina-flour mixture; ratio 1:1	as needed			

1. MAKE the dough the day before you want to serve the bread. Put the 1⅔ cups water, sour and malt in the bowl of a mixer fitted with a dough hook. Mix for 1 minute on low speed, to break up the sour (for autolyse mixing, see page 129). Add the flours, yeast and salt and mix on low speed for 4 minutes, making sure to scrape down and flip the dough over. Mix for 2 minutes on medium speed, making sure to scrape down and flip the dough over. The dough should have some (improved) gluten development. Add half of the remaining water and mix for 2 minutes on medium speed, making sure to scrape down and flip the dough over. Add the remaining half of the water and mix for 1 to 2 minutes on medium speed. The dough should be a little sticky, but with fairly good (improved) gluten development. Place the dough in a lightly oiled bowl large enough for it to double in size and cover it with plastic wrap.

2. ALLOW the dough to rest and ferment in a warm place for 45 minutes, until doubled in size.

3. PLACE the dough on a lightly floured work surface and fold it over in thirds, then leave it on the work surface, covered. Let the dough rest and ferment for 30 minutes, until when lightly touched the dough springs back halfway.

4. LINE a baking tray with a white cloth napkin or kitchen towel and dust it with some of the semolina-flour mixture.

5. UNCOVER the dough and divide it into 2 approximately equal pieces. Do this by eye, as scaling will cause some of the gas to expel, making the finished loaves denser. Roll each dough piece in a pile of the semolina-flour mixture, then gently stretch it lengthwise, being careful not to pull too hard. Place each piece upside-down on the baking tray. Continue this process with the other dough piece and then cover the tray lightly with plastic wrap. Allow the dough to rest and ferment at room temperature for 60–70 minutes, until when lightly touched the dough springs back halfway.

6. TWENTY MINUTES before the end of final fermentation, preheat the oven to 500°F with a baking stone. Ten minutes before baking the loaves, place a tray filled with 3 cups of warm water below the baking area in the oven to help produce steam.

7. UNCOVER the dough and flip the pieces onto a stiff piece of cardboard dusted with semolina, then slide them off onto an upside-down baking tray or oven peel lined with parchment paper. Spray each loaf with water.

8. TRANSFER the loaves and parchment paper to the baking stone and immediately reduce the temperature to 475°F. Bake for 12 minutes. Remove the steam tray and parchment paper and rotate each piece, then continue baking for another 16–18 minutes, until the crust has developed a deep color and doesn't give when pressed.

9. REMOVE the bread from the oven and place on a cooling rack.

Durum Sourdough

Golden durum flour gives this sourdough a tender crumb, nutty flavor and warm color. It also contributes a sweet finish to the bread. This particular loaf is chewier than regular sourdoughs and has a very firm, crispy crust.

yield: **2 loaves at 24 oz** | FDT: **78°F**

bulk fermentation: **130 minutes** | *final fermentation:* **60 minutes** | *retard:* **overnight** | *rest:* **60–75 minutes** | *bake:* **450°F** *and* **30–32 minutes**

INGREDIENT	OUNCES	GRAMS	VOLUME	BAKERS %
Water, 80°F	16.5	468	2 cups	67.3%
Durum sour (page 216)	9.6	272	•	39.2%
Malt syrup	0.2	6	1 tsp	0.8%
Bread flour	17.0	482	3½ cups	69.4%
Durum flour	7.5	213	1½ cups	30.6%
Salt	0.7	20	1 Tbsp	2.9%
TOTAL	51.5	1461	•	210.2%

1. MAKE the dough the day before you want to serve the bread. Put the water, sour and malt in the bowl of a mixer fitted with a dough hook. Mix for 1 minute on low speed, to break up the sour (for autolyse mixing, see page 129). Add the flours and mix on low speed for 2 minutes, making sure to scrape down and flip the dough over. Cover the dough in the bowl and let it sit for 15 minutes.

2. ADD the salt and mix for 2 minutes on low speed, making sure to scrape down and flip the dough over. Mix for 2 minutes on medium speed, making sure to scrape down and flip the dough over. The dough should be a little sticky, but with fairly good gluten development. Place the dough in a lightly oiled bowl that is large enough for it to double in size and cover it with plastic wrap.

3. ALLOW the dough to rest and ferment in a warm place for 60 minutes, until when lightly touched the dough springs back halfway.

4. PLACE the dough on a lightly floured work surface and fold it over in thirds, then leave it on the work surface, covered. Let the dough rest and ferment for 60 minutes, until when lightly touched the dough springs back halfway.

5. DIVIDE the dough into two 24-oz pieces. Round each dough piece against the tabletop. Place them on a lightly floured surface and cover. Allow to rest and ferment for 10 minutes.

6. LINE a baking tray or oblong baskets with white cloth napkins or kitchen towels. Dust the cloth with flour.

7. SHAPE each piece of dough into a 10-inch oblong. Place each shaped loaf seam-side up on the cloth and then bring the cloth up between each loaf on the tray. Cover the shaped dough pieces and allow the dough to rest and ferment at room temperature for 60 minutes, then refrigerate the dough overnight. (This is called retarding the bread, to help slow down fermentation and develop more flavor and acidity.)

8. REMOVE the dough from the refrigerator and leave it at room temperature for 60–75 minutes before baking.

9. TWENTY MINUTES before baking, preheat the oven to 475°F with a baking stone. Ten minutes before baking the loaves, place a tray filled with 3 cups of warm water below the baking area in the oven to help produce steam.

10. UNCOVER the dough and place each piece seam-side down on an oven peel lined with parchment paper. Spray each loaf with water and allow it to sit for 5 minutes. Then score each loaf ¼–½ inch deep and spray each loaf again.

11. TRANSFER the loaves and parchment paper to the baking stone and immediately reduce the temperature to 450°F. Bake for 12 minutes. Remove the steam tray and parchment paper and rotate each piece, then continue baking for another 18–20 minutes, until the crust has a deep color and doesn't give when pressed.

12. REMOVE the bread from the oven and place on a cooling rack.

DURUM AND WHOLE WHEAT SOURDOUGH

A sour with this combination of flours will yield breads with pronounced fermented flavor
due to the presence of the whole wheat and the sweetness of the durum.

yield: **2 loaves at 24 oz** | FDT: **78°F**

bulk fermentation: **130 minutes** | final fermentation: **60 minutes** | retard: **overnight** | rest: **60–75 minutes** | bake: **450°F** and **30–32 minutes**

INGREDIENT	OUNCES	GRAMS	VOLUME	BAKERS %
Water, 80°F	16.5	468	2 cups + 1 Tbsp	67.1%
Durum and whole wheat sour (page 217)	9.6	272	•	39.0%
Malt syrup	0.2	6	⅛ tsp	0.8%
Bread flour	17.0	482	3½ cups	69.1%
Durum flour	3.8	108	¾ cup	15.4%
Whole wheat flour	3.8	108	¾ cup	15.4%
Salt	0.7	20	1 Tbsp	2.8%
TOTAL	51.6	1464	•	209.6%

1. MAKE the dough the day before you want to serve the bread. Put the water, sour and malt in the bowl of a mixer fitted with a dough hook. Mix for 1 minute on low speed, to break up the sour (for autolyse mixing, see page 129). Add the flours and mix on low speed for 2 minutes, making sure to scrape down and flip the dough over. Cover the dough in the bowl and let it sit for 15 minutes.

2. ADD the salt and mix for 2 minutes on low speed, making sure to scrape down and flip the dough over. Mix for 2 minutes on medium speed, making sure to scrape down and flip the dough over. The dough should be a little sticky, but with fairly good gluten development. Place the dough in a lightly oiled bowl large enough for it to double in size and cover it with plastic wrap.

3. ALLOW the dough to rest and ferment in a warm place for 60 minutes, until when lightly touched the dough springs back halfway.

4. PLACE the dough on a lightly floured work surface and fold it over in thirds, then leave it on the work surface, covered. Let the dough rest and ferment for 60 minutes, until when lightly touched the dough springs back halfway.

5. DIVIDE the dough into two 24-oz pieces. Round each dough piece against the tabletop. Place them on a lightly floured surface and cover. Allow to rest and ferment for 10 minutes.

6. LINE a baking tray or oblong baskets with white cloth napkins or kitchen towels. Dust the cloth with flour.

7. SHAPE each piece of dough into a 10-inch oblong. Place each shaped loaf seam-side up on the cloth and then bring the cloth up between each loaf on the tray. Cover the shaped dough pieces and allow the dough to rest and ferment at room temperature for 60 minutes, then refrigerate the dough overnight. (This is called retarding the bread, to help slow down fermentation and develop more flavor and acidity.)

8. REMOVE the dough from the refrigerator and leave at room temperature for 60–75 minutes before baking.

9. TWENTY MINUTES before baking, preheat the oven to 475°F with a baking stone. Ten minutes before baking the loaves, place a tray filled with 3 cups of warm water below the baking area in the oven to help produce steam.

10. UNCOVER the dough and place each piece seam-side down on an oven peel lined with parchment paper. Spray each loaf with water and allow it to sit for 5 minutes. Then score each loaf ¼–½ inch deep and spray each loaf again.

11. TRANSFER the loaves and parchment paper to the baking stone and immediately reduce the temperature to 450°F. Bake for 12 minutes. Remove the steam tray and parchment paper and rotate each piece, then continue baking for another 18–20 minutes, until the crust has a deep color and doesn't give when pressed.

12. REMOVE the bread from the oven and place on a cooling rack.

RYE AND WHOLE WHEAT SOURDOUGH

The combination of the whole wheat and rye flours will give your bread
a strong fermented flavor with nutty rye overtones.

yield: 2 loaves at 24 oz | FDT: 78°F

bulk fermentation: 130 minutes | final fermentation: 60 minutes | retard: overnight | rest: 60–75 minutes | bake: 450°F and 30–32 minutes

INGREDIENT	OUNCES	GRAMS	VOLUME	BAKERS %
Water, 80°F	16.5	468	2 cups + 1 Tbsp	67.1%
Rye and whole wheat sour (page 219)	9.6	272	•	39.0%
Malt syrup	0.2	6	⅛ tsp	0.8%
Bread flour	17.0	482	3½ cups	69.1%
Rye flour, medium	3.8	108	1 cup	15.4%
Whole wheat flour	3.8	108	¾ cup	15.4%
Salt	0.7	20	1 Tbsp	2.8%
TOTAL	51.6	1464	•	209.6%

1. MAKE the dough the day before you want to serve the bread. Put the water, sour and malt in the bowl of a mixer fitted with a dough hook. Mix for 1 minute on low speed, to break up the sour (for autolyse mixing, see page 129). Add the flours and mix on low speed for 2 minutes, making sure to scrape down and flip the dough over. Cover the dough in the bowl and let it sit for 15 minutes.

2. ADD the salt and mix for 2 minutes on low speed, making sure to scrape down and flip the dough over. Mix for 2 minutes on medium speed, making sure to scrape down and flip the dough over. The dough should be a little sticky, but with fairly good gluten development. Place the dough in a lightly oiled bowl large enough for it to double in size and cover it with plastic wrap.

3. ALLOW the dough to rest and ferment in a warm place for 60 minutes, until when lightly touched the dough springs back halfway.

4. PLACE the dough on a lightly floured work surface and fold it over in thirds, then leave it on the work surface, covered. Let the dough rest and ferment for 60 minutes, until when lightly touched the dough springs back halfway.

5. DIVIDE the dough into two 24-oz pieces. Round each dough piece against the tabletop. Place them on a lightly floured surface and cover. Allow to rest and ferment for 10 minutes.

6. LINE a baking tray or oblong baskets with white cloth napkins or kitchen towels. Dust the cloth with flour.

7. SHAPE each piece of dough into a 10-inch oblong. Place each shaped loaf seam-side up on the cloth and then bring the cloth up between each loaf on the tray. Cover the shaped dough pieces and allow the dough to rest and ferment at room temperature for 60 minutes, then refrigerate the dough overnight. (This is called retarding the bread, to help slow down fermentation and develop more flavor and acidity.)

8. REMOVE the dough from the refrigerator and leave at room temperature for 60–75 minutes before baking.

9. TWENTY MINUTES before baking, preheat the oven to 475°F with a baking stone. Ten minutes before baking the loaves, place a tray filled with 3 cups of warm water below the baking area in the oven to help produce steam.

10. UNCOVER the dough and place each piece seam-side down on an oven peel lined with parchment paper. Spray each loaf with water and allow it to sit for 5 minutes. Then score each loaf ¼–½ inch deep and spray each loaf again.

11. TRANSFER the loaves and parchment paper to the baking stone and immediately reduce the temperature to 450°F. Bake for 12 minutes. Remove the steam tray and parchment paper and rotate each piece, then continue baking for another 18–20 minutes, until the crust has a deep color and doesn't give when pressed.

12. REMOVE the bread from the oven and place on a cooling rack.

CRANBERRY AND WALNUT SOURDOUGH

This loaf has a more complex flavor due to the addition of the whole wheat flour and
rye flour to the sour. It is great for toasting and making sandwiches

yield: 2 loaves at 24 oz | FDT: 78°F

bulk fermentation: 130 minutes | final fermentation: 60 minutes | retard: overnight | rest: 60–75 minutes | bake: 450°F and 30–32 minutes

INGREDIENT	OUNCES	GRAMS	VOLUME	BAKERS %
Water, 80°F	12.3	349	1½ cups	67.2%
Rye and whole wheat sour (page 219)	7.1	201	•	38.8%
Malt syrup	0.1	3	⅛ tsp	0.5%
Bread flour	12.7	360	1⅔ cups	69.4%
Rye flour, medium	2.8	79	¾ cup	15.3%
Whole wheat flour	2.8	79	⅔ cup	15.3%
Salt	0.5	14	2⅓ tsp	2.7%
Cranberries, dried	5.6	159	½ cup	30.6%
Walnuts, toasted	5.6	159	½ cup	30.6%
TOTAL	49.5	1403	•	270.4%

1. MAKE the dough the day before you want to serve the bread. Put the water, sour and malt in the bowl of a mixer fitted with a dough hook. Mix for 1 minute on low speed, to break up the sour (for autolyse mixing, see page 129). Add the flours and mix on low speed for 2 minutes, making sure to scrape down and flip the dough over. Cover the dough in the bowl and let it sit for 15 minutes.

2. ADD the salt and mix for 2 minutes on low speed, making sure to scrape down and flip the dough over. Mix for 2 minutes on medium speed, making sure to scrape down and flip the dough over. The dough should be a little sticky, but with fairly good gluten development.

3. IN A SEPARATE BOWL, toss together the cranberries and walnuts. Add the mixture to the dough in the mixer. Mix for 1 minute on low speed, making sure to scrape down and flip the dough over. If the inclusions are not mixed in well, place the dough on a lightly floured work surface and knead it the rest of the way by hand. Place the dough in a lightly oiled bowl large enough for it to double in size and cover it with plastic wrap.

4. ALLOW the dough to rest and ferment in a warm place for 60 minutes, until when lightly touched the dough springs back halfway.

5. PLACE the dough on a lightly floured work surface and fold it over in thirds, then leave it on the work surface, covered. Let the dough rest and ferment for 60 minutes, until when lightly touched the dough springs back halfway.

6. DIVIDE the dough into two 24-oz pieces. Round each dough piece against the tabletop. Place them on a lightly floured surface and cover. Allow to rest and ferment for 10 minutes.

7. LINE a baking tray or oblong baskets with white cloth napkins or kitchen towels. Dust the cloth with flour.

8. SHAPE each piece of dough into a 10-inch oblong. Place each shaped loaf seam-side up on the cloth and then bring the cloth up between each loaf in the tray. Cover the shaped dough pieces and allow the dough to rest and ferment at room temperature for 60 minutes, then refrigerate the dough overnight. (This is called retarding the bread, to help slow down fermentation and develop more flavor and acidity.)

9. REMOVE the dough from the refrigerator and leave at room temperature for 60–75 minutes.

10. TWENTY MINUTES before baking, preheat the oven to 475°F with a baking stone. Ten minutes before baking the loaves, place a tray filled with 3 cups of warm water below the baking area in the oven to help produce steam.

11. UNCOVER the dough and place each piece seam-side down on an oven peel lined with parchment paper. Spray each loaf with water and allow it to sit for 5 minutes. Then score each loaf ¼–½ inch deep and spray each loaf again.

12. TRANSFER the loaves and parchment paper to the baking stone and immediately reduce the temperature to 450°F. Bake for 12 minutes. Remove the steam tray and parchment paper and rotate each piece, then continue baking for another 18–20 minutes, until the crust has a deep color and doesn't give when pressed.

13. REMOVE the bread from the oven and place on a cooling rack.

WHOLE WHEAT SOURDOUGH

Sourdough bread is a local food, developing its flavor profile from the sourdough's "microflora"—
by-products of wild yeast and friendly bacteria found in the air. Your sourdough will develop its unique
local microflora, ranging in taste from sharp to mild. This loaf features an earthy flavor from the whole
wheat flour. The whole wheat also gives the bread less volume, creating a denser, tighter structure.

yield: **2 loaves at 24 oz** | FDT: **78°F**
bulk fermentation: **130 minutes** | *final fermentation:* **60 minutes** | *retard:* **overnight** | *rest:* **60–75 minutes** | *bake:* **450°F** *and* **30–32 minutes**

INGREDIENT	OUNCES	GRAMS	VOLUME	BAKERS %
Water, 80°F	16.5	468	2 cups	67.3%
Wheat sour (page 215)	9.6	272	•	39.2%
Malt syrup	0.2	6	1 tsp	0.8%
Bread flour	17.0	482	3½ cups	69.4%
Whole wheat flour	7.5	213	1¾ cups	30.6%
Salt	0.7	20	1 Tbsp	2.9%
TOTAL	51.5	1461	•	210.2%

1. MAKE the dough the day before you want to serve the bread. Put the water, sour and malt in the bowl of a mixer fitted with a dough hook. Mix for 1 minute on low speed, to break up the sour (for autolyse mixing, see page 129). Add the flours and mix on low speed for 2 minutes, making sure to scrape down and flip the dough over. Cover the dough in the bowl and let it sit for 15 minutes.

2. ADD the salt and mix for 2 minutes on low speed, making sure to scrape down and flip the dough over. Mix for 2 minutes on medium speed, making sure to scrape down and flip the dough over. The dough should be a little sticky, but with fairly good gluten development. Place the dough in a lightly oiled bowl large enough for it to double in size and cover it with plastic wrap.

3. ALLOW the dough to rest and ferment in a warm place for 60 minutes, until when lightly touched the dough springs back halfway.

4. PLACE the dough on a lightly floured work surface and fold it over in thirds, then leave it on the work surface, covered. Let the dough rest and ferment for 60 minutes, until when lightly touched the dough springs back halfway.

5. DIVIDE the dough into two 24-oz pieces. Round each dough piece against the tabletop. Place them on a lightly floured surface and cover. Allow to rest and ferment for 10 minutes.

6. LINE a baking tray or oblong baskets with white cloth napkins or kitchen towels. Dust the cloth with flour.

7. SHAPE each piece of dough into a 10-inch oblong. Place each shaped loaf seam-side up on the cloth and then bring the cloth up between each loaf on the tray. Cover the shaped dough pieces and allow the dough to rest and ferment at room temperature for 60 minutes, then refrigerate the dough overnight. (This is called retarding the bread, to help slow down fermentation and develop more flavor and acidity.)

Rye, Spelt and Flaxseed Loaves

Featuring whole grains and flaxseeds, this robust European-style rye is complex and hearty. Several of the ingredients—the cracked rye, cracked wheat and spelt flour—can be found at natural food stores. Cracked grains are simply whole kernels broken into fragments. Spelt flour, made from a cereal grain native to southern Europe, can be replaced with equal portions of whole wheat and rye flours. Multigrain mixture (see Resources, page 332), could be substituted for the cracked grains.

yield: **2 loaves at 24 oz** | FDT: **80°F**
soaker: **overnight** | bulk fermentation: **30–40 minutes** | final fermentation: **30–40 minutes** | bake: **450°F** *and* **31–33 minutes**

INGREDIENT	OUNCES	GRAMS	VOLUME	BAKERS %
GRAIN SOAKER				
Water, 80°F	8.3	235	1 cup	35.8%
Flaxseeds	3.8	108	¾ cup	16.4%
Cracked wheat	1.8	51	⅓ cup	7.8%
Cracked rye	1.8	51	⅓ cup	7.8%
FINAL DOUGH				
Water, 95°F	10.1	286	1¼ cups	43.5%
Grain soaker	15.7	445	•	67.8%
Rye sour (page 218)	7.4	210	•	31.9%
Malt syrup	0.1	3	½ tsp	0.4%
Bread flour	6.3	179	1⅓ cups	27.2%
Spelt flour, whole	5.2	147	1 cup	22.4%
Rye flour, medium	4.3	122	1 cup	18.5%
Yeast, instant dry	0.2	6	1½ tsp	0.9%
Salt	0.6	17	1 Tbsp	2.6%
TOTAL	49.9	1415	•	215.2%
GARNISH				
Sesame seeds	as needed			

1. **MAKE** the grain soaker by mixing the ingredients together. Cover and allow it to soak at room temperature overnight.

2. **TO MAKE THE DOUGH,** put the water, soaker, sour and malt in the bowl of a mixer. Combine the flours and yeast, then add them to the bowl. Add the salt and place the bowl on a mixer fitted with a dough hook. Mix for 4 minutes on low speed, making sure to scrape down and flip the dough over. Increase the speed to medium and mix for 2 minutes more, making sure to scrape down and flip the dough over. The dough should be wet and tacky, with partial gluten development. Place the dough in a lightly oiled bowl large enough for the dough to double in size and cover with plastic wrap.

3. **ALLOW** the dough to rest in a warm place for 30–40 minutes, until when touched the dough springs back halfway.

4. **PREPARE** a baking tray or round bowls lined with a heavy-duty paper towel, white cloth napkin or white kitchen towel for the final shape to rest in. Have a spray bottle of water nearby.

5. **PLACE** the dough on a lightly floured work surface and divide it into two 24-oz pieces. Shape each dough piece into a round, then immediately into a 10-inch oblong. Spray the loaves with water, then roll the top and sides in sesame seeds. Place each shaped loaf on the prepared cloth seam-side up and bring the cloth up

between each loaf. Or each dough piece can be shaped round, sprayed with water, then rolled in sesame seeds and placed in a prepared bowl. Use any extra cloth to cover the shaped dough pieces. Lightly cover the dough with plastic wrap and allow it to rest and ferment in a warm place for 30–40 minutes, until when touched the dough springs back halfway.

6. **TWENTY MINUTES** before the end of final fermentation, preheat the oven to 475°F with a baking stone. Ten minutes before baking the loaves, place a tray filled with 3 cups of warm water below the baking area in the oven to help produce steam.

7. **PLACE** each loaf seam-side down on a parchment paper–lined oven peel. Spray each loaf with water and allow it to sit for 5 minutes. Score the top of each loaf with a sharp razor held at a 45-degree angle to the dough, cutting ¼–½ inch deep. Spray the loaves with water again. This will help with steam in the oven and allow the loaf to expand.

8. **TRANSFER** the loaves to the baking stone and immediately reduce the temperature to 450°F. Bake for 15 minutes, then remove the water tray and parchment paper, and rotate each piece. Continue baking for another 16–18 minutes, until the crust has a dark color and doesn't give when pressed.

9. **REMOVE** the bread from the oven and place on a cooling rack.

FOCACCIA

This recipe for the classic Italian bread starts with the preferment biga, and is mixed and worked largely by hand. Stippling the dough gives each loaf its characteristic markings and keeps it from puffing too high during baking; the application of olive oil keeps the dough moist. Choices for toppings are endless—from herbs to cheeses, vegetables to meats—but make sure you top modestly so as not to lose the moist, salty flavor of the bread itself.

yield: 3 loaves at 16 oz | FDT: 82°F

biga: 1 day | bulk fermentation: 65–80 minutes | final fermentation: 30–40 minutes | bake: 450°F *and* 23–28 minutes

INGREDIENT	OUNCES	GRAMS	VOLUME	BAKERS %
BIGA				
Water, 55°F	4.0	113	½ cup	15.2%
Bread flour	6.3	177	1⅓ cups	23.8%
Yeast, instant dry	0.01	0.3	pinch	0.04%
FINAL DOUGH				
Water, 86°F	15.5	439	2 cups	59.0%
Biga	10.3	291	•	39.1%
Olive oil	1.5	43	3 Tbsp	5.7%
Malt syrup	0.2	4	⅛ tsp	0.6%
Bread flour	20.0	567	4 cups + 2½ Tbsp	76.2%
Yeast, instant dry	0.1	3	¾ tsp	0.4%
Salt	0.6	17	1 Tbsp	2.3%
TOTAL	48.2	1364	•	183.3%
GARNISHES				
Olive oil	as needed			
Selected toppings	to taste			
Coarse salt	as needed			

1. MIX the biga the day before you want to serve the bread. Put the water in the bowl of a mixer, combine the flour with the yeast, and then add the flour mixture to the bowl. Place on a mixer fitted with a dough hook and mix for 2 minutes on medium speed, or until homogenous. The biga should be stiff and slightly dry. Place the biga in a lightly oiled bowl large enough for it to double in size. Flip the biga over in the bowl to coat it lightly with oil. Cover the bowl with plastic wrap and refrigerate for 2 hours.

2. REMOVE the biga and leave it at room temperature for 10–12 hours before using. After the fermentation, the biga will be less stiff and more like an actual bread dough.

3. TO MAKE THE FINAL DOUGH, put the water, biga, oil and malt in a large bowl. Break the biga down into pebble-sized pieces by mixing by hand for about 5 minutes. Combine the flour and the yeast together, and then add them to the biga mixture while stirring (this helps to dissipate the oil on the surface and prevent lumps from forming). Next, add the salt and work the mixture with your hands for 5 minutes, making sure to scrape down and squeeze the dough with your fingers to continue to break down the biga. When it is finished, the dough should still be very tacky and will lack structure. Cover the bowl and let the dough rest and ferment in a warm place for 45–60 minutes, until double in size.

4. PLACE the dough on a lightly floured work surface and fold it into thirds. Leaving the dough on the work surface, cover it with plastic wrap and let it rest for 10 minutes.

5. LINE 2 baking trays with parchment paper.

6. UNCOVER the dough and divide it into three 16-oz pieces. Lightly flour the bottom of each piece of dough, fold it in half, then give the dough a quarter-turn and fold it in half again. Tuck the rough end under the dough to make a round loaf. Lightly round the dough against the tabletop (the dough should form a ball but not be stretched too tight). Place 2 loaves on 1 tray and the third on the second tray and brush liberally with oil. Allow the dough to rest and ferment, covered, at room temperature for 10 minutes.

7. STIPPLE the dough by dipping your fingers in oil and using them to make depressions in the dough (without going all the way through), and gently stretching it out into a 10 by 6-inch rectangle on the pan. Lightly cover the dough with plastic wrap and let it rest and ferment in a warm place for 30–40 minutes, until when lightly touched the dough springs back halfway.

8. TWENTY MINUTES before the end of final fermentation, preheat the oven to 475°F with a baking stone. Meanwhile, prepare the toppings for the focaccia. Ten minutes before baking the loaves, place a tray filled with 3 cups of warm water below the baking area in the oven to help produce steam.

9. UNCOVER the dough and lightly stipple the dough again with your fingers dipped in oil, making depressions but not stretching the dough out. Place your toppings on the dough evenly but do not apply too much (this is a bread, not a pizza).

10. TRANSFER the dough to the baking stone by bringing it to the oven on the tray and then sliding it off with the parchment paper onto the stone. Load one bread onto each rack in the oven and rotate halfway through baking. Immediately reduce the temperature to 450°F. Bake for 18–20 minutes, then remove the steam tray and bake for another 5–8 minutes, until the crust is dark and does not give when pressed.

11. REMOVE from the oven and place the focaccia on a cooling rack. Brush lightly with oil, and lightly scatter with salt.

Brush the rectangles of focaccia dough with olive oil. Then dip all five fingers into the oil and make a claw gesture before pressing them firmly into the dough. This will keep the dough from puffing up too much. Do not push all the way through the dough or your toppings will fall out the bottom.

Focaccia

Semolina Focaccia

The addition of semolina and durum flour to the basic focaccia recipe highlights the bread's close relationship to pizza dough. Produced just as a focaccia made from only bread flour, the final, garnished bread is similarly suited for sandwiches or, sliced, as an accompaniment to a meal. For something different, try adding raisins, honey or a sprinkle of sugar to create a sweet version of the savory classic.

yield: 3 loaves at 16 oz | FDT: 82°F
biga: 1 day | bulk fermentation: 65–80 minutes | final fermentation: 30–40 minutes | bake: 450°F *and* 23–28 minutes

INGREDIENT	OUNCES	GRAMS	VOLUME	BAKERS %
BIGA				
Water, 55°F	5.5	156	⅓ cup	20.4%
Semolina flour	4.5	128	¾ cup	16.7%
Durum flour	4.5	128	¾ cup + 2½ Tbsp	16.7%
Yeast, instant dry	pinch	0.3	pinch	0.04%
FINAL DOUGH				
Water, 86°F	15.7	447	2 cups	58.3%
Biga	14.5	412	•	53.8%
Olive oil	1.5	43	3 Tbsp	5.6%
Malt syrup	0.1	4	⅛ tsp	0.6%
Semolina flour	4.5	128	¾ cup	16.7%
Durum flour	4.5	128	¾ cup + 2½ Tbsp	16.7%
Bread flour	9.0	255	1 cup + 2 Tbsp	33.3%
Yeast, instant dry	0.1	4	1 tsp	0.6%
Salt	0.6	17	1 Tbsp	2.2%
TOTAL	50.5	1438	•	187.8%
GARNISHES				
Olive oil	as needed			
Selected toppings	as needed			
Coarse salt	as needed			

1. **MIX** the biga the day before you want to serve the bread. Put the water in the bowl of a mixer, combine the flours with the yeast, and then add the flour mixture to the bowl. Place on a mixer fitted with a dough hook and mix for 2 minutes on medium speed, or until homogenous. The biga should be stiff and slightly dry. Place the biga in a lightly oiled bowl large enough for it to double in size. Flip the biga over in the bowl to coat it lightly with oil. Cover the bowl with plastic wrap and refrigerate for 2 hours.

2. **REMOVE** the biga and leave it at room temperature for 10–12 hours before using. After the fermentation, the biga will be less stiff and more like an actual bread dough.

3. **TO MAKE THE FINAL DOUGH,** put the water, biga, oil and malt in a large bowl. Break the biga down into pebble-sized pieces by mixing by hand for about 5 minutes. Combine the flours and the yeast together, and then add them to the biga mixture while stirring (this helps to dissipate the oil on the surface and prevent lumps from forming). Next, add the salt and work the mixture with your hands for 5 minutes, making sure to scrape down and squeeze the dough with your fingers to continue to break down the biga. When it is finished, the dough should still be very tacky and will lack structure. Cover the bowl and let the dough rest and ferment in a warm place for 45–60 minutes, until double in size.

4. **PLACE** the dough on a lightly floured work surface and fold it into thirds. Leaving the dough on the work surface, cover it with plastic wrap and let it rest for 10 minutes.

5. **LINE** 2 baking trays with parchment paper.

6. **UNCOVER** the dough and divide it into three 16-oz pieces. Lightly flour the bottom of each piece of dough, fold it in half, then give the dough a quarter-turn and fold it in half again. Tuck the rough end under the dough to make a round loaf. Lightly round the dough against the tabletop (the dough should form a ball but not be stretched too tight). Place 2 loaves on 1 tray and the third on the second tray and brush liberally with oil. Allow the dough to rest and ferment, covered, at room temperature for 10 minutes.

7. **STIPPLE** the dough by dipping your fingers in oil and using them to make depressions in the dough (without going all the way through), and gently stretching it out into a 10 by 6-inch rectangle on the pan. Lightly cover the dough with plastic wrap and let it rest and ferment in a warm place for 30–40 minutes, until when lightly touched the dough springs back halfway.

8. **TWENTY MINUTES** before the end of final fermentation, preheat the oven to 475°F with a baking stone. Meanwhile, prepare the toppings for the focaccia. Ten minutes before baking the loaves, place a tray filled with 3 cups of warm water below the baking area in the oven to help produce steam.

9. **UNCOVER** the dough and lightly stipple the dough again with your fingers dipped in oil, making depressions but not stretching the dough out. Place your toppings on the dough evenly but do not apply too much (this is a bread, not a pizza).

10. **TRANSFER** the dough to the baking stone by bringing it to the oven on the tray and then sliding it off with the parchment paper onto the stone. Load one bread onto each rack in the oven and rotate halfway through baking. Immediately reduce the temperature to 450°F. Bake for 18–20 minutes, then remove the steam tray and bake for another 5–8 minutes, until the crust is dark and does not give when pressed.

11. **REMOVE** from the oven and place the focaccia on a cooling rack. Brush lightly with oil, and lightly scatter with salt.

OLIVE AND CHEESE BREAD

There are so many varieties of both cheese and olives that this bread can be made many times with very different and wonderful results. When choosing your olives and cheese, think of how their flavors will complement each other; provolone, mozzarella or Manchego are all good choices.

yield: **2 loaves at 24 oz** | FDT: **80°F**

pâte fermentée: **1 day** | bulk fermentation: **95–105 minutes** | final fermentation: **75–90 minutes** | bake: **450°F** *and* 30–32 minutes

INGREDIENT	OUNCES	GRAMS	VOLUME	BAKERS %
Pâte Fermentée (page 175)				
FINAL DOUGH				
Water, 90°F	14.6	414	1¾ cups	76.0%
Malt syrup	0.1	3	⅛ tsp	0.5%
Pâte fermentée	6.0	168	•	31.3%
Bread flour	15.4	437	3¼ cups	80.2%
Whole wheat flour	3.8	108	¾ cup	19.8%
Yeast, instant dry	0.1	3	1 tsp	0.5%
Salt	0.5	14	2½ tsp	2.6%
Cheese, cubed	6.0	170	½ cup	31.3%
Olives, pitted, rinsed and roughly chopped	5.0	142	½ cup	26.0%
TOTAL	51.5	1459	•	268.2%

1. MAKE the pâte fermentée the day before you want to serve the bread.

2. TO MAKE THE FINAL DOUGH, put the water and malt in the bowl of a mixer, then break up the pâte fermentée by hand and add it to the bowl. Place the bowl on a mixer fitted with a dough hook and mix for 2 minutes on low speed to break up the pâte fermentée (for autolyse mixing, see page 129). Mix the flours and yeast together, then add them to the bowl. Mix on low speed for 2 minutes, making sure to scrape down and flip the dough over twice during this time. Leave the dough in the bowl. Cover and let it sit for 15 minutes at room temperature.

3. ADD the salt and mix for 2 minutes on low speed, making sure to scrape down and flip the dough over. Mix for 2 minutes on medium speed, making sure to scrape down and flip the dough over. Add the cheese and olives, and mix for 1 minute on low speed, making sure to scrape down and flip the dough over. The dough should be a little sticky, but with fairly good gluten development. Place the dough in a lightly oiled bowl large enough for it to double in size and cover with plastic wrap.

4. ALLOW the dough to rest and ferment in a warm place for 60–70 minutes, until when lightly touched the dough springs back halfway.

5. PLACE the dough on a lightly floured work surface and fold it over in thirds, then leave it on the work surface and cover. Let the dough rest and ferment for 15 minutes.

6. UNCOVER the dough and divide it into two 24-oz pieces. Round each dough piece against the tabletop. Place them on a lightly floured surface and cover. Allow the dough to rest and ferment for 20 minutes.

7. LINE a baking tray, oblong baskets or round bowls with cloth napkins or kitchen towels. The cloth will need to be floured.

8. SHAPE each piece into a 10-inch oblong. Place each shaped loaf seam-side up on the cloth and bring the cloth up between each loaf on the tray. Or each dough piece can be shaped round, sprayed with water, and placed in a prepared bowl. Cover the shaped dough pieces. Allow the dough to rest and ferment in a warm place for 75–90 minutes, until when lightly touched the dough springs back halfway.

9. TWENTY MINUTES before the end of final fermentation, preheat the oven to 475°F with a baking stone. Ten minutes before baking the loaves, place a tray filled with 3 cups of warm water below the baking area in the oven to help produce steam.

10. UNCOVER the dough and place each piece seam-side down on an oven peel lined with parchment paper. Spray each loaf with water and allow it to sit for 5 minutes. Then score each loaf ¼–½ inch deep and spray each loaf again.

11. TRANSFER the loaves to the baking stone and immediately reduce the temperature to 450°F. Bake for 12 minutes. Remove the steam tray and rotate each piece. Continue baking for another 18–20 minutes, until the crust is dark in color and firm when pressed.

12. REMOVE from the oven and place the loaves on a cooling rack.

MUFFALETTA BREAD

Hailing from New Orleans, the oversized sandwich known as the muffaletta brings together a rich assortment of flavors—tender bread, Italian meats and cheeses, and a unique olive salad.

yield: 2 loaves at 24 oz | *FDT:* 80°F | *biga:* 1 day | *bulk fermentation:* 70–85 minutes | *final fermentation:* 40–50 minutes | *initial bake:* 450°F *and* 12 minutes | *final bake:* 425°F *and* 14–15 minutes

INGREDIENT	OUNCES	GRAMS	VOLUME	BAKERS %
BIGA				
Water, 55°F	5.5	156	⅔ cup	18.4%
Whole wheat flour	2.1	60	½ cup	7.0%
Semolina flour	2.1	60	⅓ cup	7.0%
Durum flour	4.3	122	1 cup	14.4%
Yeast, instant dry	0.01	0.3	pinch	0.03%
FINAL DOUGH				
Water, 86°F	13.8	391	1¾ cups	46.2%
Olive oil	2.2	62	¼ cup	7.4%
Malt syrup	0.1	3	½ tsp	0.3%
Biga	14.0	398	•	46.8%
Whole wheat flour	6.4	181	1½ cups	21.4%
Semolina flour	2.1	60	⅓ cup	7.0%
Durum flour	4.3	122	1 cup	14.4%
Bread flour	8.6	244	1¾ cups	28.8%
Yeast, instant dry	0.1	3	1 tsp	0.3%
Salt	0.7	20	1 Tbsp + 1 tsp	2.3%
TOTAL	52.3	1484	•	174.9%
GARNISHES				
Olive oil	as needed			
Sesame seeds, semolina flour or cornmeal (optional)	as needed			

1. **MIX** the biga the day before you want to serve the bread. Place the water in the bowl of a mixer, combine the flours with the yeast, and then add the flour mixture to the bowl. Place on a mixer fitted with a dough hook and mix for 2 minutes on medium speed, or until homogenous. The biga should be stiff and slightly dry. Place the biga in a lightly oiled bowl that is large enough for it to double in size. Flip the biga over in the bowl to coat it lightly with oil. Cover the bowl with plastic wrap and refrigerate for 2 hours.

2. **REMOVE** the biga and leave it at room temperature for 10–12 hours before using. After the fermentation, the biga will be less stiff and more like an actual bread dough.

3. **TO MAKE THE FINAL DOUGH,** put the water, oil and malt in the bowl of a mixer. Break the biga up by hand and add it to the bowl. Place the bowl on a mixer fitted with a dough hook and mix for 2 minutes on low speed to break down the biga. Mix the flours and yeast together, then add them to the bowl (for autolyse mixing, see page 129). Mix for 2 minutes on low speed, making sure to scrape down the bowl and flip the dough over. Leave the dough in the bowl, cover it, and allow it to rest for 15 minutes.

4. **ADD** the salt and mix for 2 minutes on low speed, making sure to scrape down and flip the dough over. Mix for 2 minutes on medium speed, making sure to scrape down and flip the dough over. The dough should be tacky but have some good gluten structure. Place the dough in a lightly oiled bowl large enough for it to double in size and cover with plastic wrap.

5. **ALLOW** the dough to rest and ferment in a warm place for 45–60 minutes, until when lightly touched the dough springs back halfway.

6. **PLACE** the dough on a lightly floured work surface and fold it over in thirds, then leave it on the work surface and cover it. Let the dough rest for 15 minutes.

7. **UNCOVER** the dough and divide it into two 24-oz pieces. Round each dough piece against the tabletop and place it in a heavily oiled 8-inch cake pan, then brush the top liberally with oil. Allow the dough to rest, uncovered, for 10 minutes.

8. **DIP** your fingers in oil and poke the dough all over with your fingers, but do not poke all the way through. Cover the dough with a cloth and allow it to rest and ferment in a warm place for 40–50 minutes, until when lightly touched the dough springs back halfway.

9. **TWENTY MINUTES** before the end of final fermentation, preheat the oven to 475°F with a baking stone. Ten minutes before baking the loaves, place a tray filled with 3 cups of warm water below the baking area in the oven to help produce steam.

10. **LIGHTLY** poke the top of each loaf again with your fingers dipped in oil. The tops can be garnished with sesame seeds, semolina or cornmeal, if desired. Place the loaves on the baking stone and immediately reduce the temperature to 450°F. Bake for 12 minutes, then remove the steam tray and rotate each loaf. Reduce the temperature to 425°F and continue baking for 14–15 minutes, until golden brown.

11. **REMOVE** the bread from the oven and take it out of the pans right away, then place it on a cooling rack.

NOTE: *Our muffaletta bread, baked in a round 8-inch cake pan, is made especially for this hero-style sandwich. Just slice the loaf in half widthwise, layer it up, and cut it into thick wedges for individual servings.*

Beer Bread

If you're looking for a good sandwich bread suited for loads of meat and cheese, this is it. The malty flavor goes well with a range of bold garnishes, and the chewy crust and tender crumb are mouth-watering. When selecting the beer, don't skimp on quality. Choose a fresh, good-quality dark beer—the darker, the better. The beer not only adds flavor to the bread, but helps to tenderize the dough.

yield: 2 loaves at 24 oz | FDT: 80°F
pâte fermentée: 1 day | bulk fermentation: 80–95 minutes | final fermentation: 45–60 minutes | bake: 450°F *and* 30–32 minutes

INGREDIENT	OUNCES	GRAMS	VOLUME	BAKERS %
Pâte Fermentée (page 175)				
FINAL DOUGH				
Beer, 95°F	14.0	397	1¾ cups	58.3%
Vegetable oil	3.0	85	¼ cup + 2 Tbsp	12.5%
Malt syrup	0.1	3	pinch	0.4%
Pâte fermentée	7.0	198	⅛ tsp	29.2%
Bread flour	20.0	567	4 cups + 3 Tbsp	83.3%
Rye flour, medium	4.0	113	1 cup + 2 tsp	16.7%
Yeast, instant dry	0.1	3	1 tsp	0.4%
Salt	0.6	17	1 Tbsp	2.5%
TOTAL	48.8	1383	•	203.3%

1. MAKE the pâte fermentée the day before you want to serve the bread.

2. TO MAKE THE FINAL DOUGH, put the beer, oil and malt in the bowl of a mixer. Break up the pâte fermentée by hand and add it to the mixer. Place the bowl on a mixer fitted with a dough hook and mix for 2 minutes on low speed to break up the pâte fermentée. Mix the flours and yeast together, add them to the mixer, then add the salt. Mix on low speed for 3 minutes, making sure to scrape down and flip the dough over twice. Mix on medium speed for 5 minutes, making sure to scrape down and flip the dough over twice. The dough should be a little sticky, but with fairly good gluten development. Place the dough in a lightly oiled bowl large enough for it to double in size and cover with plastic wrap.

3. ALLOW the dough to rest and ferment in a warm place for 45–60 minutes, until when lightly touched the dough springs back halfway.

4. PLACE the dough on a lightly floured work surface and fold it over in thirds, then leave it on the work surface, covered. Let the dough rest and ferment for 15 minutes.

5. **UNCOVER** the dough and divide it into two 24-oz pieces. Round each dough piece against the tabletop. Place them on a lightly floured surface, cover, and allow to rest and ferment for 20 minutes.

6. **LINE** a baking tray or oblong baskets with cloth napkins or kitchen towels. The cloth will need to be floured.

7. **SHAPE** each piece into a 10-inch oblong. Place each shaped loaf seam-side up on the cloth and bring the cloth up between each loaf on the tray. Cover the shaped dough pieces and allow them to rest and ferment in a warm place for 45–60 minutes, until when lightly touched the dough springs back halfway.

8. **TWENTY MINUTES** before the end of final fermentation, preheat the oven to 475°F with a baking stone. Ten minutes before baking the loaves, place a tray filled with 3 cups of warm water below the baking area in the oven to help produce steam.

9. **UNCOVER** the dough and place each piece seam-side down on an oven peel lined with parchment paper. Spray each loaf with water and let it sit for 5 minutes. Then score each loaf ¼–½ inch deep and spray each loaf again.

10. **TRANSFER** the loaves to the baking stone and immediately reduce the temperature to 450°F. Bake for 12 minutes. Remove the steam tray and parchment paper, and rotate each piece. Continue baking for another 18–20 minutes, until the crust is dark and does not give when pressed.

11. **REMOVE** from the oven and place the loaves on a cooling rack.

APPLE BREAD

This apple-studded bread makes a great addition to a meal, either served plain at breakfast or as part of a ham and Cheddar sandwich at lunch. The dried apples are optional, but give the bread a wonderful flavor. If you choose to include them, be sure to select crisp, tart apples such as Fuji, Gala or Granny Smith. To further enhance the flavor, substitute an equal amount of apple butter for the applesauce.

yield: **2 loaves at 28 oz** | FDT: **82°F**
pâte fermentée: **1 day** | bulk fermentation: **70–85 minutes** | final fermentation: **60–70 minutes** |
initial bake: **450°F** *and* **12 minutes** | final bake: **425°F** *and* **15–18 minutes**

INGREDIENT	OUNCES	GRAMS	VOLUME	BAKERS %
Pâte Fermentée (page 175)				
FINAL DOUGH				
Apple cider, 105°F	9.6	272	1 cup + 3 Tbsp	50.0%
Sour cream	3.7	105	½ cup	19.3%
Applesauce, smooth and unsweetened, 105°F	3.2	91	⅓ cup	16.7%
Malt syrup	0.1	3	½ tsp	0.5%
Pâte fermentée	14.9	422	•	77.6%
Bread flour	12.8	363	2⅔ cups	66.7%
Whole wheat flour	6.4	181	1½ cups	33.3%
Yeast, instant dry	0.2	6	¼ tsp	1.0%
Salt	0.4	11	2 tsp	2.1%
Apples, dried, diced (see Note)	8.5	241	1½ cups	44.3%
Cinnamon, ground	0.1	3	¼ tsp	0.5%
TOTAL	59.9	1698	•	312.0%

1. **MAKE** the pâte fermentée the day before you want to serve the bread.

2. **TO MAKE THE FINAL DOUGH,** put the cider, sour cream, apple-sauce and malt in the bowl of a mixer. Break up the pâte fermentée by hand, and add it to the bowl. Place the bowl on a mixer fitted with a dough hook and mix for 2 minutes on low speed to break up the pâte fermentée. Mix the flours and yeast together, add them to the bowl, then add the salt. Mix on low speed for 3 minutes, making sure to scrape down and flip the dough over twice while mixing. Mix for another 3 minutes on medium speed, making sure to scrape down and flip the dough over. Add the apples and cinnamon to the bowl and mix for 1 minute on low speed, making sure to scrape down and flip the dough over. The dough should be a little sticky, but with fairly good gluten development. Place the dough in a lightly oiled bowl large enough for it to double in size and cover with plastic wrap.

3. **ALLOW** the dough to rest and ferment in a warm place for 45–60 minutes, until when lightly touched the dough springs back halfway.

4. **PLACE** the dough on a lightly floured work surface and fold it over in thirds. Leave it on the work surface, cover, and allow the dough to rest and ferment for 15 minutes.

5. **UNCOVER** the dough and divide it into two 28-oz pieces. Round each dough piece against the tabletop. Place the rounds on a lightly floured surface and cover. Allow them to rest and ferment for 10 minutes.

6. **GENEROUSLY** oil 2 loaf pans.

7. **SHAPE** each dough piece into a 12-inch oblong. Place the dough in the oiled bread pans seam-side down and cover. Allow the dough to rest and ferment in a warm place for 60–70 minutes, until when lightly touched the dough springs back halfway.

8. **TWENTY MINUTES** before the end of final fermentation, preheat the oven to 475°F with a baking stone. Ten minutes before baking the loaves, place a tray filled with 3 cups of warm water below the baking area in the oven to help produce steam.

9. **UNCOVER** the dough and spray each loaf with water, then allow it to sit for 5 minutes. Spray each loaf again and then score each loaf ¼–½ inch deep.

10. **PLACE** the pans on the baking stone and immediately reduce the temperature to 450°F. Bake for 12 minutes, then remove the steam tray and rotate each pan. Reduce the temperature to 425°F. Continue baking for another 15–18 minutes, until golden brown.

11. **REMOVE** from the oven, take the loaves out of the pan immediately, and place on a cooling rack.

NOTE: To prepare your own dried apples, you will need twice the weight of the dried apples required. Preheat the oven to 400°F. Use a hard apple variety (such as Fuji, Gala or Granny Smith). Peel the apples and cut them into ½-inch dice. Spread them on a baking tray or broiler pan lined with a cooling rack and place the tray in the oven for 15–20 minutes. Make sure the apples are dried out until crunchy, then allow them to cool.

ADVANCED ENRICHED DOUGH
Breads and Rolls

Have you ever tasted something that was so good, tears came to your eyes? Prepare yourself for some strong emotions. The breads covered in this chapter are mostly indulgently delicious holiday breads, heavy on the sugar and fat—ones that you may already enjoy on special occasions.

CHAPTER NINE

CHALLAH IS A RICH AND GLOSSY BREAD that you might be tempted to make more frequently—some people bake it every week to celebrate the Jewish Sabbath. Leftover challah makes a great French toast.

Brioche is made with a super-rich dough that requires a special mixing technique called blitz (see page 130). There is so much butter and sugar in the recipe that it must be added in stages. Brioche is wonderful to eat on its own, but the dough can also be made into other elaborate breads. Craquelin, a Belgian specialty, is made from brioche dough with citrus zest and sugar cubes inserted into it.

Panettone is an Italian bread that is popular at Christmastime. It starts with a sponge and requires the blitz mixing technique, because the level of enrichment is hard to beat. Panettone not only contains milk, eggs and sugar—it is studded with orange and lemon zest, dark and golden raisins, and candied lemon and orange peel. There is also a version with chocolate and dried cherries. These breads tend to have a long shelf life because of the high sugar content.

If you're not a fan of most fruitcakes, you have some elegant alternatives. Take gugelhopf, for example, a European bread similar to a yeasted pound cake. It has a tender crumb enriched by but-ter, milk, eggs and sugar, along with candied orange peel, raisins and lemon zest. The bread is shaped into a ring and baked in an almond-lined Bundt pan. Gugelhopf is also sometimes glazed with a cream cheese and citrus zest mixture. It may sound excessive, but what the heck! You are probably going to make this only once a year.

Stollen is another European holiday bread loaded with fruit and nuts. Outwardly, stollen looks somewhat humble, but it has a complex flavor reminiscent of wine, especially when it is allowed to age for a month at room temperature. It sounds impossible that a bread could sit for that long and not go stale or grow moldy. However, stollen is very dense and contains lots of sugar and fat along with almond paste, candied fruit and raisins. Once it is baked, you roll the warm loaf in clarified butter to seal it. When it cools, it is covered in vanilla sugar, then wrapped extremely tightly to keep the air out. If you prepare this a month before you plan to eat it, you will experience it in its fullest flavor.

There are other classic recipes in this section as well, including Day of the Dead bread, hot cross buns and a variety of fruited and nut-filled breads that are great with coffee. If you already feel like you have a sugar hangover, just wait until you actually eat the special breads you bake. Be sure to share them with the people you love.

Hot Cross Buns

The historical origin of the defining cross pattern that these little breads bear is one debated amongst hungry scholars; agreed upon is the fact that the sweet buns are undoubtedly delicious. Comforting spices of nutmeg and cinnamon complement currants and candied lemon peel to create a treat that is certainly something to sing about.

yield: 12 rolls at 2 oz | FDT: 80°F
sponge: 30 minutes | bulk fermentation: 45–60 minutes | final fermentation: 45–60 minutes | bake: 375°F *and* 18–19 minutes

INGREDIENT	OUNCES	GRAMS	VOLUME	BAKERS %
SPONGE				
Milk, 90°F	11.4	323	1⅓ cups	50.4%
Malt syrup	0.2	6	⅛ tsp	0.9%
Bread flour	9.0	255	1¾ cups	39.8%
Yeast, instant dry	0.5	14	1 Tbsp	2.2%
FINAL DOUGH				
Sponge	21.1	598	•	93.3%
Butter, soft	7.5	99	½ cup	15.5%
Eggs	3.5	99	1 each	15.5%
Honey	0.8	23	1 Tbsp	3.5%
Lemon zest	0.3	9	2 tsp	1.3%
Bread flour	13.6	386	2¾ cups	60.2%
Sugar	3.5	99	½ cup	15.5%
Salt	0.5	14	2½ tsp	2.2%
Cinnamon, ground	¼ tsp	¼ tsp	¼ tsp	0.1%
Nutmeg, ground	¼ tsp	¼ tsp	¼ tsp	0.1%
Allspice, ground	¼ tsp	¼ tsp	¼ tsp	0.1%
Currants	6.7	190	½ cup	29.6%
Candied lemon peel, chopped (page 285)	2.8	79	¼ cup	12.4%
TOTAL	56.3	1596	•	249.3%

INGREDIENT	OUNCES	GRAMS	VOLUME	BAKERS %
GARNISHES				
Egg wash	as needed			
Hot Cross Topping (page 285)	as needed			
Coffe Cake Glaze (page 107)	6	170	1 cup	

1. TO MAKE THE SPONGE, combine the milk and malt in a bowl. In a separate bowl, combine the flour with the yeast, then add this mixture to the milk. Mix the sponge together by hand for 2 minutes to develop some gluten structure. Make sure all the ingredients are combined into a homogenous mass. Cover the bowl with plastic wrap, and allow the sponge to ferment in a warm place for 30 minutes, until double in size.

2. TO MAKE THE FINAL DOUGH, put the sponge in the bowl of a mixer with the butter, eggs, honey and zest. Place the bowl on a mixer fitted with a dough hook and mix the ingredients for 1 minute on low speed to break up the sponge. (The sponge can be further broken up by hand, if necessary.) Add the flour, sugar, salt and spices. Mix for 4 minutes on low speed, making sure to scrape down and flip the dough over at least twice during mixing. Increase the speed to medium, and continue to mix for another 4 minutes, making sure to scrape down and flip the dough over twice. The dough should have full gluten development. Add the currants and lemon peel and mix for 1 minute on low speed, making sure to scrape down and flip the dough over to ensure even distribution. Place the dough in a lightly oiled bowl large enough for it to double in size and cover with plastic wrap.

3. ALLOW the dough to rest and ferment in a warm place for 45–60 minutes, until when touched lightly the dough springs back halfway.

4. PLACE the dough on a lightly floured work surface and divide it into 2-oz pieces. Round each piece against the tabletop. Place the rounds seam-side down 4 by 5 on a baking tray lined with parchment paper. Brush the pieces lightly with egg wash and cover them lightly with oiled plastic wrap. Allow the dough to rest and ferment in a warm place for 45–60 minutes, until when touched lightly the dough springs back halfway.

5. PREHEAT the oven to 425°F. Prepare the topping for the hot cross buns and set aside.

6. PREPARE the buns for baking by removing the plastic wrap and lightly egg washing them again. Allow the dough to sit uncovered for 5 minutes. Place the prepared topping in a pastry bag fitted with a small, straight tip (or fill a plastic Ziploc bag with some topping and cut one of the corners from the bag to use as a tip). Pipe 1 line across the center of each roll from top to bottom and 1 line across the center, from left to right, to form a "+" on the top of each roll.

7. TRANSFER the tray to the oven and immediately reduce the temperature to 375°F. Bake for 14 minutes. Rotate the tray and bake for an additional 4–5 minutes, until light golden brown.

8. REMOVE from the oven and place the tray on a cooling rack. Prepare the glaze and lightly brush the buns with the glaze while hot. Make the topping the same day that you will bake the hot cross buns.

Candied Citrus Peel

yield: 20 citrus peels, quartered

INGREDIENT	OUNCES	GRAMS	VOLUME	BAKERS %
Lemon, orange or grapefruit peels, quartered	•	•	5 each	50.9%
Sugar	24	680	3 cups	45.2%
Light corn syrup	24	680	2 cups	50.0%
Water	16	454	2 cups	10.0%

1. Put the peels in a 4-quart saucepan and cover them with cold water. Bring to a boil, remove from the heat, and drain. Repeat this step 2 more times, using fresh water each time.

2. Bring the sugar, corn syrup and water to a simmer in a separate 4-quart saucepan. Add the blanched citrus peels, cover, and return to a simmer. Simmer for 90 minutes, stirring occasionally.

Remove the pan from the heat and allow the peels to cool to room temperature in the syrup.

3. Store the peels in the syrup in an airtight container in the refrigerator until needed, for up to 4 weeks.

Hot Cross Topping

yield: 12 oz

INGREDIENT	OUNCES	GRAMS	VOLUME	BAKERS %
Butter, melted	2.3	66	⅓ cup	50.9%
Milk, whole	2.1	59	¼ cup	45.2%
Sugar	2.3	65	⅓ cup	50.0%
Eggs	0.5	13	2½ tsp	10.0%
Vanilla extract	0.2	4	¼ tsp	3.3%
Lemon zest	0.1	2	1 tsp	1.7%
All-purpose flour	4.6	130	1 cup	100.0%
TOTAL	12.1	339	•	261.1%

PUT the butter in a mixing bowl. Add the milk, sugar, eggs, vanilla and zest. Place the bowl on a mixer fitted with a paddle attachment and mix for 1 minute on low speed. Add the flour and continue to mix until homogenous, scraping down the bowl as needed. After mixing, the topping is ready to be piped on top of the buns.

Hot Cross Buns and Gibassier

Gibassier

Named after Le Gibas, a Provençal mountain summit, these pastry-like twisted breads hail from the south of France and are a bit addictive. Characteristic flavors of sweetened orange, anise and a hint of olive oil permeate each buttered and vanilla sugar–dusted bite. Gibassiers are sure to elevate your morning bread basket or postdinner cup of coffee.

yield: **17 pieces at 3 oz** | FDT: **82°F**
sponge: **30 minutes** | bulk fermentation: **70 minutes** | final fermentation: **45–60 minutes** |
initial bake: **375°F** and **15 minutes** | final bake: **350°F** and **3–5 minutes**

INGREDIENT	OUNCES	GRAMS	VOLUME	BAKERS %
SPONGE				
Milk, 90°F	5.0	142	½ cup + 2 Tbsp	22.9%
Malt syrup	0.1	3	¼ tsp	0.5%
Bread flour	4.7	133	1 cup	21.6%
Yeast, instant dry	0.3	9	2½ tsp	1.4%
FINAL DOUGH				
Sponge	10.1	287	•	46.4%
Eggs	5.0	142	3 each	22.9%
Olive oil	2.8	79	⅓ cup	12.8%
Orange zest	0.8	21	3 Tbsp	3.4%
Bread flour	17.1	485	3½ cups	78.4%
Sugar	4.4	125	⅔ cup	20.2%
Salt	0.4	11	2 tsp	1.8%
Butter, soft	3.2	91	6 Tbsp	14.7%
Anise seed	0.2	6	2 Tbsp	0.9%
Candied orange peel, chopped (page 285)	3.3	94	½ cup	15.1%
TOTAL	47.3	1341	•	216.6%
GARNISHES				
Egg wash	as needed			
Butter, melted	8.0	227	1 cup	
Vanilla sugar (see Note)	8.0	227	1 cup	

1. **TO MAKE THE SPONGE,** combine the milk and malt in a bowl. In a separate bowl, combine the flour with the yeast, then add this mixture to the milk. Mix the sponge together by hand for 2 minutes to develop some gluten structure and ensure that all the ingredients are combined into a homogenous mass. Cover the bowl with plastic wrap and allow the sponge to ferment in a warm area for 30 minutes, until double in size.

2. **TO MAKE THE FINAL DOUGH,** put the sponge, eggs, oil and zest in the bowl of a mixer fitted with a dough hook. Mix for 1 minute on low speed to break up the sponge. (The sponge can be further broken up by hand, if necessary.) Add the flour, sugar and salt. Mix for 6 minutes on low speed, making sure to scrape down and flip the dough over twice during the mixing time. Increase the speed to high and mix for an additional 2 minutes, making sure to scrape down and flip the dough over twice. On medium speed, add the soft butter in 2 additions, making sure to scrape down and flip the dough over before each addition. Mix the dough for 1 additional minute. The dough should have developed full gluten structure. Add the anise seed and orange peel and mix on low for 30 seconds to combine. Scrape down and flip the dough over, then mix for an additional 30 seconds. Place the dough in a lightly oiled bowl large enough for it to double in size and cover with plastic wrap.

3. **ALLOW** the dough to rest and ferment in a warm place for 60 minutes, until when touched lightly the dough springs back halfway.

4. **PLACE** the dough on a lightly floured work surface and divide it into 3-oz pieces. Round each piece against the tabletop, then cover the pieces and allow them to rest on the table for 10 minutes.

5. **SHAPE** each piece into a 6-inch oblong. Using a sharp blade, make 4 widthwise cuts in the center of each piece. Place the pieces of dough on a baking tray lined with parchment paper, either left in an oblong shape or arched into a horseshoe shape. If using the horseshoe shape, you can place 3 pieces down the length of each side of the tray and 2 in the middle, offset from the other pieces. With the oblong shape, you can fit 2 rows of 4 pieces each down the length of the tray.

6. **BRUSH** the pieces of dough with egg wash and lightly cover with plastic wrap. Allow the dough to rest and ferment in a warm place for 45–60 minutes, until when touched lightly the dough springs back halfway.

7. **PREHEAT** the oven to 400°F.

8. **BRUSH** each piece again with egg wash, place the trays in the oven, and immediately reduce the temperature to 375°F. Bake for 15 minutes, then rotate the trays and lower the temperature to 350°F. Bake for an additional 3–5 minutes, until golden brown.

9. **TAKE** the bread out of the oven, allow to cool for 5 minutes on racks, then brush each piece with melted butter and roll the top in vanilla sugar. Allow the gibassiers to cool on racks over baking trays.

NOTE: To make vanilla sugar, split and scrape 2 vanilla beans into 3 pounds of sugar. Mix together with a wooden spoon and let stand for 2 weeks. Use as you would regular sugar.

GUGELHOPF

A traditional European bread, gugelhopf is known for its understated sweetness and characteristic ring shape. Gugelhopf doesn't require embellishment—this delicate yeast bread is delicious as is.

yield: 2 pieces at 20 oz | FDT: 82°F
sponge: 30 minutes | bulk fermentation: 55–70 minutes | final fermentation: 45–60 minutes | bake: 375°F and 27–30 minutes

INGREDIENT	OUNCES	GRAMS	VOLUME	BAKERS %
SPONGE				
Milk, 90°F	5.4	153	⅔ cup	31.6%
Malt syrup	0.2	6	¼ tsp	1.2%
Bread flour	6.4	181	1⅓ cups	37.4%
Yeast, instant dry	0.3	9	2½ tsp	0.8%
FINAL DOUGH				
Butter, soft	2.7	77	⅓ cup	15.8%
Sugar	2.7	77	⅓ cup	15.8%
Lemon zest	0.3	9	3 tsp	1.8%
Eggs, at room temperature	1.6	45	1 each	9.4%
Egg yolks, at room temperature	0.5	14	2 each	2.9%
Sponge	12.3	349	•	71.0%
Milk, 90°F	5.8	164	⅔ cup	33.9%
Bread flour	10.7	303	2¼ cups	62.6%
Salt	0.4	11	2 tsp	2.3%
Raisins	4.3	122	¾ cup	25.1%
Candied orange peel, chopped (page 285)	1.4	40	¼ cup	8.2%
TOTAL	42.7	1211	•	248.8%

INGREDIENT	OUNCES	GRAMS	VOLUME	BAKERS %
GARNISHES				
Almonds, sliced	2.0	57	½ cup	
Butter, soft	as needed			
Cream Cheese Glaze (page 106)	as needed			

1. TO MAKE THE SPONGE, combine the milk and malt in a bowl. In a separate bowl, combine the flour with the yeast, then add this mixture to the milk. Mix the sponge together by hand for 2 minutes to develop some gluten structure, making sure all the ingredients are combined in a homogenous mass. Cover the bowl with plastic wrap and allow the sponge to ferment in a warm place for 30 minutes, until doubled in size.

2. TO MAKE THE FINAL DOUGH, put the butter, sugar and zest in a mixer fitted with a paddle attachment. Mix on low speed for 2 minutes, making sure to scrape down the sides of the bowl twice. Mix for an additional minute on medium speed, scraping the bowl again. While the mixer is on medium speed, add the eggs and yolks in 3 additions, pausing between each addition to scrape the bowl and allow the batter to come back together. Add the sponge and milk to the bowl and mix on low speed for 2 minutes to break up the sponge. Change the attachment to a dough hook, then add the flour and salt and mix on low speed for 4 minutes, making sure to scrape down and flip the dough over twice. Mix for 4 minutes on medium speed, making sure to scrape down and flip the dough over. The dough should be pulling off the sides of the bowl and have good gluten development, but it will still be a little tacky. Add the raisins and orange peel and mix on low speed for 1 more minute to combine, making sure to scrape down and flip the dough over. Place the dough in a lightly oiled bowl large enough for it to double in size and cover with plastic wrap.

3. ALLOW the dough to rest and ferment in a warm place for 45–60 minutes, until when lightly touched the dough springs back halfway.

4. PLACE the dough on a lightly floured work surface and divide it into two 20-oz pieces. Round each piece against the tabletop, then allow the dough to rest on the table, covered, for 10 minutes.

5. PREPARE two 10-inch gugelhoph molds or bundt pans by rubbing soft butter on the sides and bottom of each pan and placing half the almond slices in each pan.

6. FLOUR each piece lightly over and under. With floured fingers, make a hole in the center of each piece of dough, working it out so that the dough will fit into the mold. Place the dough into the molds, and allow it to rest and ferment in a warm place for 45–60 minutes, until when lightly touched the dough springs back halfway.

7. PREHEAT the oven to 400°F.

8. PLACE the molds in the oven and immediately reduce the temperature to 375°F. Bake for 15 minutes. Rotate the pans and bake for an additional 12–15 minutes, until golden brown. (Note: do not bake on a baking tray; bake in the pan directly on the oven rack.)

9. REMOVE the pans from the oven and immediately transfer the bread from the pans to a cooling rack. Glaze, once cooled, with Cream Cheese Glaze.

CHALLAH

This is a traditional Jewish bread that is eaten on the Sabbath and holidays. The two loaves that are blessed at each meal reflect the restriction on cooking during the Sabbath and holidays. As such, a second loaf must be prepared ahead of time for consumption the next day. Typically challah is braided using six strands. Each strand is lightly floured before braiding, so the pieces have more definition between each strand. Here it is made with a sponge to give the yeast and gluten a chance to get going before eggs, sugar and honey are added.

yield: 2 loaves at 24 oz | FDT: 82°F
sponge: 30 minutes | bulk fermentation: 45–60 minutes | final fermentation: 75–90 minutes |
initial bake: 375°F *and* 15 minutes | final bake: 350°F *and* 10–15 minutes

INGREDIENT	OUNCES	GRAMS	VOLUME	BAKERS %
SPONGE				
Milk, 90°F	3.0	86	⅓ cup	11.3%
Malt syrup	0.1	3	⅛ tsp	0.4%
Bread flour	3.0	86	⅔ cup	11.3%
Yeast, instant dry	0.3	9	2½ tsp	1.1%
FINAL DOUGH				
Sponge	6.4	184	•	24.1%
Water, 92°F	3.4	97	⅓ cup + 2 Tbsp	12.8%
Vegetable oil	2.4	69	⅓ cup	9.1%
Honey	1.4	40	2 Tbsp	5.3%
Eggs	6.0	169	3 each	22.3%
Egg yolks	1.4	40	2 each	5.3%
Bread flour	23.7	672	5 cups	88.7%
Sugar	2.7	77	⅓ cup	10.2%
Salt	0.5	14	2½ tsp	1.9%
TOTAL	47.9	1362	•	179.7%
GARNISHES				
Egg wash	as needed			
Sesame seeds (optional)	as needed			

1. TO MAKE THE SPONGE, combine the milk and malt in a bowl. In a separate bowl, combine the flour with the yeast, and then add this mixture to the milk. Mix the sponge together by hand for 2 minutes to develop some gluten structure. Make sure all the ingredients are combined into a homogenous mass. Cover the bowl with plastic wrap and allow the sponge to ferment in a warm place for 30 minutes, until doubled in size.

2. TO MAKE THE FINAL DOUGH, put the sponge in the bowl of a mixer with the water, oil, honey, eggs and yolks. Place the bowl on a mixer fitted with a dough hook. Mix for 1 minute on low speed to break up the sponge. The sponge can also be broken up by hand a little. Add the flour, sugar and salt. Mix for 8 minutes on low speed, making sure to scrape down and flip the dough over at least 3 times during this time. The dough should have very good gluten development. Place the dough in a lightly oiled bowl large enough for it to double in size and cover with plastic wrap.

3. ALLOW the dough to rest and ferment in a warm place for 45–60 minutes, until when lightly touched the dough springs back halfway.

4. PLACE the dough on a lightly floured work surface and divide it into 4-oz pieces for a 6-strand braid or into 6-oz pieces for a 4-strand braid. Preshape the pieces into 3-inch oblongs (see illustrations in Appendix on page 326). Keep them covered with plastic wrap.

5. FOR A 4-STRAND BRAID, see page 329 for braiding instructions.

6. PLACE the 2 loaves widthwise on a baking tray lined with parchment paper. Egg wash the loaves and lightly cover with plastic wrap. Allow the dough to rest and ferment in a warm place for 45 minutes, until when lightly touched the dough springs back halfway. Egg wash again and allow it to ferment for another 30–45 minutes, until when lightly touched the dough springs back halfway.

7. PREHEAT the oven to 400°F.

8. EGG WASH the loaves a third time and roll the tops in seeds, if desired.

9. TRANSFER the tray to the oven and immediately reduce the temperature to 375°F. Bake for 15 minutes. Rotate the tray, reduce the temperature to 350°F, and bake for an additional 10–15 minutes, until a deep golden brown.

10. PLACE the tray on a cooling rack and allow to cool.

NOTE: For a 6-strand braid, roll each piece out to 12 inches (see illustrations on page 326). See illustrations on page 330 for braiding instructions.

VARIATION

CHALLAH WITH GOLDEN RAISINS

Golden raisins add an extra punch of sweetness to challah. Plump the raisins first in 12 oz or 1½ cups warm water for 15 minutes. Prepare the dough as for Challah (page 291). Once the dough has reached good gluten development, add 8.8 oz (249 g/1¾ cups) plumped golden raisins and mix for 2 minutes on low speed, making sure to scrape down and flip the dough over. Proceed as for the Challah recipe.

Challah and Gugelhopf

BRIOCHE

Brioche is an enriched bread that is similar to but usually sweeter than challah. It is used as a foundation for many desserts and is also a treat on its own. Due to its richness, it is usually served in small portions in a *tête* shape, which means "head" in French. A small ball of dough crowns the larger muffin shape below. You will need brioche molds for this, or you can use 4-oz muffin cups.

yield: 26 brioches at 2 oz or 2 loaves at 25 oz | FDT: 78°F
retard: overnight | rest: 15 minutes | bulk fermentation: 2 hours | bake: 375°F *and* 15–17 minutes

INGREDIENT	OUNCES	GRAMS	VOLUME	BAKERS %
Eggs, 40°F (cold)	8.6	244	4 each	40.2%
Butter, soft (#1)	3.5	99	½ cup	16.4%
Milk, 40°F (cold)	7.7	218	1 cup	36.0%
Malt syrup	0.1	3	⅛ tsp	0.5%
Bread flour	21.4	607	4½ cups	100.0%
Yeast, instant dry	0.3	9	2½ tsp	1.4%
Salt	0.6	17	1 Tbsp	2.8%
Butter, soft (#2)	8.0	227	1 cup	37.4%
Sugar	3.2	91	½ cup	15.0%
TOTAL	53.4	1515	•	249.7%
GARNISH				
Egg wash	as needed			

1. MAKE the dough the day before you want to serve the brioche. Place the eggs, butter #1, the milk and malt in the bowl of a mixer fitted with a paddle attachment. Combine the flour and yeast and add to the bowl. Add the salt and mix for 4 minutes on low speed, making sure to scrape down and flip the dough twice. Mix for 5 minutes on medium speed, making sure to scrape down and flip the dough twice, and replace the paddle with the dough hook attachment. Add half (4 oz) of butter #2 gradually on medium speed over 2 minutes, making sure to scrape down and flip the dough over. The dough should stay together on the hook. Add the sugar gradually on medium speed over 2 minutes, making sure to scrape down and flip the dough over. Add the remaining (4 oz) butter on medium speed over 3 minutes, making sure to scrape

down and flip the dough over twice. The dough should feel very tacky, but should have full gluten development. If you test the gluten window (see page 28), it will be able to form a very thin membrane and will be strong. Place the dough in a bowl lined with parchment paper large enough for it to double in size and cover with plastic wrap. Refrigerate overnight.

2. REMOVE the dough from the refrigerator and place it on a lightly floured work surface. Divide the dough into 2-oz pieces for a traditional *tête* shape. Lightly flour the dough and round each piece against the tabletop. Place the rounds in a lightly floured bowl. Put the dough in the freezer for 15 minutes to allow the butter in it to chill back down and to make it easier to work with.

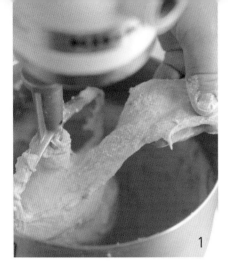

1. Mix the ingredients except the butter until they form a smooth, homogenous mass.

2. After the butter is added, the dough will become even smoother and silkier. It should begin to pull away from the sides of the bowl, sticking to itself instead of the equipment.

3. REMOVE the dough from the freezer; it should be slightly stiff. Lightly roll each piece in flour, then work it into a 3-inch oblong. Use a dough scraper to cut two thirds of the dough from each piece (see photographs on page 296). Round the larger piece and slightly flatten it. Use the end of a wooden spoon dipped in flour to poke a hole in the middle of each large piece. With your thumbs and index fingers lightly floured, work out the holes so that they are large enough to place the smaller piece of dough in the center all the way to the bottom. Place each ring of dough in a lightly oiled brioche mold, then work it into the sides, keeping your index fingers straight up and not slanted with the mold. Round the smaller pieces of dough. Lightly roll each piece in flour and knock off the excess flour. Place 1 smaller piece of dough in the hole of each larger piece. It should sit down in the hole and not be sitting on the top.

4. LIGHTLY egg wash and cover each piece, making sure not to have excess egg wash pooling down the side of the piece in the mold. Cover with oiled plastic wrap and allow to ferment for 2 hours. You will need to egg wash every 45 minutes to ensure that the surface doesn't dry out.

5. PREHEAT the oven to 425°F.

6. EGG WASH the dough, then bake at 375°F for 12 minutes. Rotate and bake for an additional 3–5 minutes, until golden brown.

7. REMOVE from the pans immediately and place on a cooling rack.

For Pan Loaves

Follow step #1 at left, and then continue as directed below.

2. REMOVE the dough from the refrigerator and place it on a lightly floured work surface. Divide the dough into two 25-oz loaves, working with a little flour, then shape each piece into an 8-inch oblong.

3. ALLOW the dough to relax for 10 minutes, covered.

4. SHAPE the oblongs tightly on a lightly floured work surface to 12 inches. Place in an oiled pan.

5. LIGHTLY egg wash and cover each piece, making sure not to have excess egg wash pooling down the side of the piece in the mold. Cover with oiled plastic wrap and allow to ferment for 2½–3 hours in a warm place. You will need to egg wash every 45 minutes to ensure that the surface doesn't dry out.

6. PREHEAT the oven to 400°F.

7. EGG WASH the dough, then bake at 350°F for 20 minutes. Rotate and bake for an additional 8–10 minutes, until golden brown.

8. REMOVE from the pan immediately and place on a cooling rack.

1. Cut one portion of a 3-inch oblong of brioche dough so that it is one third the size of the other piece. This will be your center.

2. Shape the larger piece into a disc about 1½ inches high. Use the handle of a wooden spoon to make a hole in the center of the disc for a uniform size and shape.

3. Place the disc into a lightly oiled brioche mold and gently expand the center hole until the outside edges of the dough are in the fluted grooves of the mold. Try to have an even width of dough around the whole mold.

4. Shape the center piece into a ball, lightly flour, and gently place it in the mold. Try not to flatten it as you guide it in.

5. These steps can be done as an assembly line for greater speed and accuracy. Remember to work gently with the dough so as to avoid overworking it and creating a tough crumb texture.

CRAQUELIN

Try working in an assembly-line fashion when making these rolls. Complete one step for all of the portions of dough and then continue on with the next step. This will help familiarize your muscles with the necessary motions and have a more uniform end result.

yield: **15 rolls** | FDT: **80°F**

retard: **overnight** | bulk fermentation: **2–2½ hours** | bake: **375°F** *and* 20–22 minutes

INGREDIENT	OUNCES	GRAMS	VOLUME	BAKERS %
Brioche dough #1	17.5	496	•	37.4%
Brioche dough #2	29.3	831	•	62.6%
Sugar cubes	7.4	210	1 cup	15.8%
Lemon zest	0.5	14	1 Tbsp	1.1%
TOTAL	54.7	1551	•	116.9%
GARNISHES				
Egg wash	as needed			
Coarse sugar (optional)	as needed			

1. MAKE a recipe of Brioche dough (page 294) the day before you want to serve the craquelin. Divide the dough into 2 portions: 17.5 oz and 29.3 oz. Place each portion in a container that is lightly floured and cover. Refrigerate overnight.

2. TO PREPARE THE CRAQUELIN, remove brioche dough #1 (17.5 oz) from the refrigerator and place it on a lightly floured work surface. Divide the dough into 1-oz pieces. Round each piece against the tabletop using a little flour. Place each piece on a baking tray dusted with a little flour, then put the tray in the freezer for 20 minutes.

3. REMOVE brioche dough #2 (29.3 oz) from the refrigerator and place it on a lightly floured work surface. Chop it up into 1-inch cubes.

4. PLACE half of brioche dough #2, half of the sugar cubes and half of the lemon zest in a bowl. Add the other half of brioche dough #2, sugar cubes and zest. Place the bowl on a mixer fitted with a paddle attachment and mix for 30 seconds on low speed. Scrape down and flip the dough over. Mix for another 15 seconds,

until just combined. Don't overmix; the dough should contain chunks of sugar.

5. PLACE the dough on a lightly floured work surface and divide it into 2.5-oz pieces. Round each piece against the tabletop using a little flour.

6. LINE 15 muffin cups with paper liners, then spray them with oil.

7. REMOVE brioche dough #1 from the freezer. Dip each piece in flour, then roll it out to a 4-inch disc (see photographs on page 298). Egg wash the top of the dough balls that contain the sugar cubes. Wrap 1 piece of flat dough around each brioche ball with sugar cubes, covering the top and sides but leaving the bottom exposed. Place each piece in a muffin cup with the open end on the bottom. Cover the dough and let it rest and ferment in a warm place for 2–2½ hours, until when lightly touched the dough springs back halfway. Remember that this has a lot of butter in it. If the butter gets too warm, it will melt before baking, which will prevent the dough from rising as much.

8. PREHEAT the oven to 400°F.

9. LIGHTLY egg wash each piece of dough, then use a pair of scissors to cut a slight incision across the center of each piece. Sprinkle each dough piece with a pinch of coarse sugar, if desired.

10. TRANSFER the pans to the oven and immediately reduce the temperature to 375°F. Bake for 14 minutes, then rotate the pans. Bake for another 6–8 minutes, until golden brown.

11. REMOVE from the oven and place the pans on a cooling rack. After 5 minutes, remove the craquelins from the pans and place them on the cooling rack.

NOTE: It is important to not overmix the dough while incorporating the sugar cubes. You want to have chunks of sugar throughout the dough. After baking, this leaves large sugar pockets that are unique to this bread.

1. Roll brioche dough #1 into 4-inch circles. Work on a lightly floured surface. This will help prevent the dough from sticking, but will also keep excess flour from getting in between the circles and dough #2.

2. Egg wash the circles and wrap each one most of the way around a ball of brioche dough #2. Don't stretch the circle to fit the ball.

3. Place each ball in a muffin cup with the exposed part of the ball facing down. The butter in the dough will make the bread rise beautifully in the oven.

4. Top to bottom: Craquelin dough on the left and brioche dough on the right; Roll the brioche dough into a circle; Cover the craquelin with the brioche; Pull to cover completely; Place seamside down into a paper baking form.

Craquelin and Babka

Conchas

Spanish for "shells," conchas are roll-sized baked goods named for their resemblance to a spiral shell. The slightly sweet dough is crowned with a cocoa-flavored topping scored in a concentric circular design; this recipe yields a unique pairing that is as visually whimsical as it is delicious.

This bread is a two-day process. The dough is mixed, fermented and shaped on the first day and then refrigerated to retard overnight. The Conchas Topping (pages 302–303) should also be made on the first day and kept in the refrigerator until needed.

yield: **18 rolls at 2 oz** | FDT: **82°F**
sponge: **30 minutes** | bulk fermentation: **45–60 minutes** | retard: **overnight** | final fermentation: **60–75 minutes**
initial bake: **375°F** *and* **15 minutes** | final bake: **350°F** *and* **3–5 minutes**

INGREDIENT	OUNCES	GRAMS	VOLUME	BAKERS %
SPONGE				
Milk, 90°F	8.5	241	1 cup	46.7%
Malt syrup	0.1	3	⅛ tsp	0.5%
Bread flour	9.1	258	1¾ cups + 3 Tbsp	50.0%
Yeast, instant dry	0.3	9	2¼ tsp	1.6%
FINAL DOUGH				
Eggs	3.2	91	2 each	17.6%
Sponge	18.0	511	•	98.9%
Bread flour	9.1	258	1¾ cups + 3 Tbsp	50.0%
Sugar	5.4	153	¾ cup	29.7%
Salt	0.3	9	1½ tsp	1.6%
Butter, soft	3.7	105	½ cup	20.3%
TOTAL	39.7	1127	•	218.1%
GARNISH				
Conchas Topping (pages 302–303)	as needed			

1. **TO MAKE THE SPONGE,** combine the milk and malt in a bowl. In a separate bowl, combine the flour with the yeast, then add this mixture to the milk. Mix the sponge together by hand for 2 minutes to develop some gluten structure. Make sure all the ingredients are combined in a homogenous mass. Cover the bowl with plastic wrap and allow the sponge to ferment in a warm area for 30 minutes, until doubled in size.

2. **TO MAKE THE FINAL DOUGH,** put the eggs and sponge in the bowl of a mixer fitted with a paddle attachment. Mix for 1 minute on low speed to break up the sponge. (The sponge can be broken up further by hand, if necessary.) Add the flour, sugar and salt. Mix for 6 minutes on low speed, making sure to scrape down and flip the dough over twice. Mix on medium for 2 minutes, making sure to scrape down and flip the dough over twice. The dough should have developed some gluten structure. Switch to a dough hook. While mixing on medium speed over 3 minutes, add the butter in 2 additions, scraping the bowl down and flipping the dough over before each addition. Then mix the dough for 1 additional minute. The dough should be tacky but with full gluten development. Place the dough in a lightly oiled bowl large enough for it to double in size and cover with plastic wrap.

3. **ALLOW** the dough to rest and ferment in a warm place for 45–60 minutes, until when lightly touched the dough springs back halfway.

4. **PLACE** the dough on a lightly floured work surface and divide it into 2-oz pieces. Round each piece against the tabletop. Arrange the pieces 3 by 3 on baking trays lined with parchment paper. Wrap the entire trays with plastic wrap and refrigerate overnight to retard the dough.

5. **PREPARE** the Conchas Topping on the same day as the dough and refrigerate until the next day.

6. **TO FINISH THE CONCHAS,** remove the trays from the refrigerator and allow the dough to rest at room temperature for 10 minutes.

7. **YOU WILL NEED** a spray bottle or a bowl of water with a brush and a set of round cookie cutters. Uncover the dough pieces, lightly flatten them with your hands, and spray or brush their tops with water.

8. **DIVIDE** the topping in half and refrigerate half for use later. Work 1 piece at a time and lightly flatten it with your hands. Flour the work surface and the topping. Roll the topping out into an 11 by 8-inch rectangle. Using a 4-inch round cookie cutter, cut a piece of the topping the same circumference as the dough pieces (see photographs on page 302). Place 1 topping cutout on top of 1 dough piece and flatten to adhere it. Repeat this procedure until all the dough pieces have a topping. (Work any excess topping into the unused topping and store in the refrigerator.) Using the round cookie cutters, cut concentric circles into the topping to create a shell (concha) design. Toward the end, you may wish to use a slightly smaller cutter to make the design more proportionately correct.

9. **RETURN** the dough to the trays and lightly cover with plastic wrap. Allow the dough to rest and ferment in a warm place for 60–75 minutes, until when lightly touched the dough springs back halfway.

10. **PREHEAT** the oven to 400°F.

11. **TRANSFER** the trays to the oven and immediately reduce the temperature to 375°F. Bake for 15 minutes. Rotate the trays, reduce the temperature to 350°F, and bake for an additional 3–5 minutes, until golden brown.

12. **REMOVE** from the oven and allow the conchas to cool on the trays on a cooling rack.

Flatten balls of dough to make discs and
put them on a parchment paper–lined
baking tray. Brush them lightly with water
to help the topping stick to the dough. Roll
the topping out thinly and cut it with a round
cookie cutter. Try to cut the circles as close
together as possible to avoid a lot of scraps.

Place the toppings on the discs of dough and
use the cutter to create a design of concentric circles. Or hold various sizes of cutters
together to indent a unique pattern.

Conchas

Concha Toppings

These toppings provide a variety of options to create visual interest for this dessert.

Chocolate Topping | yield: 12 oz

INGREDIENT	OUNCES	GRAMS	VOLUME	BAKERS %
All-purpose flour	4.5	128	1 cup + 1 Tbsp	91.8%
Powdered sugar, sifted	3.5	99	1 cup	71.4%
Cocoa powder, unsweetened, sifted	0.4	11	2 Tbsp	8.2%
Butter, soft	1.8	50	¼ cup	35.7%
Shortening	1.9	54	¼ cup	38.8%
TOTAL	12.1	342	•	245.9%

1. SIFT the flour, sugar, and cocoa powder together. Repeat the
sifting 2 more times, then set aside.

2. IN A MIXER fitted with a paddle attachment, cream the butter
and shortening for 3 minutes on high speed, making sure to scrape
down the bowl and paddle at least once during this process. Add the
sifted flour blend and mix on low speed until homogenous, making
sure to scrape down the bowl and paddle twice.

3. PLACE the dough on a work surface and knead it together by
hand, then flatten it into a disc. Wrap the dough in plastic wrap
and refrigerate until needed.

Vanilla Topping | yield: 12 oz

INGREDIENT	OUNCES	GRAMS	VOLUME	BAKERS %
All-purpose flour	4.7	132	1 cup + 1 Tbsp	100.0%
Powdered sugar	3.5	99	1 cup	75.3%
Butter, soft	0.9	26	2 Tbsp	19.4%
Shortening	2.7	75	⅓ cup	57.0%
Vanilla extract	0.4	11	2½ tsp	8.6%
TOTAL	12.2	343	•	260.3%

1. SIFT the flour and sugar together. Repeat the sifting 2 more times, then set aside.

2. IN A MIXER fitted with a paddle attachment, cream the butter, shortening and vanilla for about 3 minutes on high speed, making sure to scrape down the bowl and paddle at least once during the process. Add the sifted flour blend and mix on low speed until homogenous, making sure to scrape down the bowl and paddle twice.

3. PLACE the dough on a work surface and knead it together by hand, then flatten it into a disc. Wrap the dough in plastic wrap and refrigerate until needed.

Vanilla-Pecan Topping | yield: 12 oz

INGREDIENT	OUNCES	GRAMS	VOLUME	BAKERS %
All-purpose flour	4.4	125	1 cup + 1 Tbsp	100.0%
Powdered sugar	2.9	82	¾ cup + 1 Tbsp	65.9%
Pecan halves	1.3	35	⅓ cup	28.4%
Butter, soft	0.8	23	¾ cup + 1 Tbsp	18.2%
Shortening	2.3	65	⅓ cup	52.3%
Vanilla extract	0.3	9	2 tsp	6.8%
TOTAL	12.0	339	•	271.6%

1. SIFT the flour and sugar together. Repeat the sifting 2 more times, then set aside.

2. CHOP the pecans into pea-sized pieces, either by hand or using a food processor, and set aside.

3. IN A MIXER fitted with a paddle attachment, cream the butter, shortening and vanilla for 3 minutes on high speed, making sure to scrape down the bowl and paddle at least once during this process. Add the sifted flour blend and chopped pecans and mix on low speed until homogenous, making sure to scrape down the bowl and paddle twice.

4. PLACE the dough on a work surface and knead it together by hand, then flatten it into a disc. Wrap the dough in plastic wrap and refrigerate until needed.

Day of the Dead Bread

In Mexico, *pan de muerto* is made during the Day of the Dead holiday. Traditionally sweet and flavored with anise, the bread is ceremoniously placed on altars or brought to gravesites as offerings to those who have passed away.

yield: **2 loaves at 27 oz** | FDT: **82°F** | *sponge:* **30 minutes** | *bulk fermentation:* **40 minutes**
final fermentation: **45–60 minutes** | *initial bake:* **375°F** *and* **20 minutes** | *final bake:* **350°F** *and* **8–10 minutes**

INGREDIENT	OUNCES	GRAMS	VOLUME	BAKERS %
SPONGE				
Milk, 90°F	6.5	184	¾ cup	31.3%
Malt syrup	0.1	3	⅛ tsp	0.5%
Bread flour	10.4	295	2 cups + 2½ Tbsp	50.0%
Yeast, instant dry	0.3	9	2¼ tsp	1.4%
FINAL DOUGH				
Sponge	17.3	491	•	83.2%
Eggs	7.1	201	4 each	34.1%
Butter, soft	9.8	278	1¼ cups	47.1%
Bread flour	10.4	295	2 cups	50.0%
Salt	0.4	11	2 tsp	1.9%
Sugar	5.1	145	¾ cup	24.5%
Orange zest	1.1	31	1 Tbsp	5.3%
Lemon zest	0.3	9	1 tsp	1.4%
Vanilla extract	0.2	6	1¼ tsp	1.0%
Cinnamon, ground	0.1	3	1 tsp	0.5%
TOTAL	51.8	1470	•	249.0%
GARNISHES				
Bread flour	3.3	94	⅔ cup	
Egg wash	as needed			
Butter, melted	8.0	170	1 cup	
Vanilla sugar (see page 288)	8.0	170	1 cup	

1. **TO MAKE THE SPONGE,** combine the milk and malt in a bowl. In a separate bowl, combine the flour with the yeast, then add this mixture to the milk. Mix the sponge together by hand for 2 minutes to develop some gluten structure. Make sure all the ingredients are combined in a homogenous mass. Cover the bowl with plastic wrap and allow the sponge to ferment in a warm area for 30 minutes, until when lightly touched the dough springs back halfway.

2. **TO MAKE THE FINAL DOUGH,** put the sponge in the bowl of a mixer fitted with a paddle attachment. Add the eggs and about 3 oz of the soft butter (be sure that the butter is soft, but not melting), and mix for 1 minute on low speed to break up the sponge. (The sponge can also be broken up by hand, if necessary.) Add the flour and salt. Mix for 6 minutes on low speed, making sure to scrape down and flip the dough over in the bowl twice during the process. Mix for an additional 2 minutes on medium speed, making sure to scrape down and flip the dough over twice. The dough should have developed some gluten structure. Switch to the dough hook attachment. While mixing on medium speed, add 3 oz of the remaining butter in 2 additions, making sure to scrape down and flip the dough over before each addition. Reduce to medium speed, and add the sugar, orange and lemon zests, vanilla and cinnamon. Mix on medium speed for 1 minute, then increase to high speed and mix for another minute, making sure to scrape down and flip the dough over. Add the remaining soft butter and continue mixing on medium speed for 2 more minutes. Scrape down and flip the dough over twice during this time. The dough should have full gluten development but still feel slightly tacky. Take the dough out of the bowl and cut off 9 oz to make the "bones." Place the remaining dough in a lightly oiled bowl large enough for it to double in size and cover with plastic wrap.

3. **PUT** the 9 oz of dough for the bones back into the mixer, along with the bread flour for finishing, and mix on low speed until homogenous. Place the bone dough in a separate lightly oiled bowl and cover with plastic wrap. Leave it at room temperature.

4. **ALLOW** the dough to rest and ferment in a warm place for 20 minutes, until when lightly touched the dough springs back halfway.

5. **PUT** the main bread dough on a lightly floured work surface. Fold the dough over, put it back in the bowl, and cover for 20 minutes. Leave it at room temperature.

6. **PUT** the bone dough on a lightly floured work surface and divide it into 1.5-oz pieces. Keeping the dough pieces covered with a cloth while working, shape each piece into a 3-inch oblong. Roll the dough back and forth, applying slight outward pressure with the palms of your hands, until each piece is about 3 inches in length. Keep the dough pieces covered until ready to use.

7. **PUT** the main bread dough back on a lightly floured work surface and divide it into two 23-oz pieces. Round each piece against the tabletop. Place each round on a separate baking tray lined with parchment paper. Flour the center of each piece and use your fingertips to make an indent about 2 inches in diameter.

8. **MAKE** the bones (you will need 3 for each loaf) by rolling each piece to about 6 inches in length, and then use your fingers to make 3 evenly spaced depressions along the pieces. Lay 3 bones over each loaf, so that they intersect in the center and divide the loaf into 6 equal sections (see photograph). Round the additional bone dough pieces. Place a round of dough in the center of each loaf to cover where the 3 bones cross. Egg wash each loaf and cover lightly with oiled plastic wrap. Allow the dough to rest and ferment in a warm place for 45–60 minutes, until when lightly touched the dough springs back halfway.

9. **PREHEAT** the oven to 400°F.

10. **EGG WASH** each loaf again and transfer to the oven. Immediately reduce the temperature to 375°F. Bake for 20 minutes. Rotate the trays, reduce the temperature to 350°F, and bake for an additional 8–10 minutes, until golden brown.

11. **REMOVE** the bread from the oven and allow it to cool for 5 minutes, then brush each piece with melted butter and roll in vanilla sugar. Allow the loaves to cool on a cooling rack.

Use your fingers to make a 2-inch indent in the dough. These pieces will get very large, so place each one on its own baking tray.

Roll out "snakes" of dough for the bones. Place your fingers evenly apart along the snake to make indents. There should be three bones for each bread loaf. Cross the bones over the center indent. Put a small circle of dough over the top, where the bones cross.

After baking, brush each loaf with melted butter and dust it with vanilla sugar. Pour the excess sugar off over a piece of parchment paper in order to use it on other loaves.

CHOCOLATE AND PECAN BABKA

Babka is a traditional enriched Eastern European bread. It contains a sweet filling, but that filling changes between cultures. Some use only fruit, while others use a chocolate or cinnamon filling. The addition of pecans here gives an added crunch (see photograph on page 299).

yield: **4 loaves at 21 oz** | FDT: **82°F**

retard: **overnight** | rest: **30 minutes** | final fermentation: **2½–3 hours** | bake: **350°F** *and* **45–50 minutes**

INGREDIENT	OUNCES	GRAMS	VOLUME	BAKERS %
Brioche dough (page 294)	53.0	1503	•	100.0%
Chocolate Filling (page 309)	18.0	510	2 cups	34.0%
Pecans, toasted, chopped	14.0	397	4 cups	26.4%
TOTAL	85.0	2410	•	160.4%
GARNISH				
Flat Glaze (page 94)	as needed			

1. MAKE the Brioche dough the day before you want to make and bake the babka. After mixing, place the dough on a piece of floured parchment paper on a baking tray, roll out to a 10 by 12-inch rectangle, and cover. Refrigerate overnight.

2. PREPARE the Chocolate Filling the day prior also, and place in the refrigerator overnight.

3. REMOVE the dough and filling from the refrigerator and let them sit at room temperature for 30 minutes.

4. PREPARE 4 standard loaf pans by cutting parchment paper to fit across the pans in both directions, leaving the parchment paper long enough so the babka can be taken out of the pans with the parchment paper.

5. PLACE the dough on a lightly floured work surface and roll it into an 18 by 18-inch square. Spread the filling on the dough, leaving a ½-inch border at the top and bottom. If the filling is too stiff to spread, warm it slightly in the microwave. Sprinkle the pecans over the filling evenly.

6. ROLL the dough up by folding the top edge over about halfway. Keep doing this until you can't fold the dough anymore, and pinch the seam tightly to close.

7. PLACE the dough seam-side down and lightly flour the dough. Cut the dough in half lengthwise and place each half with the cut end pointing toward you. Lightly flatten each piece of dough to create more surface area, then cut each piece lengthwise into 3 strips, keeping the top end uncut. Flip each strip up so the filling shows and separate the strips a little.

8. BRAID the dough by taking the strip on the right and bringing it between the other two. Now take the strip on the left and place it between the other two on the right. Keep doing this until there is no more dough. Pinch the ends together.

9. CUT the braid in half lengthwise and place the pieces in 2 of the prepared pans.

10. **REPEAT** the braiding and cutting with the other half of the dough. Cover the pans and let the dough rest and ferment in a warm area for 2½–3 hours, until when lightly pressed the dough springs back halfway. This takes a long time due to the type of dough and the addition of the filling.

11. **AFTER 2 HOURS,** preheat the oven to 400°F.

12. **WHEN THE DOUGH HAS RISEN,** uncover and transfer the pans to the oven. Immediately reduce the temperature to 350°F. Bake for 30 minutes, then rotate the pans and bake for another 15–20

minutes, until when a skewer is inserted near the center of the loaf it comes out clean.

13. **PREPARE** the glaze while the loaves are baking.

14. **REMOVE** the loaves from the oven and let them sit in the pans for 5 minutes. Remove from the pans with hot pads by gripping the excess parchment paper on the ends, and place the loaves on a cooling rack. Brush the tops with glaze and allow them to cool thoroughly.

CHOCOLATE FILLING

yield: 2 lb

INGREDIENT	OUNCES	GRAMS	VOLUME	BAKERS %
Butter, melted	11.7	332	1½ cups	100.0%
Brown sugar	11.2	318	1½ cups	95.7%
All-purpose flour	1.5	43	¼ cup	12.8%
Cocoa powder, unsweetened	1.5	43	½ cup	12.8%
Honey	1.3	37	2 Tbsp	11.1%
Eggs	4.9	139	2 each	41.9%
Vanilla extract	dash	dash	dash	0.1%
TOTAL	32.1	912	•	274.4%

1. **PUT** the butter and sugar in the bowl of a mixer fitted with a paddle attachment. Mix for 2 minutes on medium speed, making sure to scrape down the bowl.

2. **THOROUGHLY BLEND TOGETHER** the flour, cocoa powder and honey and add to the mixer. Mix for 2 minutes on medium speed, making sure to scrape down the bowl.

3. **COMBINE** the eggs and vanilla in a separate bowl, then add to the butter mixture and mix for 2 minutes on medium speed, making sure to scrape down the bowl.

4. **TRANSFER** to a container to cool at room temperature for 1 hour. Cover and refrigerate overnight.

Panettone is scored before it is baked.

PANETTONE

This is a traditional Christmas and New Year's bread from Italy. It is distinctive in its cupola shape and its sweet and fluffy crumb texture. It can be paired with a dessert wine or dessert beverages.

yield: **2 loaves at 22 oz or 14 loaves at 3.3 oz** | FDT: **80°F** | sponge: **30 minutes** | bulk fermentation: **50–60 minutes** |
final fermentation: **50–60 minutes** | bake large loaves: **375°F** *and* **28–30 minutes** | bake small loaves: **375°F** *and* **18–20 minutes**

INGREDIENT	OUNCES	GRAMS	VOLUME	BAKERS %
SPONGE				
Milk, 88°F	4.1	116	½ cup	23.8%
Malt syrup	0.1	3	⅛ tsp	0.6%
Bread flour	5.7	162	1 cup + 3 Tbsp	33.1%
Yeast, instant dry	0.3	9	2½ tsp	1.7%
FINAL DOUGH				
Milk	4.0	113	½ cup	23.3%
Eggs	4.0	113	2 each	23.3%
Butter, soft (#1)	1.0	28	2 Tbsp	5.8%
Corn syrup, light	0.7	20	1 Tbsp	4.1%
Orange zest	0.1	3	2 tsp	0.6%
Lemon zest	0.1	3	2 tsp	0.6%
Sponge	10.2	290	•	59.2%
Bread flour	11.5	326	2⅓ cups	66.9%
Salt	0.5	14	2½ tsp	2.9%
Butter, soft (#2)	2.5	71	⅓ cup	14.5%
Sugar	2.5	71	⅓ cup	14.5%
Candied orange peel, chopped (page 285)	2.3	64	¼ cup	13.1%
Candied lemon peel, chopped (page 285)	2.3	65	¼ cup	13.4%
Dark raisins	2.3	65	½ cup	13.4%
Golden raisins	2.3	65	½ cup	13.4%
TOTAL	46.3	1311	•	269.0%

INGREDIENT	OUNCES	GRAMS	VOLUME	BAKERS %
GARNISHES				
Egg wash	as needed			
Butter, soft	as needed			

1. TO MAKE THE SPONGE, combine the milk and malt in a bowl. In a separate bowl, combine the flour with the yeast, then add this mixture to the milk. Mix the sponge together by hand for 2 minutes to develop some gluten structure. Make sure all the ingredients are combined in a homogenous mass. Cover the bowl with plastic wrap and allow the sponge to ferment in a warm place for 30 minutes, until when lightly touched the dough springs back halfway.

2. TO MAKE THE FINAL DOUGH, put the milk, eggs, butter #1, corn syrup and zests in the bowl of a mixer. Break the sponge up by hand and add to the bowl. Place the bowl on a mixer fitted with a paddle attachment and mix for 1 minute on low speed to break up the sponge. Add the flour and salt, then mix for 4 minutes on low speed, making sure to scrape down and flip the dough over. Mix on medium speed for 3 minutes, making sure to scrape down and flip the dough over. The dough should have some gluten development. It should be staying in the center of the bowl, not on the sides. Switch the attachment to the dough hook and gradually add half of butter #2 (1¼ oz) on medium speed over 2 minutes. Make sure to scrape down and flip the dough over. Add the sugar gradually while mixing over 2 minutes, making sure to scrape down and flip the dough over. Then add the remaining butter (1¼ oz) while mixing over 1 minute, making sure to scrape down and flip the dough over. The dough should have full gluten development at this point. Combine the citrus peels and raisins in a bowl and toss them together. Add them to the mixer and mix on low speed for 1 minute, making sure to scrape down and flip the dough over. Place the dough in a lightly oiled bowl large enough for it to double in size and cover with plastic wrap.

3. ALLOW the dough to rest and ferment in a warm place for 50–60 minutes, until when lightly touched the dough springs back halfway.

4. PLACE the dough on a lightly floured work surface. For large loaves, divide it into two 22-oz pieces. For small loaves, divide the dough into 3.3-oz pieces.

5. PREPARE two 6 × 4½-inch paper baking molds by spraying them with oil and placing them on a baking tray.

6. ROUND each dough piece against the tabletop. Place the pieces seam-side down in the molds and lightly egg wash them. Lightly cover the loaves with plastic wrap. Allow them to rest and ferment in a warm place for 50–60 minutes, until when lightly touched the dough springs back halfway.

7. PREHEAT the oven to 400°F.

8. UNCOVER the loaves, egg wash again, then cut an X in the top of each loaf with a sharp razor. Place a small pat of butter in each X.

9. TRANSFER the tray of bread to the oven and immediately reduce the temperature to 375°F. Bake the large loaves for 20 minutes, then rotate the tray and bake for 8–10 minutes more, until the loaves are golden brown. Bake the small loaves for 15 minutes, rotate, and bake an additional 3–5 minutes.

10. REMOVE from the oven and place the loaves, still in their paper molds, on a cooling rack.

CHOCOLATE AND ORANGE PANETTONE

Chocolate should never be melted over a direct flame. It is safer to use a double boiler or to pour a warm liquid over the chocolate, as in this recipe. Stir constantly to avoid scalding the milk while bringing it to a boil.

yield: 2 loaves at 22 oz or 14 loaves at 3.3 oz | FDT: 80°F

sponge: 30 minutes | bulk fermentation: 50–60 minutes | final fermentation: 50–60 minutes | bake: 375°F and 28–30 minutes

INGREDIENT	OUNCES	GRAMS	VOLUME	BAKERS %
SPONGE				
Milk, 88°F	3.8	108	½ cup	24.8%
Malt syrup	0.1	3	⅛ tsp	0.7%
Bread flour	5.2	147	1 cup	34.0%
Yeast, instant dry	0.3	9	2½ tsp	2.0%
GANACHE				
Milk, boiling	1.1	31	2 Tbsp	7.2%
Chocolate, 62%, chopped	2.5	71	⅓ cup	16.3%
FINAL DOUGH				
Milk, 88°F	2.8	79	⅓ cup	18.3%
Eggs	4.0	113	2 each	26.1%
Butter, soft (#1)	1.2	34	2½ Tbsp	7.8%
Corn syrup, light	1.1	31	1½ Tbsp	7.2%
Orange zest	0.3	9	1 tsp	2.0%
Sponge	9.4	267	•	61.5%
Bread flour	10.1	286	2 cups + 2 Tbsp	66.0%
Yeast, instant dry	0.1	3	1 tsp	0.7%
Salt	0.4	11	2 tsp	2.6%
Ganache	3.6	102	⅓ cup	23.5%
Sugar	2.3	65	⅓ cup	15.0%

INGREDIENT	OUNCES	GRAMS	VOLUME	BAKERS %
Butter, soft (#2)	2.5	71	⅓ cup	16.3%
Candied orange peel, chopped (page 285)	4.0	113	⅔ cup	26.1%
Chocolate, 62%, chopped	4.0	113	⅓ cup	26.1%
TOTAL	45.8	1297	•	299.2%
GARNISHES				
Egg wash	as needed			
Butter, soft	as needed			

1. TO MAKE THE SPONGE, combine the milk and malt. In a separate bowl, combine the flour with the yeast, then add this mixture to the milk. Mix the sponge together by hand for 2 minutes. Make sure all the ingredients are combined in a homogenous mass. Cover the bowl with plastic wrap and allow the sponge to ferment in a warm place for 30 minutes, until doubled in size.

2. TO MAKE THE GANACHE, bring the milk to a boil and pour it over the chopped chocolate in a bowl. Stir well with a rubber spatula. If the chocolate is not fully melted, place the bowl over a pot filled with 2 inches of water on low heat until the chocolate is fully incorporated. Remove from the heat and allow to cool to room temperature.

3. TO MAKE THE FINAL DOUGH, put the milk, eggs, butter #1, corn syrup and zest in the bowl of a mixer. Break up the sponge by hand and add to the bowl. Place the bowl on a mixer fitted with a paddle attachment and mix for 1 minute on low speed to break up the sponge. Add the flour, yeast and salt, then mix for 4 minutes on low speed, making sure to scrape down and flip the dough over. Mix on medium speed for 3 minutes, making sure to scrape down and flip the dough over. The dough should stay in the center of the bowl, not on the sides. Switch the attachment to the dough hook and gradually add half of the ganache on low speed over 1 minute, making sure to scrape down and flip the dough over. Mix for 1 minute on medium speed. Add the rest of the ganache on low speed over 1 minute, making sure to scrape down and flip the dough over. Mix for 1 minute on medium speed. Gradually add the sugar while mixing for 2 minutes, making sure to scrape down and flip the dough over. Gradually add

butter #2 while mixing over 2 minutes, making sure to scrape down and flip the dough over. The dough should have full gluten development at this point. Combine the orange peel and chocolate and toss them together. Add them to the mixer and mix on low speed for 1 minute, making sure to scrape down and flip the dough over. Place the dough in a lightly oiled bowl large enough for it to double in size and cover with plastic wrap.

4. ALLOW the dough to rest and ferment in a warm place for 50–60 minutes, until when lightly touched the dough springs back halfway.

5. PROCEED as for Panettone (page 311).

CHOCOLATE AND CHERRY PANETTONE

This delicious version of the traditional panettone is similar in flavor to a Black Forest cake. The dark bitterness of the chocolate plays against the sweet tartness of the cherries to provide a rich and interesting taste to a wonderful holiday bread. Prepare and bake the dough as for Chocolate and Orange Panettone (page 313), substituting 4 oz (113 g/¾ cup) dried cherries for the candied orange peel.

ALMOND STOLLEN

This is a wonderful variation of the German and Austrian bread made for the Christmas holiday. It is traditionally started in October and allowed to age for at least one month. It makes for a unique holiday gift. When making this, make sure the butter in the dough is soft but not too warm. Warm butter will create a greasy loaf. After removing from the oven, dip the loaves in warm clarified butter as soon as possible.

yield: 2 loaves at 25 oz | FDT: 80°F

sponge: 30 minutes | bulk fermentation: 30 minutes | final fermentation: 20 minutes | bake: 375°F and 50–55 minutes | aging time: 2 weeks

INGREDIENT	OUNCES	GRAMS	VOLUME	BAKERS %
SPONGE				
Milk, 88°F	5.0	142	½ cup + 2 Tbsp	35.7%
Malt syrup	0.1	3	1 tsp	0.7%
Bread flour	7.1	201	1⅓ cups	50.7%
Yeast, instant dry	0.3	9	¼ tsp	2.1%
Salt	0.1	3	pinch	0.7%
ALMOND FILLING				
Almond paste	4.7	133	½ cup	•
Sugar	1.5	43	3 Tbsp	•
Egg whites	0.6	17	1 each	•
Almonds, sliced	2.4	68	½ cup	•
FINAL DOUGH				
Almond paste	0.8	23	2 Tbsp	5.7%
Sugar	1.6	45	3 Tbsp	11.4%
Orange zest	0.3	9	2 Tbsp	2.1%
Vanilla extract	0.2	6	2 tsp	1.4%
Butter, soft	6.9	196	⅔ cup	49.3%
Sponge	12.6	358	•	89.9%
Bread flour	6.9	196	1½ cups	49.3%
Salt	0.2	6	1 tsp	1.4%

Almond Stollen and Panettone

INGREDIENT	OUNCES	GRAMS	VOLUME	BAKERS %
Candied orange peel, chopped (page 285)	1.6	45	¼ cup	11.4%
Candied lemon peel, chopped (page 285)	1.6	45	¼ cup	11.4%
Dark raisins	3.1	88	¼ cup	22.0%
Golden raisins	3.1	88	¼ cup	22.0%
Almonds, sliced	3.5	99	¼ cup	22.0%
TOTAL	42.4	1204	•	299.3%
GARNISHES				
Clarified butter	as needed			
Vanilla sugar (page 288)	as needed			
Powdered sugar	as needed			

1. **TO MAKE THE SPONGE**, combine the milk and malt in a bowl. In a separate bowl, combine the flour with the yeast, add this mixture to the milk, then add the salt. Mix the sponge together by hand for 2 minutes to develop some gluten structure. Make sure all the ingredients are combined in a homogenous mass. Cover the bowl with plastic wrap and allow the sponge to ferment in a warm place for 30 minutes, until doubled in size.

2. **TO MAKE THE ALMOND FILLING**, place the almond paste and sugar in the bowl of a mixer fitted with a paddle attachment. Mix for 2 minutes on medium speed, making sure to scrape down the bowl. With the mixer running, add the egg whites gradually, making sure to scrape down the bowl. Add the almonds and mix for 1 minute to blend completely.

3. **DIVIDE** the filling into 2 equal pieces and roll each into a 7-inch cylinder. Cover and reserve at room temperature.

4. **TO MAKE THE FINAL DOUGH**, place the almond paste, half the sugar, orange zest and vanilla in the bowl of a mixer fitted with a paddle attachment. Mix for 2 minutes on medium speed, mak-

ing sure to scrape down the bowl. Add the remaining sugar and mix for 1 minute on medium speed, making sure to scrape down the bowl. Add the butter gradually while mixing on low speed over 2 minutes, making sure to scrape down the bowl. Break the sponge up by hand and add to the mixer, then mix for 1 minute on low speed. Add the flour and salt. Mix for 4 minutes on low speed, making sure to scrape down the bowl and flip the dough over 2 times. Mix for 3 minutes on medium speed, making sure to scrape down and flip the dough over. The dough should have slight gluten development. Leave the dough in the bowl and cover it. Allow the dough to rest in a warm place for 30 minutes, until when lightly touched the dough springs back halfway.

5. **TOSS** together the candied orange and lemon peel, raisins and almonds. Place the dough on a lightly floured work surface and chop it up with a scraper. Add the fruit and nut mixture, and work it in by hand.

6. **DIVIDE** the dough into two 25-oz pieces. Shape each piece into a 6-inch oblong.

7. SLIGHTLY FLATTEN each dough piece. Roll each piece out to 6 by 8 inches. Place a cylinder of almond filling in the center of each piece, then bring the dough over this to cover and encase the filling. Make sure to close the ends and the seam. Place the loaves seam-side down on a baking tray lined with parchment paper. Slightly flatten the loaves and cover lightly. Allow the dough to rest in a warm place for 20 minutes.

8. PREHEAT the oven to 425°F.

9. TRANSFER the baking tray to the oven and immediately reduce the temperature to 375°F. Bake for 20 minutes, then rotate the tray and bake for 30–35 minutes. The bread will have a dark color and the fruit on the exterior may be burnt, but this is correct.

10. REMOVE from the oven and let the bread cool on the tray set on a cooling rack for 5 minutes.

11. REMOVE any burnt fruit from the outside of each loaf and dip each loaf completely in warm clarified butter, making sure to be careful when picking up each loaf. Use both hands and keep them under the center of the bread. Place the loaves on a cooling rack with parchment paper underneath it. Allow them to cool for 1 hour and then roll them in vanilla sugar. Allow to cool fully. Wrap the loaves well in plastic wrap and let them age at room temperature for a minimum of 2 weeks.

12. WHEN ready to serve, remove the plastic wrap and lightly sift powdered sugar over the bread. This bread should be sliced thin due to its richness.

Roll the dough out to a 6 by 8-inch rectangle. For almond stollen, insert the filling, which is in log form, leaving a border with which to handle the dough. Pinch the dough closed over the filling, making a cylindrical shape. Pinch the ends closed to add a taper to the dough. Place the dough on a baking tray lined with parchment paper and flatten it slightly at the top.

While still fairly hot, remove each loaf from the baking tray and throw away any burnt pieces of fruit from the outside. Dip the loaf in clarified butter. It is important to handle the bread carefully since it is still hot and can crack easily.

ORAHNJACHA

Croatian in origin, orahnjacha, a sweetened nut bread flecked with lemon zest, is a delicious treat any time of year. Either walnuts or pecans can be used to prepare the filling.

yield: one 9-inch loaf | *sponge:* 30 minutes | *bulk fermentation:* 45 minutes | *bake:* 350°F *and* 45 minutes

INGREDIENT	OUNCES	GRAMS	VOLUME	BAKERS %
SPONGE				
Water, 85°F	1.2	35	3 Tbsp	12.9%
Bread flour	1.0	30	¼ cup	11.1%
Yeast, dry	0.3	10	2½ tsp	3.0%
FILLING				
Milk	7.2	205	¾ cup	75.0%
Sugar	5.3	150	¾ cup	55.0%
Walnuts or pecans, ground	10.5	300	2½ cups	111.0%
FINAL DOUGH				
Sponge	2.5	75	•	27.0%
Eggs	2.3	66	1 each	24.0%
Butter, melted, cooled	5.6	160	¾ cup	59.0%
Lemon zest	0.2	6	1 Tbsp	2.0%
Bread flour	9.5	270	2 cups	100.0%
Salt	0.2	6	1 tsp	2.0%
Sugar	2.1	60	⅓ cup	22.0%
TOTAL	22.4	643	•	236.0%

1. TO MAKE THE SPONGE, in a large bowl, mix all the ingredients for the sponge by hand until well combined. Cover and let ferment for 30 minutes.

2. MEANWHILE, MAKE THE FILLING. Bring the milk and sugar to a boil over medium-high heat. Remove from the heat, stir in the ground nuts, and let cool.

3. TO MAKE THE FINAL DOUGH, place the sponge in the bowl of a mixer fitted with a paddle attachment. Add the rest of the ingredients for the final dough. Mix on low speed for 5 minutes, scraping down the sides of the bowl frequently.

4. TRANSFER the dough to an oiled bowl and let ferment for about 45 minutes. The dough will not increase drastically in size.

5. PREHEAT the oven to 400°F.

6. TURN the dough out onto a lightly floured work surface. Using a rolling pin, roll the dough out into a very thin 24 x 12-inch rectangle.

7. SPREAD the nut filling across the dough, leaving ½ inch clean around the edge of the dough.

8. ROLL UP the dough, beginning with one of the 24-inch sides and rolling to the other side. Then form the finished roll into a snail shape, creating a large spiral.

9. BUTTER a 9-inch cake pan. Place a 9-inch parchment paper circle in the center, then flour the pan. Place the dough in the pan.

10. TRANSFER the pan to the oven and immediately reduce the temperature to 350°F. Bake for 45 minutes, until lightly browned.

11. UNMOLD the finished bread and let cool completely on a cooling rack. Dust the finished loaf with powdered sugar.

UTOPLJENICI

Also known as "drowned cookies," these Croatian yeast-raised pastries are best
eaten the same day they are baked and are perfect with a cup of coffee.

yield: 13 pastries | bulk fermentation: 30–60 minutes | final fermentation: 60–75 minutes | bake: 350°F and 25–30 minutes

INGREDIENT	OUNCES	GRAMS	VOLUME	BAKERS %
Milk	2.8	80	⅓ cup	16.0%
Water, 85°F	1.9	55	¼ cup	11.0%
Bread flour	17.6	500	3⅔ cups	100.0%
Yeast	0.2	7	1¾ tsp	1.0%
Eggs	2.3	66	1 each	13.0%
Lemon zest	0.2	6	1 Tbsp	1.0%
Vegetable oil	3.3	95	⅓ cup	19.0%
Salt	0.1	4	⅔ tsp	1.0%
Walnuts, coarsely chopped	1.7	50	½ cup	10.0%
Sugar	5.3	150	¾ cup	30.0%
TOTAL	35.4	1013	•	202.0%

1. **HEAT** the milk and water together in a small pot until they reach 85°F.

2. **COMBINE** the flour and yeast in the bowl of a mixer fitted with a paddle attachment. Add the milk and water mixture, eggs, lemon zest, oil and salt and mix on low speed for 5 minutes, scraping down the sides of the bowl frequently.

3. **PLACE** the dough in the center of a large cloth and tie a knot at the top. Submerge the cloth-wrapped dough in 85°F water and let it ferment until the dough rises to the surface, 30–60 minutes.

4. **PREHEAT** the oven to 400°F.

5. **PLACE** the walnuts and sugar in a bowl and stir to combine.

6. **DIVIDE** the dough into 2.2-oz pieces. Gently twist each piece of dough, then roll it in the nut and sugar mixture. Twist the dough again and form it into a crescent. Place the finished pieces on a parchment paper–lined baking tray.

7. **ALLOW** to ferment for 60–75 minutes in a warm place until the dough springs back halfway when touched.

8. **TRANSFER** the baking tray to the oven and immediately reduce the temperature to 350°F. Bake for 25–30 minutes, until lightly browned.

Sauces and Dips

GUACAMOLE

yield: 8 servings

INGREDIENT	AMOUNT
Ripe avocados	5 each
Plum tomatoes, seeded, diced	2 each
Jalapeño, seeded, minced	1 each
Cilantro, roughly chopped	2 Tbsp
White onion, diced	1 each
Lime, juiced	1 each
Salt	as needed
Tabasco	as needed
Black pepper	as needed

1. **PEEL** the avocados and roughly cut into a medium dice.

2. **COMBINE** the avocados with the rest of the ingredients in a medium bowl and mix well. As you mix, slightly mash the avocados to form a rough paste.

HARISSA (TUNISIAN HOT CHILI PASTE)

yield: 1 cup

INGREDIENT	AMOUNT
Dried hot chilies, stemmed, seeded	3 oz
Garlic clove, peeled, roughly chopped	1 each
Salt	1 tsp, plus more as needed
Coriander seeds, ground	¼ tsp
Caraway seeds, ground	¾ tsp
Extra-virgin olive oil	as needed
Limes, juiced	3 each
Tabasco	as needed
Black pepper	as needed

1. **SOAK** the chilies in cold water for 15 minutes. Drain them well, wrap them in cheesecloth, and press out the excess moisture. Using the side of a chef's knife, rub the garlic and 1 tsp salt together to form a paste.

2. **PUT** the chilies, garlic paste, coriander, caraway, oil and lime juice in the bowl of a food processor and grind to a paste. Season with salt, Tabasco and pepper as needed. Transfer the mixture to a bowl and add enough oil to thinly cover the paste. Cover tightly and keep refrigerated.

NOTE: In Tunisia, fiery hot red peppers play a role in almost every dish, usually in the form of the famous harissa, a paste made of sun-dried peppers pounded with spices and garlic, and packed into jars under a coating of olive oil.

Hummus

yield: 10 servings

INGREDIENT	AMOUNT
Chickpeas, dried	8 oz
Onion, cut in half	1 each
Tahini paste	½ cup
Garlic cloves, peeled, roughly cut	3 each
Lemons, juiced	2 each
Extra-virgin olive oil	¼ cup
Salt	as needed
Black pepper	as needed
GARNISHES	
Extra-virgin olive oil	¼ cup
Hot paprika	2 tsp
Cumin, ground	1 tsp

1. SOAK the chickpeas the day before you want to serve the hummus. Place them in a bowl with three times their volume of water and let them soak overnight.

2. RINSE the chickpeas and add more water to cover. Add the onion and place in a medium pot and cook until the chickpeas are tender, 25–30 minutes. Remove and discard the onion. Drain the chickpeas, reserving the cooking liquid, and allow them to cool slightly.

3. ADD the chickpeas to the bowl of a food processor along with the tahini paste, garlic, lemon juice, oil, salt and pepper. Process the ingredients, adding enough of the bean cooking liquid to form a thick puree.

4. TO SERVE, form a small well in the center and drizzle with the oil, paprika and cumin to garnish.

Lima/Fava Bean Spread

yield: 1 lb

INGREDIENT	AMOUNT
Onions, diced	1 each
Garlic, minced	2 tsp
Lima or fava beans	2 lb
Vegetable stock	1 cup
Extra-virgin olive oil	1 cup
Parsley, chopped	2 Tbsp
Rosemary, minced	1 tsp
Salt	as needed
Black pepper	as needed

1. SWEAT the onions in a large pot, 3–4 minutes, or until translucent. Add the garlic and cook until it is aromatic, 1 minute more.

2. ADD the beans and stock. Simmer until the beans are tender, about 30 minutes.

3. DRAIN the beans, reserving the liquid.

4. PUT the beans, in small batches, in the bowl of a food processor and fully puree. Transfer each batch of pureed beans to a large bowl. Add the rest of the ingredients to the large bowl and combine. Add more salt and pepper if needed. Cool and serve.

PESTO

yield: 1 cup

INGREDIENT	AMOUNT
Basil leaves, washed, dried	1 cup packed
Sea salt	1 pinch
Garlic, minced	2 tsp
Pine nuts, lightly toasted	3 Tbsp
Extra-virgin olive oil	3–4 Tbsp
Pecorino Romano cheese, grated	2 Tbsp
Parmigiano-Reggiano cheese, grated	2 Tbsp

PUT the basil, salt and garlic in the jar of a blender. Blend into a paste. Add the pine nuts and slowly pour in half the oil. Add the cheeses and the remaining oil. Blend until the mixture becomes a homogenous, creamy paste. Overblending will cause the pesto to become bitter.

ROMESCO SAUCE

yield: 2 cups

INGREDIENT	AMOUNT
Garlic cloves, peeled	2 each
Bread slices	2 each
Almonds	1 cup
Hazelnuts	1 cup
Tomatoes	2 each
Red bell peppers	3 each
Parsley, chopped	2 Tbsp
Extra-virgin olive oil	3 Tbsp
Sherry vinegar	2 Tbsp

1. PREHEAT the oven to 350°F.

2. PLACE the garlic, bread, almonds and hazelnuts on a baking tray and roast until lightly browned, 5 to 10 minutes. Cool completely.

3. PLACE the tomatoes and peppers, unpeeled, in a stovetop smoker. Smoke them on high heat for 5 minutes. Remove the skins of both the tomatoes and peppers. Cool slightly before peeling so they are not too hot to handle. Cool completely.

4. TRANSFER all the cooled ingredients to the bowl of a food processor and puree. Stir in the parsley, oil and vinegar.

Salsa Cruda

yield: 5 cups

INGREDIENT	AMOUNT
Plum tomatoes, seeded, diced	20 each
Spanish onion, diced	1 each
Jalapeños, seeded, minced	3 each
Limes, juiced	2 each
Cilantro, roughly chopped	3 Tbsp
Salt	as needed

COMBINE all the ingredients in a medium bowl. Cover tightly and keep refrigerated.

Tapenade

yield: 1½ cups

INGREDIENT	AMOUNT
Black olives, pitted	8 oz
Capers, drained	¼ cup
Garlic, chopped	1 tsp
Tuna packed in olive oil, drained	⅓ cup
Brandy	2 Tbsp
Extra-virgin olive oil	½ cup
Lemon juice	¼ tsp
Tabasco	as needed
Black pepper	as needed

COMBINE all the ingredients very briefly in a blender or food processor (tapenade should be a rather coarse-textured paste).

Appendix

Braiding and Knotting

PRESHAPING STRANDS OBLONG

STEP A: To preshape the dough, first fold the left and right edges of the dough inward so that they just touch in the center.

STEP B: Fold the top edge one third of the way over the dough and press firmly. Then tightly fold the top edge over two more times to create an oblong.

STEP C: Roll until the oblong is the desired length as per the recipe.

SHAPING STRANDS FOR BRAIDING/KNOTTING

STEP A: With the seam facing up, gently flatten the piece of dough with your fingertips.

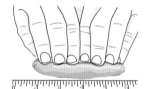

STEP B: Fold the top edge one third of the way over the dough and press along the edge to create a seam.

STEP C: With the seam pinched securely closed, the dough should be smooth and taut, but not stretched too tightly.

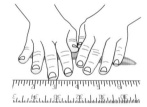

STEP D: Roll the dough back and forth against the tabletop, pressing down and outward with the palms of your hands to elongate the dough.

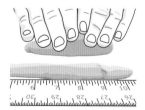

STEP E: Roll until the strand is the desired length as per the recipe.

SINGLE KNOT

STEP A: Grasp one third of the strand between your thumb and fingers and allow the remaining two thirds to drape over the back of your hand.

STEP B: Bring the two-thirds length around and secure under your thumb.

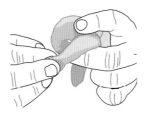

STEP C: Continue bringing the two-thirds length over and through the dough wrapped around your fingers.

STEP D: Pull the strand all the way through to form an even knot.

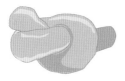

STEP E: Finish the knot.

FIGURE EIGHT

STEP A: Form a loop with two thirds of the strand, pressing the end into the strand to connect.

STEP B: Take the end of the strand and bring it through the top of the loop.

STEP C: Take the bottom of the loop and twist to the right.

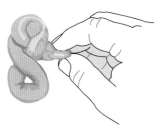

STEP D: Bring the end of the strand over and through the bottom loop.

STEP E: Finished figure "eight" knot.

KAISER ROLL

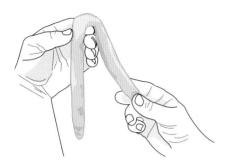

STEP A: Grasp two thirds of the strand between your thumb and fingers and allow the remaining one third to drape over the back of your hand.

STEP B: Bring the one-third length around and secure under your thumb.

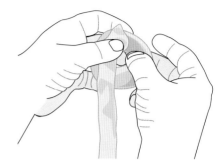

STEP C: Continue bringing the one-third length over and through the dough wrapped around your fingers.

STEP D: Bring the two-thirds length through the front of the loop twice.

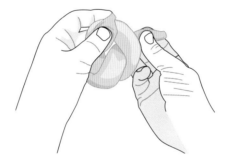

STEP E: Shape into an even round.

STEP F: Finished kaiser knot.

CHALLAH: 4-STRAND

STEP A: Roll each piece out to 16 inches. Arrange the strands side by side and pinch one end of all the strands together. Lightly flour the pinched strands.

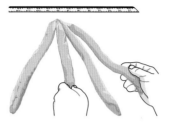

STEP B: Place the pinched end at the top. With your right hand hold the outer strand and with your left hand hold the 2nd strand from the left (this should leave one strand to the left of each of your hands).

STEP C: Take the right hand and go under the left-hand strands, then place the left-hand strand where the right hand was, so that the pieces have now switched positions, and the right strand is now under the left-hand strand.

STEP D: With your left hand hold the outer strand on the left, and with your right hand hold the 2nd strand from the right (this should leave one strand to the right of each of your hands).

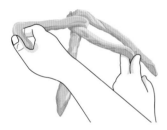

STEP E: Take the left hand and go under the right-hand strands, then place the right-hand strand where the left-hand strand was. The strands should have switched exact positions so that the right-hand strand is over the left-hand strand.

STEP F: Repeat these steps until no more dough is left. Make sure to lay the strands tightly together, but do not pull on them. An easy way to remember the steps is with this mnemonic: Step 1: right hand under left hand. Step 2: right hand over left hand.

STEP G: Finish the braid and pinch off any excess dough, then place the top of the braid parallel to you.

STEP H: Place each hand at the end with your small finger pressing the dough into the table and roll the dough back and forth to close off the ends.

STEP I: The braid for 4 strands should be about 11–12 inches long.

CHALLAH: **6**-STRAND

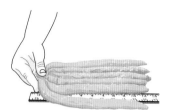

STEP A: Roll each piece out to 12 inches. Arrange the strands side by side and pinch one end of all the strands together. Lightly flour the pinched strands.

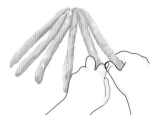

STEP B: Place the pinched end at the top. With your right hand hold the outer strand on the right and with your left hand hold the 2nd strand from the right. This should leave your hands holding the outer two strands on the right.

STEP C: Take your left hand and move it to the outside of the last strand on the left.

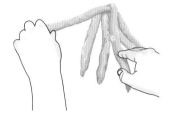

STEP D: Then take your right-hand strand to the middle of the four that you have not touched.

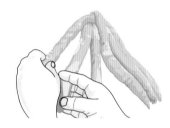

STEP E: With your left hand hold the outer strand on the left and with your right hand hold the 2nd strand from the left. This should leave your hands holding the outer two strands on the left.

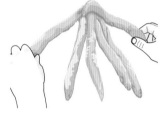

STEP F: Take your right hand and move it to the outside of the last strand on the right.

STEP G: Take your left-hand strand to the middle of the four strands that you have not touched. Make sure to lay the strands in tight together but don't pull on them.

STEP H: Continue repeating these steps until the loaf is completely braided. An easy way to remember the steps is with this mnemonic: Step 1: 2 outer strands on right / inside to outside / outside to middle. Step 2: 2 outer strands on left / inside to outside / outside to middle.

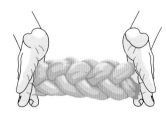

STEP I: Finish the braid, pinch off any excess dough, then place the braid parallel to you. Place each hand at the end with your small finger pressing the dough into the table and roll back and forth to close off the ends.

STEP J: The braid for 6 strands should be 9–10 inches.

Readings and Resources

Books

The Culinary Institute of America. *Baking at Home with The Culinary Institute of America.* Hoboken, New Jersey: John Wiley and Sons, Inc., 2004.

The Culinary Institute of America. *Baking and Pastry: Mastering the Art and Craft.* Hoboken, New Jersey: John Wiley and Sons, Inc., 2004.

Figoni, Paula. *How Baking Works: Exploring the Fundamentals of Baking Science.* Hoboken, New Jersey: John Wiley and Sons, Inc., 2004.

Hamelman, Jeffrey. *Bread: A Baker's Book of Techniques and Recipes.* Hoboken, New Jersey: John Wiley and Sons, Inc., 2004.

Jacob, H. E. *Six Thousand Years of Bread: Its Holy and Unholy History.* New York: Doubleday, 1945.

Leader, Daniel, and Judith Blahnik. *Bread Alone: Bold Fresh Loaves from Your Own Hands.* New York: William Morrow and Company, Inc., 1993.

Reinhart, Peter. *Crust and Crumb: Master Formulas for Serious Bread Bakers.* Berkeley, California: Ten Speed Press, 2006.

Robertson, Laurel, with Carol Flinders and Bronwen Godfrey. *The Laurel's Kitchen Bread Book: A Guide to Whole Grain Baking.* New York: Random House, Inc., 1984.

Silverton, Nancy. *Nancy Silverton's Breads from the La Brea Bakery.* New York: Villard Books, Random House, Inc., 1996.

Treuille, Eric, and Ursula Ferrigno. *Bread.* New York: DK Publishing, Inc., 2007.

Magazines and Web Sites

Cook's Illustrated
www.cooksillustrated.com

This magazine tests recipes, techniques, ingredients and equipment relevant to bakers and chefs. No advertising is accepted. You may subscribe to the magazine itself or to the Web site.

bbga.org Bread Bakers Guild of America

theartisan.net

artisanbakers.com

Resources: Ingredients and Equipment

King Arthur Flour
www.kingarthurflour.com
135 Route 5 South, Norwich, VT 05055
To order baking supplies: 800-827-6836
To request a catalog: 800-777-4434

King Arthur sells flour, grains (including multigrain mixture), barley malt, yeast and other baking supplies, pans and accessories. It also sells books and publications.

Bob's Red Mill
www.bobsredmill.com
13521 SE Pheasant Court, Milwaukie, OR 97222
To order: 800-349-2173

Bob's Red Mill carries flour and other baking supplies.

Chicago Metallic Bakeware
www.cmbakeware.com

This Web site is for retailers and food-service bakers, but provides an overview of the product line. Chicago Metallic pans can be ordered from www.cooking.com, www.chefsresource.com, www.chefscatalog.com and www.surlatable.com among others.

Fibrament-D Baking Stone
www.bakingstone.com
AWMCO, Inc., 11560 West 184th Place, Orland Park, IL 60467
To order: 708-478-6032

At ¾ inch, these baking stones are thicker than most of those available to the home baker. Measure your oven carefully before ordering.

Epicurean Cutting Surfaces
www.epicureancs.com
1325 North 59th Avenue, West Duluth, MN 55807
To order: 218-740-3500 or toll free 866-678-3500

Offers heat-resistant pizza peels and cutting surfaces good for both loading bread and as a work surface. The products are made from eco-friendly paper and can be washed in the dishwasher.

The Super Peel
www.superpeel.com
EXOProducts, Inc., 9 Reed Lane, Clifton Park, NY 12065
To order: 518-371-3173

This conveyor belt–style peel is small enough for home use. It is great for transferring delicate bread doughs to the oven. It may be ordered online.

TMB Baking
www.tmbbaking.com

Index

Page numbers in *italics* indicate illustrations

K

Kaiser Rolls, 47–48, *49*
    braiding and knotting, *328*, 328
Knives, 21
Knot rolls, shaping, 69, *70*, *327*, 327
Knotting. *See* Braiding and knotting

L

Lactic acid, 124
Lames, 3, *21*, 21, 40
Lavash, 141–142, *143*
Lean Breads, 4, 44–65
    autolyse method for, 129
    gluten development, 28, 30
    hand mixing, *29*, 29
    Multigrain, *60*, 61–62, *109*
    Oatmeal, 54–55
    Rolls
        Durum and Rosemary, 56–57, *57*
        Durum, Rosemary and Lemon,
            58–59
        Hoagie, 47–48, *49*
        Kaiser, 47–48, *49*
    Rye, Rustic, 64–65, *65*
    Whole Wheat, 51–52, *53*
Lemon
    in Candied Citrus Peel, 285
    Durum and Rosemary Rolls, 58–59
Levain. *See* Sour
Lima Bean Spread, 323
Loaf pans, *22*, 22. *See also* Pan Loaves
Lye solution, in Pretzels, 209, 210

M

Maillard reaction, 41
Malted barley, 4–5, 13
Margherita Pizza (variation), 150
Masa harina, *9*, 12, 134, 153
    in Corn Tortillas, 153
Measuring cups and spoons, 19
Milk
    in bread making, 18
    in Flat Glaze, 94
    in Hot Cross Topping, 285
Mixers, 18–19, 28
Mixing methods
    autolyse, 28, 114, 116, 129
    blitz, 28, 116, 130
    double hydration, 28, 114, 130–131
    and gluten development, 27–28, *28*, 30
    hand mixing, *29*, 29
    straight mixing, 28
Molds, 22
Mozzarella
    in Herb, Pepper and Cheese Buns,
        82–83
    in Margherita Pizza (variation, 150
    in Pesto Pizza (variation), *149*, 150
    in Pretzel Stuffing, Pesto and Cheese
        (variation), 212
    in Pretzel Stuffing, Sun-Dried Tomato
        and Cheese (variation), 213
    in White Pizza (variation), *149*, 151
Muffaletta Bread, 274–275
Multigrain Bread, *60*, 61–62, *109*
    English Muffins (variation), 162–163
    Rolls, Soft, 84–85, *109*
    and Rye, 260–261

N

Naan, 146–147

O

Oatmeal Bread, 54–55
Oat soaker, 54
Oblong loaves
    preshaping, *34*, 34
    scoring, 41
    shaping, 37–38, *38*
Olive(s)
    and Cheese Bread, 272–273
    and Cheese Bread, Semolina
        (variation), 173
    in Tapenade, 325
Olive oil, in bread baking, 17
Onion(s)
    Bialy Filling, Roasted, 191
    in Bialy Filling, Traditional, 191
    -Cheddar Rye Rolls, 75–76, *77*
    and Rye Loaves, 256–257, *264*
    -Rye Sour, 256, 257
    Sourdough, 238–239
    in Sourdough, Everything, 232–233
Orahnjacha, 319–320
Orange
    Almond and Currant Sourdough,
        226–227
    in Candied Citrus Peel, 285
    and Chocolate Panettone (variation),
        313–314
Ovens, 22–23
    loading, 23, *42*, 42
    preheating, 5
    steaming, 5, 22, 41
Oven-spring, 3, 41